Outsider art

The modernist era was marked by a continual breaching of distinctions regarding what is or is not art, and the breakdown of the hierarchies which had traditionally demarcated them. Today, the arts are characterized by an unprecedented openness to new possibilities, a shifting of established genres, a melding of unlikely forms, and far greater inclusiveness. How then, without an art world establishment with formal authority over outcomes, do we determine what constitutes art and judge different artistic works? *Outsider art* explores the historical roots of this post-modern condition and analyzes how artistic recognition is attained. Sociologists, art historians, policy-makers, and artists themselves analyze cases from the visual and performing arts, taking as their starting point the "classic" outsiders – asylum inmates, "naïve artists," and African "primitives" – and turning to other "outsider" group members, from prison inmates to tango artists, to reveal aspects, stages, and strategies of artistic transformation.

AZE - 1 by Anna Zemankova, ink and colored pencil on paper (11¾″ × 16″). Reproduced by kind permission of the Judy A. Saslow Gallery, Chicago.

Cambridge Cultural Social Studies

Series editors: JEFFREY C. ALEXANDER, *Department of Sociology, University of California, Los Angeles,* and STEVEN SEIDMAN, *Department of Sociology, University at Albany, State University of New York.*

Titles in the series

ILANA FRIEDRICH SILBER, *Virtuosity, charisma, and social order*
LINDA NICHOLSON AND STEVEN SEIDMAN (EDS.). *Social postmodernism*
WILLIAM BOGARD, *The simulation of surveillance*
SUZANNE R. KIRSCHNER, *The religious and Romantic origins of psychoanalysis*
PAUL LICHTERMAN, *The search for political community*
ROGER FRIEDLAND AND RICHARD HECHT, *To rule Jerusalem*
KENNETH H. TUCKER, *French revolutionary syndicalism and the public sphere*
ERIK RINGMAR, *Identity, interest and action*
ALBERTO MELUCCI, *The playing self*
ALBERTO MELUCCI, *Challenging codes*
SARAH M. CORSE, *Nationalism and literature*
DARNELL M. HUNT, *Screening the Los Angeles "riots"*
LYNETTE P. SPILLMAN, *Nation and commemoration*
MICHAEL MULKAY, *The embryo research debate*
LYNN RAPAPORT, *Jews in Germany after the Holocaust*
CHANDRA MUKERJI, *Territorial ambitions and the gardens of Versailles*
LEON H. MAYHEW, *The New Public*

Outsider art

Contesting boundaries in contemporary culture

EDITED BY

Vera L. Zolberg

and

Joni Maya Cherbo

PUBLISHED BY THE PRESS SYNDICATE OF THE UNIVERSITY OF CAMBRIDGE
The Pitt Building, Trumpington Street, Cambridge CB2 1RP, United Kingdom

CAMBRIDGE UNIVERSITY PRESS
The Edinburgh Building, Cambridge CB2 2RU, United Kingdom
40 West 20th Street, New York, NY 10011-4211, USA
10 Stamford Road, Oakleigh, Melbourne 3166, Australia

First published 1997

Printed in the United Kingdom at the University Press, Cambridge

Typeset in 10/12½ Monotype Times [SE]

A catalogue record for this book is available from the British Library

Library of Congress cataloguing in publication data

Outsider art: contesting boundaries in contemporary culture / edited by Vera L. Zolberg and Joni Maya Cherbo.
p. cm. – (Cambridge cultural social studies)
ISBN 0 521 58111 7 (hardback). – ISBN 0 521 58921 5 (paperback)
1. Arts, Modern – 20th century. 2. Arts and society – History – 20th century. 3. Outsider art. I. Zolberg, Vera L. II. Cherbo, Joni Maya, 1941– . III. Series.
NX456.092 1997 700′.9′045–dc21 96-52184 CIP

ISBN 0 521 58111 7 hardback
ISBN 0 521 58921 5 paperback

Contents

Figures

Notes on contributors

Anne Bowler is an Assistant Professor of Sociology at the University of Delaware. Her most recent publication, "Methodological Dilemmas in the Sociology of Art," appears in *The Sociology of Culture: Emerging Theoretical Perspectives*. Her current research examines changing cultural definitions of race, class and gender in the social construction of female sexual deviance in early twentieth-century New York.

Joni Maya Cherbo is a sociologist who specializes in the arts and arts policy. She has taught at a number of universities, including the State University of New York at Purchase and New York University. Her publications include "A Department of Cultural Resources: A Perspective on the Arts" in the *Journal of Arts Management and Law*, and she has coauthored *Arts Education Beyond the Classroom* and *American Participation in Opera and Musical Theater 1992* for the National Endowment for the Arts.

Juan E. Corradi is Professor of Sociology and Acting Dean of the Graduate School of Arts and Science at New York University. Born and raised in Buenos Aires, he was trained professionally in the United States. He has specialized in the sociology of development, the sociology of culture, and social theory. His more recent books include *The Fitful Republic: Fear at the Edge*, and the forthcoming *Imaginary Mimicries: Buenos Aires and Paris 1880-1930*. An avid ocean sailor, he will also publish a book of nautical adventures, titled *Swan Sail*.

Steven C. Dubin is Associate Professor of Sociology at Purchase (State University of New York), where he directs the Social Sciences and the Arts Program, and is also Adjunct Associate Professor of Sociology at Columbia University. He is the author of *Arresting Images: Impolitic Art and Uncivil Actions* and *Bureaucratizing the Muse: Public Funds and the Cultural Worker*.

Henry C. Finney, who retired in 1994 from the sociology faculty at the University of Vermont, is a professional artist, sociologist and writer. His recent published essays deal with art criticism, Zen Buddhism, and the social organization of the contemporary art world. They include "Mediating Claims to Artistry: Social Stratification in a Local Visual Arts Community," *Sociological Forum*, and "The Stylistic Games that Visual Artists Play," *Boekmancahier*. His art has been widely exhibited in the United States, including New York and Santa Fe, New Mexico.

Nathalie Heinich is a researcher in sociology at the Centre National de la Recherche Scientifique (CNRS, Paris). Her specialty in the field of culture has led her to investigate artistic professions, aesthetic perception, and conflicts about contemporary art. Her recent books include *The Glory of Van Gogh: An Anthropology of Admiration* and *Etats de femme: L'Identité féminine dans la fiction occidentale*.

Judy Levine is an adjunct faculty member at New York University. As an organizational development consultant, she has instructed, trained, and written for more than one thousand non-profit organizations, in senior positions with the Cultural Council Foundation, Cause Effective, the Support Center of New York, and independently. Her article, "New York City Department of Cultural Affairs: Art as Municipal Service," appears in *Paying the Piper: Causes and Consequences of Art Patronage*.

Irit Rogoff teaches in the program of critical analysis of visual culture, which she developed at the University of California, Davis. Her intent is to understand how power relations and epistemic values circulate through visual information and the attempt to refract visual imagery through the critical models of gender and sexual difference, race and cultural difference. Her publications include *The Divided Heritage – Themes and Problems in German Modernism* and *Terra Infirma: Geography and Spectatorship*.

Maria Shevtsova is Professor of Contemporary Performance and Theatre Studies at Lancaster University, and has held academic positions at the Universities of Paris, Rome, Sydney, and Connecticut. She has also taught at the Ecole des Hautes Etudes en Sciences Sociales, Paris, and at the Academy of Theatre Arts in St. Petersburg. Her research methodologies in the sociology of theatre have considerably developed the field, combining theories and methodologies of the social sciences with theatre practice and the humanities. Her most recent book is *Theatre and Cultural Interaction*.

András Szántó is presently Research Manager at the Media Studies Center, New York City. His doctoral dissertation in sociology examined transformations in the New York art world in the 1980s. Co-author of a book about Stalinist persecution policies in the 1950s in his native Hungary, he has also conducted research on professional pianists, American and European media, and other subjects in the field of cultural sociology.

Vera L. Zolberg is a Senior Lecturer in the Department of Sociology of the Graduate Faculty of the New School for Social Research. Holder of the Boekman Foundation Chair in Sociology of the Arts at the University of Amsterdam (1992–94), she has taught at the Ecole des Hautes Etudes en Sciences Sociales, and was visiting researcher at the Centre National de la Recherche Scientifique. Author of *Constructing a Sociology of the Arts*, her recent work is on the role that museums play in constructing social memory.

Acknowledgments

This book owes its existence to the intellectual and moral support of a number of colleagues whose longstanding and abiding interest in culture and the arts has provided years of stimulation and comraderie.

Special thanks to Anne Bowler, who was deeply involved in formulating ideas that became the foundation of this book. We value as well the seasoned advice of Judith H. Balfe and Richard A. Peterson, the cogent comments by the anonymous readers which guided our revisions, and the close reading of the introduction by Aristide R. Zolberg. Our posthumous thanks to our late colleague, Muriel Cantor, who was a welcome source of encouragement. Vera Zolberg expresses her appreciation to the American Council of Learned Societies, whose travel grants facilitated her participation in colloquia where the general outlines for this book were initiated.

We would like to extend our particular appreciation to Catherine Max of Cambridge University Press, who has been unfailingly helpful in moving this project forward. Our thanks as well to the many sources who provided us with the visual materials that enhance many of the essays in the collection. Finally, a note of gratitude to our contributors for their searching essays and unfaltering eagerness and commitment to this mapping of cultural change in the late twentieth century.

Introduction

Vera L. Zolberg and Joni M. Cherbo, Editors

The construction of a new genre

Outsider art began inauspiciously when asylum inmates, such as the Swiss peasant, Adolf Wölfli, confined as a schizophrenic from the late 1890s until his death, were encouraged to express themselves through drawing. Although their works were of interest primarily to therapist-physicians, they fascinated artists as well. The transformation of these works from therapy into art began in the 1920s when avant-garde artists became intrigued with them (Bowler, this volume). Convinced that artistic creativity was a universal human gift capable of flourishing outside the confines of traditional artistic practice, artists such as Jean Dubuffet collected the works, giving them the name *art brut* – literally, "raw art" – in the sense that they represented uncultivated, unrefined, spontaneous expression.

Despite their obvious pictorial appeal, asylum works remained on the margins of the artworld. Nevertheless, Dubuffet's thesis was not disparaged by modern art sympathizers, who found artistic expression of interest even in works by madmen, primitives, and children. But most were convinced that it could not flower without professional association and guidance. An unlettered, untutored artist was a fluke – or a fiction.

By the 1970s the British critic, Roger Cardinal, expanded the notion of outsiders beyond mental patients to include a variety of persons making art outside the mainstream (Hall and Metcalf 1994). Cardinal's yardstick for recognizing an outsider as an artist was the presence of an untrained impulse for making works that defied art historical classification (Bowler, this volume).

Over the years the cast of players ballooned. Besides asylum inmates and the makers of primitive art, whose works had long been recognized by the avant-garde (Zolberg, this volume), outsider artists came to encompass folk and ethnic artists, the homeless, prison inmates, elderly people in nursing homes, hospice patients, and others, confined or isolated, who produce objects or performances of aesthetic interest.

The growing pool of outsider artists further expanded the notion of outsiderness itself. Some outsiders, rather than being completely detached from existing, traditional, artistic practice, received some form of artistic training through family or community sources. Others had been apprenticed to artists, and as inmates were given artistic instruction of sorts. Furthermore, a number of outsider artists aspired to recognition in the larger art world and had few qualms about seeking and accepting publicity and remuneration (Dubin, this volume). Gone are the noble savages (Goldwater 1986 [1938]), the peasants of Toennies (1963), and proletarians. Gone, too, with deinstitutionalization and drug treatment, are many of the long-term asylum inmates (Bowler, this volume).

In the face of a booming art market in the 1960s and 1980s (Szántó, Dubin, this volume), dealers and collectors began looking beyond established artistic institutions for promising new forms and creators. Outsider art appealed to art world cognoscenti, not only visually, but because of its congruence with Romantic notions of the authentic, misunderstood, creative genius. Outsiders possessed purity, spontaneity, sincerity, authenticity, as opposed to the contrivance, artificiality, and insincerity of civilized society (Goldwater 1986 [1938]). Given today's world, these outsiders came to represent our lost soul. As outsider art became fashionable, outsiders became insiders.

The success of outsider art is illustrated by the fourth annual Outsider Art Fair, held at the Puck Building in New York City in 1996. Thirty-five exhibitors from the United States and other countries over a four-day period drew crowds paying an admission of ten dollars to see the latest outsider discoveries as well as those already known. Many of the works were priced in line with mainstream art. A 1992 piece by Wölfli was marked at $40,000. Drawings by the Mexican painter, Martin Ramírez, who spent the last years of his life in a California asylum, were listed at $35,000. Recently, a Ramírez drawing fetched $180,000 (Bowler, this volume). Clearly, outsider art has migrated from an existence beyond the pale, acquired its green card, and become naturalized into the art world.

The import of this latest newcomer is that it is a snapshot of an ongoing process. From a historical perspective, the incorporation of outsider art into the mainstream is the latest manifestation of the valorization of new forms of expression and creators, an essential hallmark of modern and postmodern art, particularly in the visual arts.

The arts today exhibit a degree of fluidity, openness to new possibilities, and inclusiveness that is historically unprecedented. The barriers between high and low art, art and politics, art and religious rite, art and emotional expression, art and therapy, art and life itself have been signficantly breached. Led by a changing body of practitioners, art can be intended or unintended, made by professionals or non-professionals (Rosenberg 1964).

Genres we now accept unquestionably as art were once not part of the mainstream. Photographs, prints, lithographs, modern dance and jazz once existed on the outskirts of what was accepted as art. Craft, ethnic dance, rap, new age music, video art, kinetic art, happenings, site specific performances are recent entrants into the artistic fold. Tattoo art and computer art are waiting in the wings.

We have grown accustomed to crossovers in the arts – the opera singer, Barbara Cook, who records Disney favorites, or trumpet virtuoso, Wynton Marsalis, who moves with ease between jazz and Bach. Hybrid arts, a cross between an art form and a previously unrelated domain, such as computer art, have come into vogue. Once distinctive types within an art form have become melded into artistic mutants. Jazz, once a variety of rhythm and blues, gospel, and dance accompaniment, has evolved into a distinct musical genre. The mixing of diverse arts with other cultural forms into a unique expression stands as the creolization of the arts. Zingaro, for example, is a classical dressage troupe that unites horsemanship, circus acrobatics, ethnic music, and dance into an uncommon theatricality.

Late twentieth century art has incarnated a continuing process of absorbing, sampling, appropriating and amalgamating new and unusual forms. When piles of bricks are displayed in museums, when music is composed for performance under water, the boundaries between genres have become so fluid that once conventional understandings of art are suspended or nullified. When the periphery becomes valorized beyond all expectations, how can we speak about an aesthetic center?

Today, we would be hard pressed to identify a center as distinct from a periphery. While we could trace the biographies of successful artistic practitioners, identify social forces that contribute to artistic recognition, and situate strategically placed art-world actors empowered in the social construction of what is art/non art, the center would still remain elusive.

What then are the historical roots of this phenomenon?

The aesthetic canon

Outsider art implies an insider art. Insider art implies a canon around which artistic products and their makers are evaluated, along with a body of work that represents those standards.

In the western European tradition, the domain of fine art came to be conceived of as an elevated autonomous sphere, structured with a hierarchical ranking of artistic genres and techniques. While other civilizations have glorified the arts, none has produced such a distinctive and lofty aesthetic realm (Alsop 1982; Geertz 1983: 95–98). Indeed, without such a social construction, there would be no outsider art. It can only arise where art itself is constructed with clearly delineated boundaries, in which an aesthetic canon mandates the modalities and outcome of creation. A sociology of outsider art starts from this premise.

The historical and institutional roots of this unique conception and practice hark back to the rise of the French Academic system and its valorization of the fine arts. This institutional structure became the prototype of the idea of an artistic core (Boime 1971).

Although its underlying ideas originated with the decentralized, powerful cities and families of Renaissance Italy, the Academic system attained its greatest importance in France. Its development started through the efforts of guild and independent painters and carvers to improve their standing by association with monarchical patronage, at a moment coinciding with the centralizing agenda of the absolutist French kings. By the eighteenth century, the stature of Academic art had come to be on a par with the intellectual, liberal arts, rather than the lesser, artisanal, craft guilds (Heinich 1993).

The Academy flourished over the better part of the nineteenth century, maintaining a monopoly over the practice of art. It fostered a topical hierarchy dominated by history painting, inspired by classical motifs, portraits and scenic works depicting the achievements of monarchs and nobles, while relegating landscape and genre painting, often of domestic scenes, to lesser stature. It mandated correct painting techniques. And it guided and sustained substantial professional careers for most of those who came into its fold.[1]

However, in the course of creating a defined and dominant aesthetic center, the Academy excluded alternative expressions and creators. While space for experimentation existed, straying too far from the established canon meant consignment to relative oblivion and financial insecurity (Corvisier 1978; Hauser 1951; Kempers 1992). Regardless, many painters became disenchanted with the Academy's rigidity and narrowness, perceiving it as fossilized in style, cherishing predictable art, and unresponsive to innovation and experimentation. Almost by definition, the academic structure made it likely that a class of refusés would emerge.

In fact, the nineteenth century was replete with outsiders: the Barbizon painters with their revalorization of the landscape genre, Courbet's Realism, the Impressionists' *plein air* painting, color experiments by Neoimpressionists, Van Gogh's expressionism, Gauguin's exoticism, Cézanne's structuralism, Cubism, Fauvism, and so on. Initially these innovators brought their works to the official salon. Some were accepted. When rejected, these painters found alternative means of support, aligning themselves with independent dealers, writers/critics, and newly moneyed patrons (Graña 1964; White and White 1965).

Gradually a pattern became established: creative newcomers produced challenging visions that found their support outside the traditional Academic practice (Zolberg 1990: 59–61). By the end of the nineteenth century, entry into the Academy stopped being the goal of avant-garde artists, for whom the institution had become all but irrelevant.

Outsider/insider art in the postmodern condition

Modernism undermined not only the Academic monopoly over career and aesthetics, both in France and in the countries where similar institutions had been established, but inadvertently it threw into question the presumption of legitimacy for *any* absolutist aesthetic and agreed-upon standard as to what constitutes art. The very notion of an official canon became obsolete.

Whatever else it was, modernism is the history of the dismantling of a guiding canon and a governing center. It is the history of the boundaries of art/non art being contested and re-contested, of recurring waves of outsiders struggling to become insiders.

It is understandable in this light that the New York School of Abstract Expressionists and their supporters such as Clement Greenberg made a last stab at retaining a rarified, autonomous sphere for the fine arts. They took the position that the abstractionist trend represented the inevitable, unfolding unidirectionality of modern art (Rose 1967: 235). This modernist bent – an exclusionary stance pitted against inclusivist tendencies – prevailed as an unofficial canon. It denigrated most figurative painting, narrative, regional or ethnic content and styles. But the 1960s confronted abstractionism with a challenge that Andreas Huyssen sees as the onset of postmodernism.

For Huyssen, the 1960s represent the Great Divide and the beginning of postmodernism – the elimination of distinctions and the demise of the autonomous sphere of fine art (Huyssen 1986: viii). The importation of technological inventions such as print, color lithography, and photography initiated the breakdown of the barrier between fine and commercial art. With the inclusion of everyday subject-matter and commercial techniques into easel painting, the notion of a separate fine art sphere was fatally fractured (Cherbo, this volume). Despite all efforts made by the detractors of postmodernism, primarily the older vanguard artists and their cohorts, the boundaries between fine and other arts became increasingly fuzzy (Gans 1992: viii). Anything could potentially be art.

Commentators on the modern and post-modern condition note broad socio-cultural patterns and sensibilities wherein universal, fixed categories and hierarchical renderings inherited from the Enlightenment are being continually breached and reordered. The postmodern turn is characterized by a loss of certainty, a unifying center, agreed-upon standards of cultural excellence, morality, and types of knowledge. In its place are hybrid forms, an eclectic mixing of codes, validity granted to a wide range of outsider activities and mentalities, shifting power centers, and greater tolerance of ambiguity (Huyssen 1986; Seidman 1994). Not surprisingly the arts reflect this condition.

Given this new frontier, how do we conceive of outsider/insider art? What do we mean by legitimacy, recognition, and who are the gatekeepers of success? Reality has intruded on some of our governing concepts: they are ready to be revisited.

Toward a sociology of outsider art

Artistic recognition does exist, but it is no longer an all or nothing affair, identifiable and situated in a single institution such as the Academy. Rather, it inhabits the domain of a plurality of gatekeepers – organizations, influential individuals, publications, and media, popular and commercial or elite and scholarly. These gatekeepers variously have an impact at local, national or international levels. Insider/outsider distinctions have become multilayered, multidimensional, and must be conceptualized as matters of degree rather than of kind. Recognition, for instance, may be founded on the fame and glamor of stardom, sales based on commercial success, or critical or scholarly appreciation. Furthermore, because recognition is fluid, the stature and reception of any art work, artist, or movement are likely to change.

Artistic forms and makers achieve and lose varying degrees of repute over time (Lang and Lang 1990). Large-scale history paintings that once graced the walls of mansions and official buildings during the peak years of the French Academy may now be relegated to lesser spots in museums or their storage areas; they may also be revived.[2] Photography, once considered an artistic stepchild, now commands a significant following, financial success, a secondary auction market, and a separate department in all major museums. Rock music is a commercially successful, internationally renowned, historically recognized movement, as witnessed by the founding of the Rock Music Hall of Fame. But it is still considered no more than a popular form of entertainment by musicologists. At its inception Pop Art garnered popular, financial and media recognition, but repute among critics, historians, and museums came later (Cherbo, this volume). Recognition today can only be understood as multilayered and multidimensional.

Depending upon their theoretical concerns, sociologists have interpreted the arts from divergent, sometimes conflicting, standpoints. Despite their differing assumptions, frameworks, levels of analysis, and political orientations, almost all see art as a social construction. Social scientists do not focus primarily on the work of art itself, leaving that to humanistic and aesthetic scholarship.[3] The individual artist, artistic product, and art worlds are studied not for their own sake, but as embodiments of society, created and recreated over time, rather than fixed and unproblematic. The arts are treated as part of the social fabric of the worlds in which they are embedded (Becker 1982). In that sense the arts are integrally intertwined with the production and reception of value (Bourdieu 1995; Hauser 1951).

Artistic change may be compared to the processes of transformation discerned by sociologists of science. Like sociologists of the arts, they do not conceive of science as a closed sphere, in which change takes place through internalist processes alone. Sociologists see cultural products in the contexts of their communities of production, networks of influence (in which ideas are transmitted over successive cohorts), mechanisms of dissemination, reward, and reception (Crane 1976: 57–72). The role that outsiders play may be as important in bringing about change as is that of established participants (Merton 1972; Szántó, this volume). Thus, while Thomas Kuhn saw change as the process of exhaustion of a prevalent paradigm when confronted with anomalies (Kuhn 1970), Michael Mulkay emphasized the importation of ideas from other scientific domains by risk-taking, creative outsiders (Mulkay 1972).

Although the contesting of artistic boundaries that so vividly marks contemporary aesthetics is applicable to all the arts, it is beyond the scope of this volume to generalize about the arts as a whole. Because each art form has its own unique characteristics, history and organization, each warrants independent attention (Zolberg 1990: 171). Furthermore, within each art form differences can be dramatic. Consider the many forms of music that permeate our present, each distinctive, with its own audiences, creative centers, distribution networks, commercial and noncommercial status. This also applies internationally, where governmental bodies and laws can impinge upon artistic products. Yet, for all the arts in the postmodern era the transgression and maintenance of artistic boundaries coexist in a state of chronic tension.

This collection addresses cases and issues surrounding contemporary artistic outsiderness and shifts in genre boundaries. Our contributors are sociologists, art historians, critics, policy analysts. One is a creative artist. Some wear more than one hat. None takes for granted the established categories of art. All are acutely aware of the flux and flow of artistic genres, the continual construction of new artistic expressions, and the role of creators, gatekeepers, audiences, and other influences in the making and unmaking of artists, art, and art worlds. Each writer contributes to an enlarged understanding of the fluidity of artistic taste, practice and stylistic succession in the last century. Their interests range from the works of classic outsiders – the insane, the primitive, the naïves – through forms and genres that transgress the boundaries between art and therapy, social welfare, ethnicity, the underworld, gender empowerment, and public reception as part of the art work itself. By this exploration, we hope to increase sensitivity to, and understanding of, the factors and forces that affect the permeability of artistic taste and genres. Outsider art is the cultural entity in which these processes are most clearly seen and delineated.

Notes

1 Albert Boime (1970) provides a detailed analysis of the French institution. On music in Paris, which followed a different path, see Elaine Brody (1987).
2 For example, the prominence given to dusty Academic works at the Musée d'Orsay in Paris fosters ongoing dispute.
3 See, for example, Pierre Bourdieu's analysis of Baudelaire and Flaubert (Bourdieu1995: 40–54), and how Tia DeNora and Nathalie Heinich examine two important artists of the nineteenth century, Beethoven (DeNora 1995) and Van Gogh (Heinich 1996).

References

Alsop, Joseph 1982, *The Rare Art Traditions: The History of Art Collecting and Its Linked Phenomena Wherever They Have Appeared*, New York: Harper and Row.
Becker, Howard S. 1982, *Art Worlds*, University of California Press.
Boime, Albert 1971, *The Academy and French Painting in the 19th Century* (translated by Richard Nice), London: Phaidon Press.
Bourdieu, Pierre 1984, *Distinction: A Social Critique of the Judgement of Taste,* Cambridge, MA: Harvard University Press.
1995, *The Rules of Art: Genesis and Structure of the Literary Field* (translated by Susan Emanuel), Stanford University Press.
Brody, Elaine 1987, *Paris: The Musical Kaleidoscope, 1870–1925*, New York: George Braziller.
Corvisier, André 1978, *Arts et sociétés dans l'Europe du XVIII° Siècle*, Paris: Presses Universitaires de France.
Crane, Diana 1976, "Reward Systems in Art, Science, and Religion," *The Production of Culture*, ed. R. A. Peterson, Sage Publications, 57–72.
DeNora, Tia 1995, *Beethoven and the Construction of Genius: Musical Politics in Vienna, 1792–1803*, University of California Press.
Gans, Herbert J.1992, Preface to *Cultivating Differences: Symbolic Boundaries and the Making of Inequality*, ed. Michèle Lamont and Marcel Fournier, University of Chicago Press, vii-xv.
Geertz, Clifford 1983, "Art as a Cultural System," *Local Knowledge: Essays in Interpretive Anthropology*, New York: Basic Books, 94–120.
Goldwater, Robert 1986, *Primitivism in Modern Art* (enlarged edition), Cambridge, MA: The Belknap Press of Harvard University Press [originally 1938].
Graña, César 1964, *Bohemian and Bourgeois: French Society and the French Man of Letters in the 19th Century*, New York: Basic Books.
Hall, Michael D. and Metcalf, Eugene W., Jr., eds., 1994, *The Artist as Outsider: Creativity and the Boundaries of Culture*, Washington, DC: Smithsonian Institution Press.

Hauser, Arnold 1951, *The Social History of Art* (four vols), New York: Alfred A. Knopf.
Heinich, Nathalie 1993, *Du peintre à l'artiste: Artisans et Académiciens à l'âge classique*, Paris: Editions de Minuit.
1996, *The Glory of Van Gogh: An Anthropology of Admiration* (translated by Paul Leduc Browne), Princeton University Press.
Huyssen, Andreas 1986, *After the Great Divide: Modernism, Mass Culture, Postmodernism*, Bloomington: Indiana University Press.
Kempers, Bram 1992, *Painting, Power, and Patronage: The Rise of the Professional Artist in the Italian Renaissance* (translated by B. Jackson), London: Allen Lane/Penguin Press.
Kuhn, Thomas 1970, *The Structure of Scientific Revolutions*, University of Chicago Press.
Lang, Gladys Engel and Lang, Kurt 1990, *Etched in Memory: The Building and Survival of Artistic Reputation*, Chapel Hill: University of North Carolina Press.
Merton, Robert K. 1972, "Insiders and Outsiders: A Chapter in the Sociology of Knowledge," *American Journal of Sociology,* 78 (July): 9–47.
Mulkay, Michael J. 1972, *The Social Process of Innovation: A Study in the Sociology of Science*, London: Macmillan.
Rose, Barbara 1967, *American Art Since 1900: A Critical History*, New York: Praeger.
Rosenberg, Harold 1964, *The Anxious Object: Art Today and Its Audience*, New York: Horizon Press.
Seidman, Steven 1994, *The Postmodern Turn, New Perspectives on Social Theory*, Cambridge University Press.
Toennies, Ferdinand 1963, *Community and Society*, New York: Harper & Row.
White, Harrison C. and White, Cynthia 1965, *Canvases and Careers: Institutional Change in the French Painting World*, New York: John Wiley.
Zolberg, Vera L. 1990, *Constructing a Sociology of the Arts*, Cambridge University Press.

PART I

Traditional outsiders

Here we address traditional outsiders, creators first identified as "outsider artists" – nineteenth-century asylum inmates, African "primitives" and contemporary naïves, unschooled artists working outside the artistic mainstream.

Anne Bowler shows how the rationales, images, and visual creativity of asylum artists were appropriated by nineteenth- and twentieth-century avant-gardists in reconstituting their artistic practice and goals. In this way they transformed a therapeutic into an aesthetic activity. She notes that in the light of deinstitutionalization and drug therapies, "true" mentally ill art may become an artifact or genre of the past.

Steven Dubin focuses on the concept of marginality in sociology and the art world with an eye to its psychological and social functions. He views naïves as representing the extreme triumph of untrained personal vision. As such they are a source of sympathetic identification for young aspiring artists, the majority of whom will not become successful in an overcrowded art market. Endorsement of select naïves shows a willingness to admit alternative visions, and channels off some of the steam of those left outside the traditional reward system. Dubin presents biographical and career data on three recognized contemporary outsider artists to exemplify this process.

In the next chapter Vera Zolberg analyzes the processes by which objects made by "primitive" peoples for ancestral or utilitarian purposes, and relegated to institutions lacking the prestige of art museums, came to be transformed into works of purely aesthetic value. After tracing key moments in their trajectory, she relates the process to the changing outsider status of contemporary African American artists. As new opportunities open up to them, they find themselves faced with the dilemma of identifying with universal aesthetic themes, as opposed to embracing their African heritage.

1

Asylum art: the social construction of an aesthetic category

Anne E. Bowler

> But is it not essential that in a movement of amused indulgence, a personage of unreason is allowed back into daylight at the very moment he was believed to be most profoundly hidden in the space of confinement? . . . As if, at the moment of its triumph, reason revived and permitted to drift on the margins of order a character whose mask it had fashioned in derision – a sort of double in which it both recognized and revoked itself.
>
> Foucault (1973: 201–2)

Outsider art is a somewhat broad term applied to the artistic products of a variety of self-taught artists, including naïves, visionaries, patients in mental hospitals and, more recently, prisoners. While a more precise definition remains the subject of some debate, use of the term is generally reserved for the work of artists with little or no formal artistic training, in particular, socially marginal individuals who, for various reasons and without prior instruction, begin to paint, sculpt or draw; artists thus presumed to be both "outside" the influence of the established art world and "outside" mainstream society.[1] This chapter is constructed as a critical history of one category of outsider art, the art of the asylum patient or, as it is more widely termed, the art of the insane.[2]

Recent developments in the reception of the art of the insane suggest the timeliness of this project. Exhibition tours of the Prinzhorn Collection of the Art of the Mentally Ill in Europe in 1980–81 and, for the first time, the United States in 1984–85, merited extensive coverage by art critics in both specialized journals and the popular press.[3] Assembled by the psychiatrist and art historian Hans Prinzhorn at the Heidelberg Psychiatric Clinic in the early 1920s, the collection has been until now something of an obscure footnote in the development of modern art, most noteworthy for its influence on established artists ranging from the Expressionists Paul Klee and Alfred Kubin to the Surrealist artists André Breton and Max Ernst.

The question of influence assumed a more explicit role as the organizing principle of a 1992 exhibition tour sponsored by the Los Angeles County Museum of Art. "Parallel Visions" juxtaposed the work of some thirty-four outsider artists, approximately one-half with a history of psychiatric incarceration (including eight artists from the Prinzhorn Collection), with the work of forty professional artists influenced by outsider art. Like the Prinzhorn Collection exhibition, "Parallel Visions" was the subject of reviews in forums ranging from *Art in America* to *The New York Times*.[4] Additionally, both exhibitions were accompanied by elegant exhibition catalogs featuring essays by recognized experts in outsider art, alongside reproductions of works, thus suggesting an established area of specialization.

Taken together, the exhibition tours of the Prinzhorn Collection and "Parallel Visions" may constitute a signal event in the reception of works traditionally the purview of the medical expert, occasional devotee, or private collector. Recent interest in the art of the insane belongs to the more general surge of interest in outsider art that surfaced in the 1980s and shows little sign of abatement at present. Yet even within this more general trend, the asylum artist occupies a position of considerable significance. Amidst the proliferation of gallery exhibitions of outsider art, the one-man exhibition of Swiss artist Adolf Wölfli in 1988–89, a critically acclaimed "outsider genius" who produced all of his work as an inmate in a Bern psychiatric clinic, is important as a departure from the standard presentation of asylum artists (and outsider artists more generally) in anonymous groups.[5] Asylum artists like Wölfli, Martin Ramírez, and Johann Hauser occupy prominent positions in the canon of outsider "masters" (elsewhere referred to as outsider "geniuses" and "superstars") that has emerged (Smith 1992; Wells 1992: A1). Scholarly interest has produced the first comprehensive history of asylum art, *The Discovery of the Art of the Insane*, by art historian John M. MacGregor.

Indications abound that the art of the insane has attained a firm, recognized niche in the art market. Dealers report sharp rises in sales. While prices for asylum art generally remain well below that of established, conventional artists, collectors are now paying six-figure prices for works by artists whose commercial viability twenty years ago remained uncertain (DeCarlo and Dintenfass 1992: 36; Wells 1992). As the *Wall Street Journal* reported, the art of the insane has emerged as a "major art trend of the 1990s" (Wells 1992: A1).

This chapter presents a sociological analysis of the social construction of the "art of the insane." The history of this process is mapped through the intersection of a set of shifting discourses and practices in the nineteenth and early twentieth centuries marked by changing definitions of insanity in the context of the emerging sciences of psychopathology; the rejection of traditional systems of representation in the theory and practice of modern art; and the rise of a new institutional framework for the production, distribution and reception of art in response to the development of a commercial, capitalist market. In the last section of the chapter, the critical implications of this history for the contemporary reception of the art of the insane are assessed.

The "mad artist" of the nineteenth century

The social construction of the art of the insane is the product of a constellation of factors which crystallized in the early twentieth century. It was in this period that the principal collections of asylum art were amassed, the first exhibitions of the art of the insane were organized, and the first major studies of patient art were published. This interest was not limited to medical circles. Beginning around 1912, a growing number of artists perceived in the art of the insane a new model of creativity untainted by established aesthetic conventions, conventions which they sought to transform, revolutionize, or reject. It was during this period that the creative products of the insane began to be defined as art.

Interest in the artistic activity of the insane predates the twentieth century. Medico-scientific attention to the artistic production of the insane in the early nineteenth century arose with the emergence of the sciences of psychopathology and the modern asylum. In 1801 French asylum reformer Philippe Pinel made passing reference to the artistic activity of patients, individuals who had displayed artistic ability prior to the onset of illness. Artistic activity by the asylum patient signified for Pinel a vestigial link to sanity, an insight which subsequently led the famous reformer to a nascent recognition of the potential therapeutic value of art. In an influential textbook published in 1812, the American physician Benjamin Rush, in contrast, noted the sudden appearance of artistic activity in patients with no prior history of involvement in the arts, a matter that has since become a major theme in writings on the art of the insane (Gilman 1985: 220; MacGregor 1989: 26–32).

Broadly speaking, early nineteenth-century interest in the question of insanity and creativity owes much to the cultural influence of Romanticism. For the Romantic poet, insanity (as well as extra-normal states of consciousness like the hallucination or nightmare) stood as a source of creative vision unconstrained by social or artistic convention. The French poet Lamartine, for example, wrote of "the mental illness called genius" (quoted in MacGregor 1989: 77). Charles Lamb, despite his later antipathy toward the idea of the "mad genius," stated in a letter to Coleridge in 1796, "I look back upon madness at times with a gloomy kind of envy. For while it lasted I had many hours of pure happiness. Dream not, Coleridge, of having tasted all the grandeur and wildness of Fancy, till you have gone mad."[6]

The connection between insanity and creative genius was neither specific to Romanticism nor new to the nineteenth century. Rather, it is an idea which can be traced back to Plato and Aristotle, was revitalized in the Renaissance, and thematized again in the mid-eighteenth century by Diderot (Gilman 1985: 219–20; Gisbourne 1992: 231; MacGregor 1989: 72). Nevertheless, for both Classical and Renaissance thinkers, the association of genius with melancholia, "pazzia," or madness did not necessarily denote insanity in the modern, clinical sense of the term. As sociologist George Becker (1978: 24) notes, a distinction was drawn "between the sane melancholics capable of rare accomplishments and those condemned to insanity." Similarly, "assessments of scholars and artists in terms of 'pazzia' were generally not intended to convey the notion of insanity. 'Pazzia' actually had numerous shades of meaning ranging from insanity to strangeness and eccentricity."

The Romantic contribution to the tradition linking genius and madness was first, to narrow the definition of genius to artistic genius; second, to associate artistic genius and madness more closely through giving the imagination greater significance than reason; and finally, to extend this reconfiguration into the general cultural vocabulary through the trope of the isolated, misunderstood artist. "Unlike the pre-Romantic analysis where genius for the arts and genius for science were assessed as being similarly constituted," Becker (1978: 26) writes, "Romantic thought dissociated the two, elevating the artist, and particularly the poet, to a position of preeminence." The effect of this redefinition, in which the artist appears as the ultimate exemplar of genius, is to strengthen the association of genius with madness. For whereas the Enlightenment view of genius stressed the importance of imagination and creativity tempered or balanced by judgment, Romantic poets and philosophers sought to free the imagination from reason as the path to unbridled aesthetic creativity. As the Schlegel brothers declared, "The beginning of all poetry is to suspend the course and the laws of rationally thinking reason . . . The free will of the poet submits to no law" (quoted in Becker 1978: 27).

As portraits of the insane by painters such as Fuseli, Goya, and Géricault demonstrate, the "madman" served as an object of fascination in Romantic thought as well (Gilman 1982). Particularly noteworthy was the figure of the "mad artist." Consider, for example, Delacroix's famous portrait of the poet Tasso, *Tasso in the Madhouse* (1839) – a popular subject for Romantic painters, poets and dramatists alike (Honour 1979: 264–67). But this metaphorical identification of the artist with the madman found its fullest development in the literary glorification of the mad artist embodied in the Romantic heroes of such writers as Byron, Novalis, and E. T. A. Hoffman. The artist, cut off from the prosaic character of everyday life, seeks transcendence in the realm of the aesthetic. Like the madman, the artist is an "outsider," exiled or otherwise estranged from society.

As an aesthetic philosophy, Romanticism simultaneously presupposes and further cultivates a sharp opposition between art and social life. Historically, this opposition arises out of the decline by the late eighteenth century of traditional systems of artistic patronage and the rise of the modern capitalist market. In practice, as Wolff (1981: 11) observes, this shift meant the "separation of the artist from any clear social group or class and from any secure form of patronage, as the older system of patronage was overtaken by the dealer-critic system, which left the artist in a precarious position in the market." In this context Romantic themes of alienation, isolation, and the retreat to the subjective world of the imagination can be read, in part, as a reaction to specific historical changes in the social and economic conditions of artistic production and reception. But the "achievement" of Romanticism was ultimately to de-historicize the relationship between alienation and creativity, to construct isolation as the essential condition from which all great art is produced and to "romanticize" marginality as the mark of the authentic artist.

If Romanticism plays a significant role in the link drawn between insanity and creativity, it is nevertheless limited. The focus of the Romantic artist is on the symbol of the madman and the condition of insanity, rather than the artistic product of the asylum patient. Moreover, many Romantics remained ambivalent toward the purported link between insanity and artistic genius (Becker 1978; Cubbs 1994; Furst 1979, 1969; MacGregor 1989). In any case, irrationality is heralded as a link to creative insight and renewal but nowhere is it put forth as a set of systematic aesthetic principles, as it appears in the writings of later nineteenth-century figures like Rimbaud or Alfred Jarry, or twentieth-century avant-garde movements like Dada or Surrealism. As

MacGregor (1989: 76) observes, "The Romantic view of madness was seldom based on any real experience of the insane. It was a fantasy, a dream of madness as a treasure trove of the imagination free of reason and constraint."

Nevertheless, it is the nineteenth century, specifically the second half of the century, which remains distinct as the period during which the trope of the "mad genius" is elevated to the status of an ontological truth through the emerging sciences of psychopathology. In 1864, criminologist and psychiatrist Cesare Lombroso published the first of what would become an enormously influential set of arguments linking genius (and artistic inclinations more generally) with insanity (Becker 1978: 28–29, 38–39; Gilman 1985: 221–22; MacGregor 1989: 93–102). By 1882, the year his (in)famous volume *Genio e follia* appeared in its fourth edition, the topic had blossomed into a major international debate (Becker 1978: 35–53). The vast majority endorsed the link between madness and genius, including German physician Max Nordau, whose widely read volume, *Entartung*, published in 1892, has been cited as an important source for the later National Socialist (Nazi) theory of degeneracy and its defamation of avant-garde art in particular (Barron 1991: 11–12; Mosse 1991: 26).[7]

Early nineteenth-century interest in the "mad artist" focused on either the role of insanity in the creative process or the Romantic symbol of the "madman" as tragic hero and social outsider. The legacy of the "mad genius" debate in the later nineteenth century is to shift focus to the artistic products of the insane, as illustrative evidence of their illness or as a diagnostic tool through which the nature of insanity might be revealed. French psychiatrist Paul-Max Simon, for example, has been credited by MacGregor (1989: 103, 113) as being the first psychiatrist to undertake a serious study of the art of the insane, *L'imagination dans la folie* published in 1876, as well as one of the first psychiatrists to have amassed a large collection of drawings and paintings by asylum patients. Unlike Lombroso, Simon did not assume the existence of a link between creativity and insanity. The purpose of his study was diagnostic, concerned with the construction of a classificatory schema of formal qualities characteristic of patient art corresponding to psychiatric categories of diagnosis. Lombroso, whose published writings on the art of the insane began to appear in 1880, was similarly nosological in orientation.[8] In Foucauldian terms, the diagnostic classification of the art of asylum patients during this period is part of a containment process in which insanity is "produced" as a scientifically isolatable phenomenon whose absolute distance from normality functions, in part, to legitimate medico-scientific rationality as the guardian of social order. The potential status of the creative products of asylum patients as art was inherently compromised by their proximity to mental disease.

Prinzhorn and the discovery of the art of the insane

As in the case of the first studies of patient art which appeared in the later nineteenth century, medicine and psychiatry were the institutional vehicle for the "discovery" of the art of the insane in the early twentieth century. For it is in this period that we find publications by psychiatrists which not only reproduced patients' works but analyzed them in artistic as well as clinical terms. By all accounts, the most influential remains

Bildnerei der Geisteskranken (*Artistry of the Mentally Ill*) by German psychiatrist Hans Prinzhorn, first published in 1922. The study was based on an analysis of works amassed at the Heidelberg Psychiatric Clinic where Prinzhorn assumed a staff position in 1919 and where the study of psychotic art had already begun under the supervision of Clinic director, Karl Wilmanns (Jadi 1984: 2; von Baeyer 1972: v). Between 1919 and late 1921, when Prinzhorn left Heidelberg, the collection had been expanded to some five thousand drawings, paintings, and sculptures executed by approximately 450 patients, 70 percent of whom had been diagnosed as schizophrenic. With few exceptions, the majority had no artistic training or history of artistic activity prior to the onset of illness.[9]

Several factors distinguished *Artistry of the Mentally Ill* and its author from previous studies of patient art. A degree in art history from the University of Vienna preceded Prinzhorn's turn to the study of medicine and psychiatry. Throughout the volume, he speaks with authority on a wide variety of art, including the work of artists of his own day, and draws on scholarship in fields ranging from psychiatry and art history to philosophy. Three influences are most notable: the recently developed theory of schizophrenia from Swiss psychiatrist Eugen Bleuler; a theory of the unconscious roots of expression derived from psychologist and philosopher Ludwig Klages; and a phenomenological theory of configuration advanced by art historian and critic Conrad Fiedler (Foy 1972: xi-xii). Finally, an introductory statement that "[m]ost of the reports published to date about the works of the insane were intended only for psychiatrists," suggests that Prinzhorn sought for his study a broader audience beyond medical circles (1972: 1).

The first portion of the book is devoted to the construction of what might be characterized as a general psychology of art, a theory of a universal, innate expressive urge that satisfies itself in configuration. Prinzhorn identifies six basic "drives" or urges that govern the character of pictorial configurations: an expressive urge, the urge to play, an ornamental urge, an ordering tendency, a tendency to imitate, and the need for symbols (1972: 11–28). By far the bulk of the book is concerned with a detailed analysis of ten "schizophrenic masters" chosen from the Collection (1972: 7). Prinzhorn's thesis is that these works are best understood or grasped through a formalist theory of configuration rather than diagnostic categories. Works are analyzed in terms of the degree to which they deviate from, or exhibit unorthodox traits relative to, configurative tendencies. A pencil drawing, for example, composed of intricately rendered shapes repeated across the page until no space has been left undecorated is categorized in terms of a preponderance of the playful urge in combination with an ornamental urge and ordering tendency (1972: 44–47).

Although Prinzhorn avoided using the word "art" (*Kunst*), adopting the more neutral term *Bildnerei* or "image-making," he appears, at least in part, to have done so strategically: "It sets up a distinction between one class of created objects and another very similar one which is dismissed as 'nonart'" (1972: 1). In the concluding pages of his study he declared, "The differentiation of our pictures from those of the fine arts is possible today only because of obsolete dogmatism. Otherwise there are no demarcation lines" (1972: 271). This debate over terminology and its larger implications shed light on Prinzhorn's descriptions of specific images from the collection and the comparisons he makes with established works of art. The fact that the volume contained no fewer than 187 reproductions, including 20 plates, is noteworthy by itself. But it is Prinzhorn's identification of ten "masters" that remains most significant. For each, he combined biographical and clinical information with detailed descriptions of specific works. In a passage devoted to the sculpture of Carl Genzel (or "Karl Brendel," the pseudonym Prinzhorn used), the reader is informed of the "compelling execution" of a carving and the "feeling of mystery" it evokes among viewers. "[W]e are touched by a breath of that simplicity which stills us," Prinzhorn writes, "whenever we meet it, whether in the eyes of an animal, a child, or in the works of primitives and earlier cultures" (1972: 108).

Even more striking is the comparison Prinzhorn draws between Genzel's carving and *Der Blaue Reiter* artist Franz Marc:

> His animal relief contains an element of the emotion usually called the new animal myth, which we associate with Franz Marc . . . His [Genzel's] work maintains in its formal aspects a sovereign plastic balance of masses, a touching composition, a sure and convincing use of his unique relief technique without slipping into vulgar realism. *It has qualities, in short, which one can describe only by using the language of art.* (1972: 108; emphasis added)

The comparison of Genzel with a representative of what was considered in certain artistic and intellectual circles to be the most advanced art of the day – a comparison repeated throughout the book with different artists, schizophrenic and established – was not incidental. As Inge Jadi, current curator of the Collection confirms, materials chosen for inclusion were preselected in a very specific way. In a letter soliciting contributions from major psychiatric institutions in Germany, Austria and Switzerland, Prinzhorn requested above all "drawings, paintings and sculptures by the mentally ill that do not merely reproduce prototypes or remembrances from times when they were healthy, but rather are the expression of personal experience during illness." In a particularly telling line he asks potential donors to look for "outstanding isolated achievements" (quoted in Jadi 1984: 2). Additionally, Prinzhorn is said to have withheld or suppressed weaker images, "emphasizing through size or color those images he knew would be unforgettable" (MacGregor 1989: 199). As Gilman observes,

> The fascinating nature of [the] material is the result not only of the psychopathology of the patients but also of the preselection by the institutions that supplied it. The Heidelberg project was interested in the insane as artist, with all of the ideological implications which that term had for the educated bourgeoisie. (1985: 231)

As the example of Genzel indicates, Prinzhorn's field of comparison included primitive as well as contemporary art. Carved figures from West Africa, for example, were reproduced in order to illustrate detailed points of similarity with works by Genzel such as those shown in Figure 2 (Prinzhorn 1972: 250–54).

This comparison is significant in the context of a period notable for the "discovery" of primitive art by Western artists and intellectuals or, more precisely, its movement from the category of "scientific (cultural) artifacts" to "(aesthetic) works of art" (Clifford 1988: 222). Expressionist artists' involvement with primitive art is well known

Figure 1. Carl Genzel, *The Gentle Animal* (wood). Reproduced in Hans Prinzhorn, *Artistry of the Mentally Ill*, 1972 (1922). Reproduced here with the kind permission of Springer-Verlag.

Figure 2. Carl Genzel, *Three Head-and-Feet Figurines*, front view (wood). Reproduced in Hans Prinzhorn, *Artistry of the Mentally Ill*, 1972 (1922). Reproduced here with the kind permission of Springer-Verlag.

and was certainly known to Prinzhorn. At the same time, he clearly was aware of the potential hazards of a comparative form of analysis, stating:

The conclusion that a painter is mentally ill because he paints like a given mental patient is no more intelligent than another; *viz.*, that Pechstein and Heckel are Africans from the Camerouns because they produce wooden figurines like those by Africans from the Camerouns. (1972: 271)

It is interesting then that Prinzhorn concludes on a distinctly Romantic note, suggesting an affinity between the "schizophrenic outlook and our age," on the one hand, and on the other, the contemporary artist's renunciation of society in favor of "a decisive turn inward upon the self" (1972: 270–71). The "schizophrenic outlook" of the present, he seems to imply, may require a "schizophrenic art."

Artistry of the Mentally Ill was neither the first nor the only publication to discuss the artistic products of the insane in artistic terms. In 1921, one year before the appearance of Prinzhorn's study, psychiatrist Walter Morgenthaler published a monograph on Waldau Asylum patient Adolf Wölfli. Like Prinzhorn, Morgenthaler (1992) combined biographical history with a detailed description of works. By many accounts, the center of interest in the art of the insane at the turn of the century lay in France, revolving around the collection of patient art amassed by French alienist Auguste Marie. Under the rubric of the "Mad Museum," Marie opened the collection to the public in 1905, an event which inspired commentary in the British press who compared it to a 1900 exhibition of patient art at the Bethlem Royal Hospital ("Bedlam") (MacGregor 1989: 166).[10] The lasting importance of the collection, however, remains its status as the source for studies of asylum art by Rogues de Fursac, Jean Vinchon, and Marcel Réja, this last being the pseudonym, when he wrote as an art critic, of psychiatrist Paul Meunier, whose *L'Art chez les fous* published in 1907 is considered to be the first book to analyze the art of the insane in artistic terms (MacGregor 1989: 172–73, 177, 182; Samaltanos 1984: 87–88).

Réja was interested in the art of the insane for the potential glimpse it offered into the "genesis of artistic activity," claiming that "it is in insanity, perhaps, that this genesis is to be recognized in its purest form" (quoted in MacGregor 1989: 174). Like Vinchon, whose volume *L'Art et la folie* appeared in 1924, Réja rejected a simple equation between the artistic products of the insane and the "fine arts." Nevertheless, each author offered a serious analysis of works and, especially important by many accounts, featured reproductions from the collection of Auguste Marie. The significance of both books is generally attributed to their influence on contemporary artists of the day. Samaltanos (1984: 85–89) emphasizes the impact of Marie's collection on the poet, critic, and impresario, Guillaume Apollinaire, and the critical role played by Réja and Vinchon as intermediaries in introducing the poet to the art of the insane. Apollinaire, already famous in Paris art circles for his passion for tribal art, naïve art and Douanier Rousseau, immediately identified the art of the insane as an important source of creative inspiration. In addition, according to Samaltanos (1984: 84–100), it is likely that Duchamp, Picabia, and Breton were all influenced by Marie's collection through their association with Apollinaire.

Although Morgenthaler's study of Wölfli is said to have "attracted enormous attention in European art circles" and the publication of Réja's *L'Art chez les fous* was "sufficiently well received to require a second printing within the year," neither provoked the kind of response occasioned by *Artistry of the Mentally Ill* (MacGregor 1989: 182, 208). By all accounts, the publication of Prinzhorn's book constituted a critical moment in the history of the art of the insane. James L. Foy (1972: xiv), in a preface to the 1972 edition, cites the "favorable and enthusiastic reviews of the book [which] appeared throughout Central Europe," including a largely positive review in Freud's journal *Imago*. But it is the reception within artistic circles that remains most noteworthy, the publication provoking enthusiastic responses from artists ranging from the Dadaist Sophie Tauber and Expressionist painter Paul Klee to the Surrealist artists André Breton, Hans Bellmer, Paul Eluard and Max Ernst.[11] Eluard characterized it as "the most beautiful book of images there is" (quoted in Cardinal 1992: 105). Cardinal (1979: 20) reports that Bellmer considered its publication "to be one of the major intellectual events of this century." And as Jean Dubuffet, the modern artist most closely associated with championing the art of the insane, later recalled, "Prinzhorn's book struck me very strongly when I was young. It showed me the way and was a liberating influence. I realized that all was permitted, all was possible. I wasn't the only one . . . The book had an enormous influence on modern art" (quoted in MacGregor 1989: 292).

The influence to which Dubuffet refers can be measured by the emergence in this period of a set of practices which attempt to integrate the art of the insane into the various institutional settings of established art: gallery exhibitions, collections by established artists, and publications on the art of the insane in specialized journals. Among the early gallery exhibitions, a 1928 show at the Paris Galerie Vavin was "said to have been attended by all of Montparnasse" (MacGregor 1989: 281). Breton, who drew explicit connections between insanity and creativity in the First Surrealist *Manifesto* (1924), is thought to have begun his collection of psychotic art during this period (Breton 1969; MacGregor 1989: 288–89). Similarly, Eluard included works by psychotic artists in his collection of contemporary and tribal art (Cardinal 1992: 102). The most prominent collection by far, of course, remains that of Jean Dubuffet, the Collection de l'Art Brut, a significant portion of which comprises the art of the insane.[12]

Among the earliest publications by an artist on asylum art, Expressionist painter Alfred Kubin's article "The Art of the Insane" which appeared in the German art journal *Das Kunstblatt*, recorded the impressions of his visit to the Heidelberg Collection in 1922. On a painting by one of Prinzhorn's "schizophrenic masters," Franz Pohl (the pseudonym Prinzhorn assigned Franz Karl Bühler), Kubin wrote:

> Unquestionably a gift of genius (in which) an exceptional power of invention in color and form finds expression. One senses an unmistakable development, an intensification of the ability to make use of the means of painterly expression, to the point of unheard of symphonies of color.
> (quoted in MacGregor 1989: 236)

Artists' declarations of psychotic art as a new model of creativity also served to bring the art of the insane into artistic discourse and practice. As early as 1912 Klee had

Figure 3. Franz Karl Bühler, *Self-portrait* (crayon). Reproduced in Hans Prinzhorn, *Artistry of the Mentally Ill*, 1972 (1922). Reproduced here with the kind permission of Springer-Verlag.

declared the importance of asylum art for the development of modern art, a conviction apparently strengthened by the images reproduced in *Artistry of the Mentally Ill* which he compared favorably with his own work (Klee 1964: 266; 1962: 183). For the Surrealists, as Cardinal (1992: 101) has observed, the psychotic artist constituted the "paradigm of the creative subject," a position Breton set out perhaps most systematically in the 1953 essay "L'Art des fous, la clé des champs," where he invoked several of Prinzhorn's "schizophrenic masters" as examples of the new model of art (1953: 225).

The degree to which these declarations resulted in instances of direct influence remains open to question and debate. Art historian James Smith Pierce (1978) has identified the wooden sculpture of Genzel (Figure 2) as a specific source of influence on a series of drawings and lithographs executed by Klee in 1922, the year Prinzhorn's book was first published. Similar conclusions have been drawn by Goldwater (1986: 193–95). Elsewhere Pierce (1977) suggests instances during the same period where Klee may have actually "borrowed pictorial ideas" from the pencil drawings of Heidelberg patient Heinrich Welz (the pseudonym of H. H. V. Wieser). Cardinal (1992: 100) cites the influence of the 1928 Galerie Vavin exhibition on the visual work of Breton. Werner Spies (1982) has documented striking similarities between the pencil drawing *Miraculous Shepherd* (Figure 4) by Heidelberg patient August Neter (the pseudonym of August Natterer) and Ernst's 1931 collage *Oedipe*, a work later chosen by the artist for the cover of a special issue of *Cahiers d'art* devoted to his work (Prokopoff 1984: 17).

Several sculptural works by Ernst have been similarly scrutinized for the influence of Genzel (Cardinal 1992: 104–05; MacGregor 1989: 280–81; Prokopoff 1984: 18). If, as Cardinal (1992: 114–15) has suggested, many experts remain wary of the search for direct points of influence, examples such as these indicate that it is a debate which remains unresolved.

In sum, the significance of Prinzhorn's publication and its reception is evinced by the changing discourse surrounding the artistic products of the insane – from the category of artefact to art – and the appropriation of the art of the insane by modernist artists as sources of inspiration and influence. Taken together, these changes constitute what I have termed the social construction of the art of the insane. This process did not simply evolve out of Romanticism and the emerging sciences of psychopathology in the nineteenth century. Rather, it is necessary to place it in the broader social context of three inter-related shifts: (i) an epistemological shift in the definition of insanity and mental functioning more generally; (ii) an aesthetic shift centering on artists' rejection of traditional modes of representation; and (iii) a social-institutional shift involving twentieth-century avant-garde artists' appropriation of the art of the insane as a device in their attack on modern society and the institution of art.

Schizophrenia, the unconscious and the concept of originality

Within medicine and psychiatry, the early twentieth century is characterized by important changes in the basic definition of mental illness, changes generally described as a gradual move from a view of mental illness as an abnormality or disease of the brain

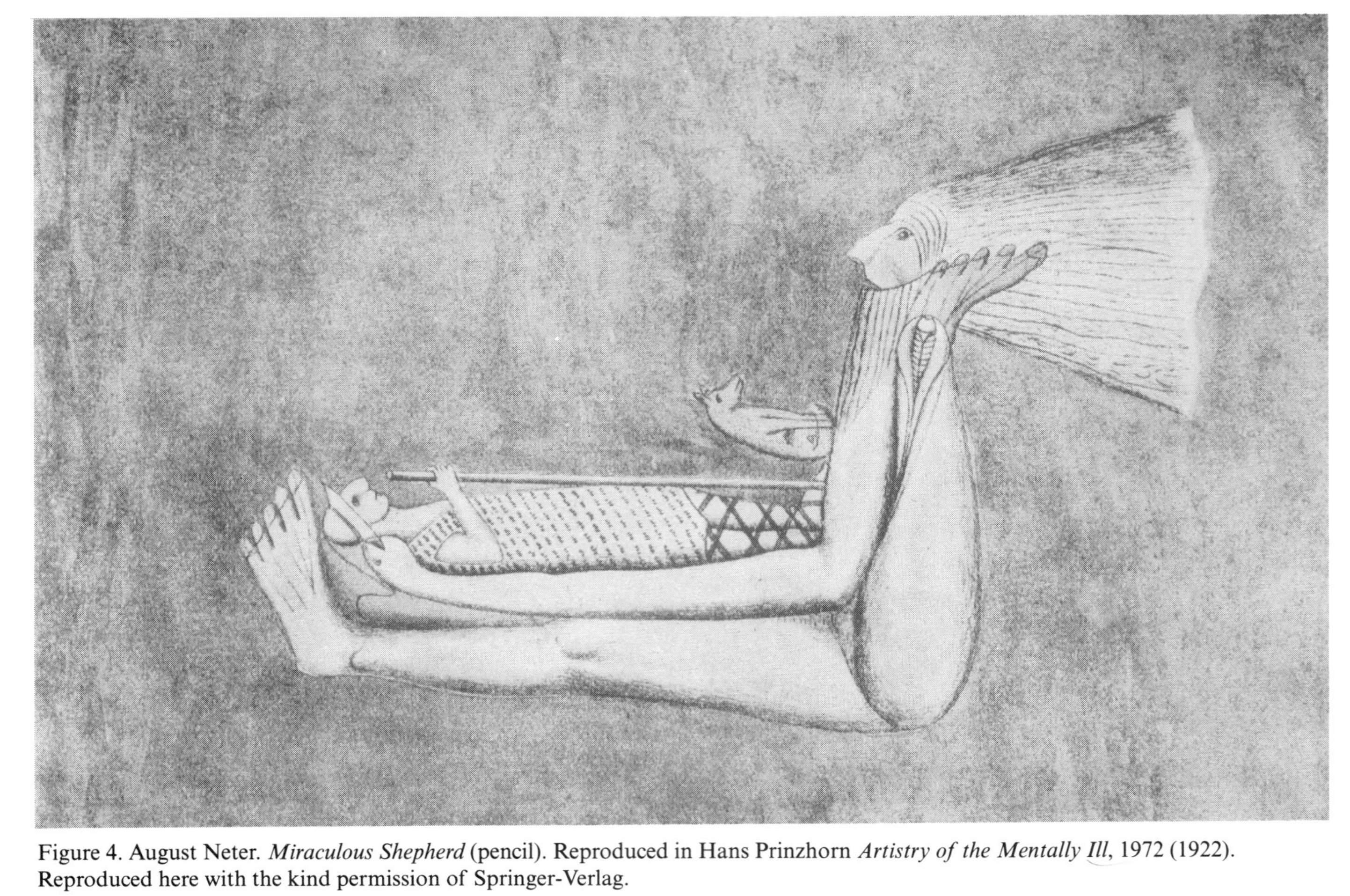

Figure 4. August Neter. *Miraculous Shepherd* (pencil). Reproduced in Hans Prinzhorn *Artistry of the Mentally Ill*, 1972 (1922). Reproduced here with the kind permission of Springer-Verlag.

to a growing interest in the psyche and the study of the emotions (Gilman 1985: 225). This complex history does not follow a single line of development and can be only sketched here with specific reference to the reception of the art of the insane. Two points remain particularly relevant: the popularization of the concept "schizophrenia," a term introduced by Bleuler in 1911, and an increasing interest in the nature and dynamics of the unconscious.

Based on a reformulation of Kraeplin's theory of dementia praecox, the category of schizophrenia has since come to occupy a central place in twentieth-century psychopathology. The impact of the concept in the history of the art of the insane may be no less significant. As Gilman (1985: 225–26) has observed:

> Interest in the artistic production of the insane was not lacking in the decades preceding Kraeplin's and Bleuler's works, but was greatly heightened with the popularization of the concept "schizophrenia"... Schizophrenics were perceived as suffering from some type of alteration in their relation to their sense of self. According to the new theories, this relationship could be extrapolated from the nature of their art.

Artists' interest in asylum art appear to have been equally heightened by the concept of schizophrenia. Modern artists like Kubin or Breton, however, emphasized the potential liberating effects of schizophrenia as a condition of isolation from established social and aesthetic conventions. MacGregor (1989: 235), commenting on Kubin's fascination with schizophrenia, cites specific remarks by the artist on the benefits of the isolating effects of psychosis for creativity:

> Kubin was intrigued by the schizophrenic state precisely because it involved a rich fantasy life evolved by individuals, "permanently and completely closed up within themselves, . . . closed off from outer experience . . . Confined within the impenetrable circle of his imagination."

Bauhaus artist Oskar Schlemmer, who attended a lecture by Prinzhorn in 1920, expressed a similar conviction: "The Madman lives in the realm of ideas which the sane artist tries to reach; for the madman it is purer, because completely separate from external reality" (quoted in MacGregor 1989: 234).

Expressionist artists' fascination with the link between creativity and insanity has been well documented in histories of the movement and is generally understood as part of an aesthetic which emphasized heightened emotional states and a retreat into the self as both a reaction to and a protest against the alienation of modern life. Equally significant, perhaps, is the influence of Van Gogh, regarded by a number of art historians as an artist of singular importance for the development of the Expressionist aesthetic. For some, there appeared an intimate connection between Van Gogh's brilliance as a painter and the "exemplary tragedy" of his life, a phrase applied to the artist by Paul Klee who believed that Van Gogh's most important work had been executed under the influence of insanity (Paul Klee 1964: 220, 224).

It is with the Surrealists, however, that schizophrenia is elevated to the status of an artistic doctrine. Vinchon, commenting on Breton's experiences as a medical assistant at various psychiatric hospitals during the First World War, noted: "The observation of schizophrenics revealed to him the possibilities of the imagination" (quoted in Samaltanos 1984: 85). In practice, Breton's conviction about the power of schizophrenia to unleash new creative forces informed Surrealist experiments with techniques designed to imitate the effects of psychosis. Experiments with "automatic" writing and drawing, for example, were intended to wrest the imagination from rational control and elicit the spontaneous creative eruptions that the Surrealists associated with insanity (Breton 1969: 3–47; Nadeau 1965: 79–84).

The impact of the theory of the unconscious expounded in psychoanalytic circles in the early decades of the century is no less important. Although the term itself predates Freud, it is only with the development of psychoanalysis that the notion of the unconscious entered the larger cultural vocabulary. Within artistic and literary circles it signified a source of creativity unspoiled by conventional social or artistic norms. As Emil Nolde stated, "In art, I fight for unconscious creation. Labour destroys a painting" (quoted in MacGregor 1989: 223). Noting early twentieth-century avant-garde artists' turn to asylum art as inspiration for formal experimentation in language as well as painting, curator Ann Temkin (1989: 139) observes, "On a psychological level, the art of the insane held an additional allure as raw manifestation of the newly labeled realm of the unconscious."

Interest in the unconscious was intimately bound up with modern artists' search for "origins" – of art, the psyche and, at the broadest level, civilization. As Goldwater (1986: 217) argues, the Surrealists drew an intimate link between the unconscious and the desire, in Eluard's words, to "give back to civilized man the force of his primitive instincts." This search for "origins" informed modern artists' fascination not only with the art of the insane but also with tribal art and the art of children. For the Expressionists, as Heller (1992: 78) has noted, interest in the art of the insane formed part of a quest for the *Uranfange* ("original beginnings") of art. As Klee stated in a lecture delivered in 1924:

> The artists with real vocations nowadays are those who travel to within fair distance of that secret cavern where the primal law is hidden; where the central organ of all temporal and spatial movement – we may call it the brain or the heart of creation – makes everything happen. What artist would not wish to dwell there? . . . Our own instinct drives us downward, deep down to the primal source. (Felix Klee 1962: 177)

Prinzhorn (1972: 271), describing the reaction of a group of artists to the Heidelberg Collection, noted that they "were shaken to their foundations and believed they had found the original process of all configuration, pure inspiration, for which alone, after all, every artist thirsts."

The modernist work of art

Important shifts in the conception and definition of the work of art directly informed early twentieth-century artists' interest in the art of the insane. At the center of this reconceptualization lay the rejection of traditional modes of pictorial representation. For the modernist artist, traditional bases of aesthetic authority – the Academy, the imitation of "Masters," Classical or otherwise – appeared exhausted. In place of tradition, artists emphasized "originality," an aesthetic value which, having appeared to arise first in the middle of the sixteenth century, was reinvigorated in the latter part of the seventeenth century with the famous "Quarrel of the Ancients and the Moderns," and solidified during the course of eighteenth-century debates over the concept of genius (Becker 1978: 23–24, 108–09). In the twentieth century "originality" is elevated to the status of a maxim, one of the defining features or "myths" of aesthetic modernism as Krauss has argued (1985: 151–70).

In practice this meant the rejection of a representational system in painting that had dominated Western art since the Renaissance, a system characterized by linear perspective, the uniform organization of the space of the canvas, and the placement of figures according to principles of Euclidean geometry. While the authority of this traditional system had begun to break down in the nineteenth century, by the early twentieth century, as Bürger (1984: 116 n.13) has argued, its "obligatory value" was lost. In its place, artists experimented with perspective, distance, scale, the reorganization of the pictorial space of the canvas, and the juxtaposition of seemingly disparate or incongruous objects and media.

Modern artists' turn to the art of the insane as a source of inspiration, in this context, becomes clearer. A common characteristic of much asylum art, like the art of children, naïves or other individuals untrained in the academic and historical conventions of Western art, is precisely the absence of this traditional representational system at work: two eyes stare out from the side of a face drawn in profile; the stick-like figure of a man walks a dog three times his size; a crowded landscape seemingly inverts conventional rules of scale and depth – all compositional schemes familiar to the late twentieth-century eye accustomed to the modernist repertoire. But to artists in the early decades of the twentieth century seeking "new models of creativity," as art critic Roberta Smith (1992: 33) has noted, "the spontaneous creations of the insane and other outsiders seemed to open a new door on the human imagination."

Modern society and the institution of art

While the Romantic poets' metaphorical identification of the artist and the madman as social "outsiders" contained a nascent protest against society at the beginning of the industrial age, the early twentieth-century avant-garde's appropriation of the art of the insane played an integral role in its open revolt against modern bourgeois society. To the avant-garde artist, bourgeois values subordinate the imagination to reason and threaten to destroy the creative capacity of the individual. But the "rational" organization of bourgeois society, particularly after the onset of the First World War, appeared increasingly like madness to many artists and writers. In this context, the asylum patient functions as a principle of inversion for the avant-garde artist. It is modern society, not the "madman" (or the artist derided for painting like a madman) which is insane. Dada poet Hugo Ball, for whom the "the death-throes and death-drunkenness" of war-torn Europe in 1916 revealed a world "gone to pieces," utilized precisely this principle of inversion in his poem "The Schizophrenic":

> A victim of dismemberment, completely possessed
> I am – what do you call it – a schizophrenic.

> You want me to disappear from the scene,
> In order that you may forget your own appearance
> (1963: 37, author's own translation)[13]

As Gilman incisively observes, "the schizophrenic becomes a device, used in much the same way as other exotics have been traditionally used to present a critique of society" (1985: 229).

The avant-garde attack on modern, bourgeois society was simultaneously an attack on the institution of art, not simply established on artistic norms and standards but on the institutional framework for the production, distribution and reception of art in modern society (Bürger 1984; Huyssen 1986; Williams 1989). In practice, this meant a rebellion against the material conditions of a commercial, capitalist market; the commodification of the work of art; the intermediary figure of the dealer-critic as arbiter of style and taste; and the bourgeois consumption of cultural products as markers of class and status. In this context, asylum art becomes an effective weapon against prevailing artistic conventions. Goldwater (1986: 219), for example, cites Dada artists' exultation over the art of children and the insane as proof that no acquired technique or training is necessary for artistic creation. A 1919 exhibition marking Dada's debut in Cologne organized by Max Ernst and Johannes Baargeld may be illustrative in this context. Visitors to the exhibition viewed works by Ernst, Baargeld, Arp, Klee and others displayed next to the art of children and folk painters, African sculpture, found objects and works by psychotics (Cardinal 1992: 104; Temkin 1987: 19). According to Cardinal (1992: 104), the exhibit had been organized as a deliberate provocation against an exhibition of more conventional contemporary art shown in the same building.

The art of the insane thus appears as part of a field of socially debased objects (the "primitive," the scatological, the perverse) cultivated by the avant-garde for shock value. This can be placed within the larger tradition of nineteenth-century Bohemia. Indeed, both the Dada and Surrealist movements enshrined nineteenth-century figures like Jarry, Rimbaud and Lautréament whose works were celebrated as an affront to bourgeois taste and decorum. But the attraction of asylum art lies in something more than its capacity to shock. The avant-garde, as Gilman (1985: 228) notes, constructs a "mythopoesis of mental illness" transforming insanity into an aesthetic doctrine. The schizophrenic creates without regard for – or even knowledge of – the established aesthetic criteria of the gallery, museum or academy. Rather, the mad artist creates out of the pure "inner necessity" of his own experience, uncontaminated by the conventions or trends of the market. The isolating effects of madness and the sequestered space of the asylum thus appear as a guarantee of the art of the insane as a pure, spontaneous manifestation of the imagination.

Dubuffet provides the most systematic articulation of this view. Like the use of asylum art in the avant-garde attack on modern society, Dubuffet's approach to the art of the insane operates according to a principle of inversion: asylum art is the "true" art in contrast with "l'art culturel," the "official" art of museums, galleries, salons and "intellectuals" (1988a: 31–33[1949]). In the famous statement *L'art brut préféré aux arts culturels* which accompanied a 1949 exhibition at the Galerie René Drouin, Dubuffet set forth his definition of "art brut":

> We understand by this term works produced by persons unscathed by artistic culture, where mimicry plays little to no part . . . These artists derive everything – subjects, choice of materials, means of transposition, rhythms, styles of writing, etc. – from their own depths, and not from the conventions of classical or fashionable art. We are witness here to a complete pure artistic operation, raw, brute, and entirely reinvented in all of its phases solely by means of the artists' own impulses. It is thus an art which manifests an unparalleled inventiveness, unlike cultural art, with its chameleon- and monkey-like aspects. (1988a: 33[1949])

While the term "art brut" has become to a great extent synonymous with the art of the insane, Dubuffet did not confine the term to asylum artists alone. Additionally, Dubuffet rejected conventional distinctions between sanity and insanity, a position which led him to repudiate the suggestion that there could be an "art of the insane," averring "there is no more an art of the insane than there is an art of dyspeptics or of those with knee problems" (1988a: 33). Nevertheless, Dubuffet consistently invoked insanity as the paradigmatic basis from which "true" art springs. In a statement accompanying a 1967 exhibition, he characterized insanity as the "temperament [which] is precisely the mainspring of all creativity and inventiveness" (1988b: 35). Similarly, MacGregor (1989: 303) reports a 1976 conversation with the artist wherein he declared, "Insanity is the great art."

The politics of appropriation: the ideology of authenticity

The art of the insane is constructed as an aesthetic category through a set of discourses and practices which turn on the question of authenticity: the art of the asylum patient is valorized as an "authentic" art through which the "inauthentic" character of bourgeois society and the modern institution of art is revealed. Free of exterior influence, free of the contaminating effects of the market, the madman seeks neither profit nor prestige. The asylum artist thus casts an aura of authenticity on an avant-garde whose own self-proclaimed "outsider" status became increasingly difficult to sustain as one vanguardist gesture after another was absorbed into the modernist canon. Only insanity, Breton declared in 1953, provides a guarantee of authenticity, "les garants de l'authenticité totale qui fait défaut partout ailleurs et dont nous sommes de jour en jour plus altérés" (1953: 227).

This mode of appropriation has had distinct effects on the contemporary reception of the art of the insane. The most notable of these effects may be the consistency with which the work of art is displaced from view. Because the question of authenticity hinges, ultimately, on the social condition of the artist, biography supersedes the aesthetic analysis to which works by conventional artists are subjected. A survey of critical responses to the European and American tours of the Prinzhorn Collection by Perin (1994), for example, documents reviewers's preoccupation with psychiatric background and issues. Elsewhere, the briefest reference to Wölfli occasions an allusion to the deviant sexual acts for which he was incarcerated (see, for example, DeCarlo and Dintenfass 1992: 36; Johnson 1993: 87; Marks 1989: 6). Perhaps most striking in this context is the reviewer who criticizes the juxtaposition of works by "outsiders" and "insiders" in the "Parallel Visions" exhibition:

Looking at the show, you didn't get a feeling for just how strange the outsiders are, how far they diverge psychologically and biographically from the conventional model of the professional artist. Everything looked like art in about the same way. (Johnson 1993: 88)

Preoccupation with biography is not peculiar to critics. As New York dealer Randall Morris reports, "When I speak to audiences, if I talk about surface tension, or even say that the artist can paint, I lose them. If I talk about how strange the artist is, they love me. The stranger the human being, the more they like it" (quoted in DeCarlo and Dintenfass 1992: 38).

As curator Joanne Cubbs (1994: 85) has noted, at the core of this approach lies a tendency to "conflate social and artistic nonconformity, to re-code social marginality as a willful act of creative individualism." Put differently, this "re-coding," or "clinicization" as Perin (1994: 183) terms it, can be understood as an *aestheticization* of madness, a process wherein insanity is constructed as a form of artistic strategy with little or no regard for the injurious effects of mental illness in the life of the asylum artist. Insanity becomes, rather, a state of artistic "emancipation" and "liberation" (Dubuffet (1988b: 35); the asylum a place of "revolt" and "contestation . . . conducive to free expression" (Thévoz 1976: 32).

The extent to which the work of art enters critical discourse is marked by a proliferation of terms largely absent from the description and assessment of the established artist. This difference derives, in part, from the frequent attempt to discern signs of psychopathology in the work, a process referred to by Perin (1994: 185) as "psychologizing the content." It is not, however, the dispassionate language of the clinician one encounters but rather the vocabulary of the exotic and sensational, at times reminiscent of the sideshow barker. Characterizing the Prinzhorn exhibition as "a haunting treasure trove of 'mad' art," for example, one prominent critic issues a "warning to the viewer" about the "terror of unanswerable riddles" it poses (Ashbery 1985: 61–63). The "Parallel Visions" exhibition is characterized as a "troubling" and "mysterious" "crazyquilt" (DeCarlo and Dintenfass 1992: 35). Wölfli's drawings are described as a "voluptuous delirium" (Wye 1989: 87). "Terrifying," "raw," "mysterious," "uncanny" – all (and more) appear with a striking regularity. Thus, even when received in the institutions of established art (the museum, gallery), the art of the insane does not share in the same discourse.

Attempts to provide a systematic, comprehensive explanation of the contemporary surge of interest in the art of the insane, and in outsider art more generally, have been largely unsuccessful. According to one expert, the current popularity of outsider art can be attributed to the reaction against a "postmodernism dedicated to dismantling Romanticist myths that informed modernism" (Cubbs 1994: 83–84). At the same time, a prominent critic characterizes the popularization of marginal art in the last decade as part of a postmodern fetishization of "incoherence" and "nostalgia" for novelty (Kuspit 1991: 135–36). Less dramatically, interviews with dealers, critics and buyers indicate an interest that appears to stem from an art market without clear direction and the search for an "innocent," uncontrived art (see De DeCarlo and Dintenfass 1992: 40; Slesin 1995: C1, 6; Wells 1992: A1).

If the element of protest so central to the avant-garde's approach to the art of the insane is no longer in evidence, a trace of vanguardism nevertheless remains. Ownership of asylum art appears to confer a particular type of status on the buyer: entry into the cutting edge of marginality. As Kuspit (1991: 134) notes, the market "garners sociopolitical credit for its 'discovery' of and 'responsibility' to the 'lesser' art, almost as though to bring alien art into the fold were a civic service."

As this chapter has demonstrated, the art of the insane is constructed as an aesthetic category through a set of discourses and practices which turn on the question of authenticity. At present the stakes on authenticity have risen as a consequence of an attempt to redefine the "art of the insane" in the context of changing psychiatric practices. The de-institutionalization of the mentally ill, the development of new psychotropic drugs, and art therapy programs within hospitals have led several prominent experts to conclude that true asylum art is now largely a thing of the past. According to MacGregor, "most images made by [the mentally ill], especially now that treatment involves the use of anti-psychotic and mood altering drugs, and the procedures of art therapy, [are] simply amateur art; mediocre, cliché-ridden and dull" (1990: 12). Similar judgments are shared by Cardinal (1979: 39) and prominent collector Sam Farber (1990: 7). The use of psychotropic drugs, according to Thévoz (1994: 67–68), has had a "fatal impact on artistic creativity within the clinical context," wherein "patients have moved from a condition of exaltation and possession to one of drugged stupor." The pursuit of the truly authentic thus becomes, as Cubbs (1994: 89) and Metcalf (1994) have suggested, a form of ethnographic collecting from a "vanishing" world. The effect of this redefinition will be to create a rarified market for a limited number of "authentic" works. Current evidence that this process is already under way can be found in the rising prices for works once considered largely unmarketable. Wölfli paintings now regularly sell for $30,000 and a drawing by Martin Ramírez recently sold for $180,000 (Wells 1992: A1, A14).

The art of the insane enters the domain of art on the basis of a paradox: the terms of its inscription demand that it remain marginal. It is, however, a paradox which operates according to a specific cultural logic. As Metcalf (1994: 218) writes, "[w]ithin their binary relationship, 'inside' and 'outside' are never equal terms." The social construction of the art of the insane belongs to a history in which the "otherness" of marginal individuals or groups is celebrated in order to mark off their distance from the dominant culture. To the extent that this mode of reception displaces the work of art from view may constitute another means by which, as Foucault (1973) has argued, madness has been silenced.

Notes

For their helpful comments and suggestions on an earlier version of this paper, I would like to thank Jeffrey C. Goldfarb and the late Ferenc Feher. Very special gratitude is extended to Nancy Weiss Hanrahan, David Weisberg and Vera L. Zolberg.

1 The term "outsider art" has been credited to British art historian Roger Cardinal. For an overview of the debate surrounding questions of definition, see Cardinal (1994).

2 A cautionary note about terminology is necessary here. My use of the term "insane" and "mad" imply no judgment about the mental status of any individual or set of individuals under discussion. They are used for purposes of consistency with the existing literature. As Gilman (1992: 224n.1) has stated: "I am using the terms 'madness' and 'creativity' in this context to categorize two traditions of labeling individuals and their products as different and unique. I am not taking any position on the validity of those labels. What 'madness' is may well relate to questions of commodification or the fascination with ideas of original genius."

3 The European tour consisted of museum and gallery exhibitions in, respectively, Heidelberg (where the collection permanently resides); Hamburg; Stuttgart; Berlin; and Basel. The United States tour, limited to university galleries, consisted of the Krannert Museum, University of Illinois; the Lowe Art Museum, University of Miami; the Johnson Museum, Cornell University; and the Smart Gallery, University of Chicago. For a complete listing of locations and dates see the exhibition catalog, *The Prinzhorn Collection* (1984). On the reception by art critics in specialized journals, see Kuspit (1986), Moehl (1985), and Schwabsky (1986). On the reception by art critics in the popular press, see, for example, Ashbery (1985) and Brenson (1985).

4 In addition to the Los Angeles County Museum of Art where the exhibition originated, "Parallel Visions" was shown at the Museo Nacional Reina Sofia, Madrid, the Kunsthalle, Basel, and the Setagaya Art Museum, Tokyo. For the complete exhibition itinerary, see the exhibition catalog edited by Tuchman and Eliel (1992). On the reception by art critics in specialized journals and the popular press, see, respectively, Johnson (1993) and Smith (1992).

5 See Temkin (1989) on the exhibitions of Wölfli in Philadelphia and New York, and Smith (1992) for the reference to Wölfli as an "outsider genius". Titles of several recent exhibitions provide an example of the conventional presentation of outsider artists in anonymous groupings: "Portraits from the Outside," a 1990 exhibition at the Parsons School of Design in New York; "European Outsiders," a 1986 exhibition at the Rosa Esman Gallery in New York; and "In Another World: Outsider Art from Europe and American," a 1987 exhibition tour in Britain.

6 Quoted in Dinnage (1993: 33). See also the discussion of Lamb, in particular, his later antipathy for the concept of the "mad genius," in MacGregor (1989: 75–76).

7 Beginning in 1933 the Nazi German government mounted a series of exhibitions which juxtaposed works by contemporary artists deemed "degenerate" with that of asylum patients and children (Barron 1991: 12; Zuschlag 1991: 84, 98). In July 1937, the infamous "Entartete Kunst" exhibition opened in Munich, where over six hundred works by artists ranging from Expressionist painters Klee and Nolde to Dada, Constructivist, and Bauhaus artists were displayed with the intention of demonstrating a link between modern art, Judaism, Marxism, degeneracy, and madness. The exhibition catalog, published in November 1937 further emphasized this link. One-quarter of the catalog's illustration pages featured reproductions from the Prinzhorn Collection next to the work of various contemporary artists. See Zuschlag (1991: 92) and "Facsimile of the 'Entartete Kunst' Exhibition Brochure" in Barron, ed. (1991: 356–90). For details of the 1937 exhibition see the collected essays and illustrative tables in Barron, ed. (1991).

8 According to MacGregor (1989: 94, 333 n.8), Lombroso's reputation as the author of the first serious study of the art of the insane has been overemphasized. As MacGregor's careful research demonstrates, Lombroso's first writing on the art of the insane, an essay entitled "L'Arte nei pazzi," did not appear until 1880, four years after the publication of Simon's

"L'Imagination dans la folie." Lombroso's essay was subsequently included as a chapter in the fourth edition of *Genio e folio*, published in 1882.

9 There is some discrepancy in current reports about the size of the collection and the number of patients whose works are represented therein. My numbers are taken from Prinzhorn (1972: 2) on the assumption that they accurately reflect the size of the collection at the time of publication. According to Inge Jadi (1984: 2), the current curator, the collection now includes some six thousand objects produced by 516 patients. Presumably, the difference arises from works added to the Collection after Prinzhorn's departure from the Heidelberg Clinic in late 1921.

10 According to MacGregor (1989: 161–66), the exhibition at the Bethlem Royal Hospital in 1900 may be significant as the first public exhibition of patient art. Contents of the exhibition are likely to have been compiled from the collections of British physicians Theophilus Hyslop, an enthusiastic supporter of Nordau's theory of degeneracy, and George Savage. A second exhibition at the Bethlem in 1913, organized by Savage, is noteworthy for the inclusion of works by Richard Dadd.

11 On Tauber, see Prokopoff (1984: 16) On Klee, see MacGregor (1989: 235) and Pierce (1977). On Breton, see Breton (1953: 225); Polizzotti (1995: 353); and Samaltanos (1984: 207n.145). On Bellmer, see Cardinal (1979: 20). On Eluard, see Cardinal (1992: 105) and Polizzotti (1995: 353).

12 Dubuffet's serious collecting is said to have begun around 1945 He subsequently acquired the collections of August Marie and Swiss psychiatrist Charles Ladame. See Thévoz (1976: 35).

13 On the "death-throes and death-drunkenness" of modern society, see Ball (1967: 51). My translation of "The Schizophrenic" differs slightly from that of Gilman (1985: 228).

References

Ashbery, John 1985, "Visions of the Insane: A Haunting Treasure Trove of 'Mad Art' Goes on Tour," *Newsweek* 105 (February 11): 61, 63.

Ball, Hugo 1967, "Dada Fragments," *The Dada Painters and Poets*, ed. Robert Motherwell, (translated by Eugene Jolas), New York: George Wittenborn; 51–54.

1963, "Der Schizophrene," *Gesammelte Gedichte*, Zurich: Peter Schifferli Verlag.

Barron, Stephanie, ed., 1991a, *"Degenerate Art": The Fate of the Avant-Garde in Nazi Germany*, Los Angeles: Los Angeles County Museum of Art and New York: Harry N. Abrams.

1991b, "1937: Modern Art and Politics in Prewar Germany," in Barron (ed.); 9–23.

Becker, George 1978, *The Mad Genius Controversy: A Study in the Sociology of Deviance*, Beverly Hills and London: Sage Publications.

Brenson, Michael 1985, "The Need to Communicate in a World That Does Not Listen," *New York Times* (June 23): Section 2, 27, 30.

Breton, André 1969, "The First Surrealist Manifesto," in *André Breton: Manifestos of Surrealism* (translated by Richard Seaver and Helen R. Lane), Ann Arbor: University of Michigan Press, 3–47 [originally 1924].

1953, "L'Art des fous, le clé des champs," *Le Clé des Champs*, Paris: Les Editions du Sagittaire, 224–27.

Bürger, Peter 1984, *Theory of the Avant-Garde* (translated by Michael Shaw), Minneapolis: University of Minnesota Press, 1984.

Cardinal, Roger 1979, *Outsider Art*, New York and Washington: Praeger Publishers.

1992, "Surrealism and the Paradigm of the Creative Subject," in Tuchman and Eliel (eds.), 94–119.

1994, "Toward an Outsider Aesthetic," in Hall and Metcalf (eds.): 20–43.
Clifford, James 1988, "On Collecting Art and Culture," *The Predicament of Culture: Twentieth-Century Ethnography, Literature, and Art*, ed. Clifford, Cambridge, MA and London: Harvard University Press, 215–51.
Cubbs, Joanne 1994, "Rebels, Mystics, and Outcasts: The Romantic Outsider," in Hall and Metcalf (eds.), 77–93.
DeCarlo, Tessa and Susan Subtle Dintenfass 1992, "The Outsiders," *Los Angeles Times Magazine* (October 11): 34–40.
Dinnage, Rosemary 1993, "The Scream Behind the Pattern," *New York Review of Books* (April 8): 33–36.
Dubuffet, Jean 1988a, "Art Brut in Preference to the Cultural Arts" (translated by Paul Foss and Allen S. Weiss), *Art Brut: Madness and Marginalia*, special issue of *Art & Text* 27 (December-February): 31–33 [originally 1949].
1988b, "Make Way for Incivism," translated by Chantal Khan Malek and Allen S. Weiss, in *Art Brut: Madness and Marginalia*, Special Issue of *Art & Text* 27 (December–February): 34–36 [originally 1967].
Farber, Sam 1990, "Portraits from the Outside: Figurative Expression in Outsider Art," *Portraits from the Outside: Figurative Expression in Outsider Art*, eds. Carr et al., New York: Groegfeax Publishing, 1990, 7–9.
Foucault, Michel 1973, *Madness and Civilization: A History of Insanity in the Age of Reason* (translated by Richard Howard), New York: Vintage [originally 1961].
Foy, James L. 1972, Introduction to the English translations of Prinzhorn, ix-xvi.
Furst, Lilian R. 1969, *Romanticism in Perspective*, London: MacMillan and New York: St. Martin's Press.
1979, *The Contours of European Romanticism*, Lincoln: University of Nebraska Press.
Gilman, Sander 1982, *Seeing the Insane*, New York: John Wiley & Sons in association with Brunner/Mazel.
1985, "The Mad as Artists," *Difference and Pathology: Stereotypes of Sexuality, Race, and Madness*, Ithaca: Cornell University Press, 217–38, 280–83.
1992, "Constructing Creativity and Madness: Freud and the Shaping of the Psychopathology of Art," in Tuchman and Eliel (eds.), 230–45.
Gisbourne, Mark 1992, "Playing Tennis with the King: Visionary Art in Central Europe in the 1960s," in Tuchman and Eliel (eds.), 174–97.
Goldwater, Robert 1986, *Primitivism in Modern Art*, Cambridge, MA: Harvard University Press.
Hall, Michael D. and Metcalf, Jr., Eugene with Roger Cardinal, eds., 1994, *The Artist Outsider: Creativity and the Boundaries of Culture*, Washington and London: Smithsonian Institution Press.
Heller, Reinhold 1992, "Expressionism's Ancients," in Tuchman and Eliel (eds.), 78–93.
Honour, Hugh 1979, *Romanticism*, New York: Harper and Row.
Huyssen, Andreas 1986, *After the Great Divide: Modernism, Mass Culture, Postmodernism*. Bloomington and Indianapolis: University of Indiana Press.
Jadi, Inge 1984, "The Prinzhorn Collection and its History," in *The Prinzhorn Collection*, 2–4.
Johnson, Ken 1993, "Significant Others," *Art in America* Vol. 81, no. 6 (June): 84–91.
Klee, Felix 1962, *Paul Klee: His Life and Work in Documents*, translated by Richard and Clara Winston, New York: George Braziller.
Klee, Paul 1964, *The Diaries of Paul Klee 1898–1918*, ed. Felix Klee, Berkeley: University of California Press.

Krauss, Rosalind E. 1985, *The Originality of the Avant-Garde and Other Modernist Myths*, Cambridge, MA: MIT Press.
Kuspit, Donald 1986, "Selections from the Prinzhorn Collection: The Art of the Mentally Ill," *Artforum* Vol. xxiv, no. 5 (January): 94–95.
1991, "The Appropriation of Marginal Art in the 1980s," *American Art* Winter/Spring: 133–41.
MacGregor, John M. 1989, *The Discovery of the Art of the Insane*, Princeton: Princeton University Press.
1990, "Marginal Outsiders: On the Edge of the Edge," *Portraits from the Outside: Figurative Expression in Outsider Art*, ed. Carr et al., New York: Groegfeax Publishing, 1990, 11–17.
Marks, Ben 1989, "Regressions Toward the Primordial," *Artweek* 20: 6 (October 21): 6.
Metcalf, Eugene W. Jr. 1994, "From Domination to Desire," in Hall and Metcalf (eds.), 212–27.
Moehl, Karl 1985, "Selections from the Prinzhorn Collection of the Art of the Mentally Ill," *New Art Examiner* (January): 66.
Morgenthaler, Walter 1992, *Madness and Art: The Life and Work of Adolf Wölfli* (translated by Aaron H. Esman in collaboration with Elka Spoerri), Lincoln and London: University of Nebraska Press [originally 1921].
Mosse, George L. 1991, "Beauty without Sensuality: The Exhibition Entartete Kunst," in Barron (ed.), 25–31.
Nadeau, Maurice 1965, *The History of Surrealism*, translated by Richard Howard, New York: MacMillan [originally 1945].
Perin, Constance 1994, "The Reception of New, Unusual, and Difficult Art," in Hall and Metcalf (eds.), 173–97.
Pierce, James Smith 1977, "Paul Klee and Baron Welz," *Arts Magazine* 52 (September): 128–31.
1978, "Paul Klee and Karl Brendel," *Art International* 22, no. 4: 8–20.
Polizzotti, Mark 1995, *Revolution of the Mind: The Life of André Breton*, New York: Farrar, Straus and Giroux.
The Prinzhorn Collection: Selected Work from the Prinzhorn Collection of the Art of the Mentally Ill 1984, Exhibition Catalog, Champaign, IL: Krannert Art Museum, University of Illinois at Urbana-Champaign.
Prinzhorn, Hans 1972, *Artistry of the Mentally Ill* (translated by Eric von Brockdorff), introduction by James Foy, New York, Heidelberg and Berlin: Springer-Verlag [originally 1922].
Prokopoff, Stephen 1984, "The Prinzhorn Collection and Modern Art," in *The Prinzhorn Collection*, 15–20.
Samaltanos, Katia 1984, *Apollinaire: Catalyst for Primitivism, Picabia and Duchamp*, Ann Arbor: UMI Research Press.
Schwabsky, Barry 1986, "Between Art and Schizophrenia: Reflections on the Prinzhorn Collection," *Arts Magazine* Vol. 60, no. 6 (February): 72–3.
Slesin, Suzanne 1995, "Outsider Art Comes In," *New York Times* (January 26): C1, C6.
Smith, Roberta 1992, "How 'Outsiders' Opened a Door on Imagination," *New York Times* (December 13): H33, H35.
Spies, Werner 1982, "Getting Rid of Oedipus: Max Ernst's Collages: Contradiction as a Way of Knowing," *Focus on Art*, ed. Spies, New York: Rizzoli, 96–103.
Temkin, Ann 1987, "Klee and the Avant-Garde, 1912–1940," *Paul Klee*, ed. Carolyn Lanchner, New York: Museum of Modern Art, 13–37.
1989, "Wölfli's Asylum Art," *Art in America* Vol. 77 (March): 132–40, 162.
Thévoz, Michel 1994, "An Anti-Museum," in Hall and Metcalf (eds.), 63–74.
1976, *Art Brut* (translated by James Emmons), forward by Jean Dubuffet, New York: Rizzoli.

Tuchman, Maurice and Eliel, Carol S., eds., 1992, *Parallel Visions: The Modern Artist and the Outsider*, Exhibition Catalog, Los Angeles: Los Angeles County Museum of Art and Princeton: Princeton University Press.

von Baeyer, W. 1972, "Preface to the Reprint of 1968," in Prinzhorn, v-vii.

Wells, Ken 1992, "'Outsider Art' Becomes the Rage Among Art Insiders of the World," *Wall Street Journal* (February 25): A1, A14.

Williams, Raymond 1989, *The Politics of Modernism*, ed. Tony Pinkney, London and New York: Vergo, 1989.

Wolff, Janet 1981, *The Social Production of Art*, New York: St. Martin's Press.

Wye, Pamela 1989, "Adolf Wölfli" in *Arts Magazine* 63 (March): 87.

Zuschlag, Christopher 1991, "An 'Educational Exhibition': The Precursors of Entartete Kunst and Its Individual Venues," in Barron (ed.), 83–103.

2

The centrality of marginality: naïve artists and savvy supporters

Steven C. Dubin

> The artist of our dreams is possessed; he may be totally nuts, but he's a hero.
> (Goodman 1987: 20)

Now, more than ever, outside is in. From thrift store paintings to works done by the mentally ill or the socially dispossessed, a myriad of previously overlooked or underrated creations are being accorded value by parts of the art world .

Marginality is also a dominant social science concern. It is not a residual category. Marx mapped it primarily along an economic axis. Durkheim located it outside the confluence of religious, domestic, economic and political circumstances. And for Simmel it appeared beyond the intersection of circles of sociability. Each plots a geometry of marginality as the complement to conformity and integration. It is one of those contrastive conditions that accentuates rather than diminishes the norm.

A great deal of emotion typically accompanies such discussions. Durkheim most certainly feared this condition, for "without mutual relationships, [individuals] tumble over one another like so many liquid molecules, encountering no central energy to retain, fix and organize them" (1951: 389[1897]). Simmel, on the other hand, celebrates it to a substantial degree. His stranger is freer from social constraints and prejudices (1971 [1908]).

Marginality can be a burden or an asset. If it is structurally determined (i.e. an expected social category), it probably denotes low power, low discretion and choice, a limited ability to secure desired goods, and a high degree of frustration. Yet when others are similarly situated, as Marx notes, the marginalized can potentially band together to effect change.

If marginality is self-chosen, it is generally more desirable. Marginality may be accompanied by a heightened sense of power and choice when it is voluntary and singular, but any psychological burdens it spawns cannot be as readily shared with others. When structurally determined and enforced, marginality is a less attractive state.

Social scientists have typically examined the more obvious cases of marginality. For example, there are classic studies of individuals straddling two cultural worlds because of immigration, or those who are marginal even though they share the same culture with a dominant racial group (Dickie-Clark 1966; Park 1950; Stonequist 1937).

However, some groups are marginal not because they display certain sexual, religious or racial attributes, but because of achieved statuses such as their occupations.

Conformity might command society's respect. Marginality often captures its heart. There are probably more Babbitts than Walter Mittys in this world, but the former elicit disdain whereas the latter allow us to honor the loser and enjoy his small triumphs. Conformity may heighten the chances for success, yet marginality can be a far from devalued stance. In fact, it may be deliberately cultivated and suggest models for what eventually will be embraced by many others.

My goal is to examine how marginality can be contained and controlled within one specific world of work, and to analyze the interaction between that world's various segments.

Marginality in the social world of art

Over the past several years, considerable sociological attention has been devoted to the collective nature of artistic pursuits and the social dimensions of art worlds. The focus has been on activities and events, not objects. The emphasis has increasingly become that of systems and their interconnections.

However, one type of artist evokes an interest beyond what its numbers alone might lead us to expect. Naïve artists, "outliers" to the complexities of the artistic world, are intriguing anomalies relative to many general formulations. For present purposes naïve artists are defined as individuals who have not undergone formal artistic training and do not orient their creations towards organized artistic worlds. They tend to work in relative isolation, and their output expresses individual and not collective themes and concerns. Nevertheless, they can be recognized by the art world for creating products with aesthetic dimensions[1] (Becker 1976; 1982).

Naïves are commonly considered to be bizarre at best, insane at worst. They live and work beyond many cultural constraints. They seldom participate fully in either their own local cultures or in organized artistic ones.

While the fascination with naïves is widespread, it may be heightened for certain other groups of artists, particularly students or those struggling with their own artistic careers. Such an interest is somewhat ironic: naïve artists are untrained, which implies that anyone could become an artist without having to undergo the formal instruction their admirers themselves receive. But naïve artists are not revered because they are central, but precisely because they are marginal.

Those naïve artists who garner recognition and attract a following are an extreme example of the triumph of the individual vision. They commonly generate fascination and admiration instead of eliciting resentment. They are generally cast as models, not competitors, since they embody a situation all artists must confront: there is little guarantee that their own individual expressions will ever be hailed by the art establishment.

These unconventional practitioners and their art have a symbolic appeal that conventional expression typically does not. In significant respects the naïve artist is a twentieth-century analog of the artist of Romantic myth, the nineteeth-century garret being replaced by either a secluded rural or urban retreat, or even the nomadic existence of a baglady/virtuoso. This is largely due to the thematic and stylistic nature of their work (its non-adherence to established forms), in conjunction with a structural problem (the low probability of success many individuals confront in the socially regulated world of art).

The social circumstances of naïve artists and the responses they summon closely correspond to the experiences of many young artists and those in the early stages of their careers. Naïves in effect represent the collective concerns and anxieties of these other individuals, and can offer a symbolic vindication of their own struggles. The fate of naïve artists dramatizes the structural predicament of a much larger group of individuals who – even though they are actively orienting themselves toward the art world – have little guarantee of future rewards.

For artists who do find success, their interest in and identification with naïve artists can provide a temporary release from the pressures inherent in their situation. For those whom success eludes, the naïves they champion offer a reserve of hope for the possibility of eventual triumph.

Artistic types and the intersection of artistic worlds

Idiosyncratic art and its equally idiosyncratic creators have been widely documented. However, the criteria for inclusion in this category are imprecise, mushy. The most compelling definition comes from Howard Becker's discussion of art worlds and social types (1976), where naïve artists are considered in relation to the larger art world, even though they essentially stand apart from it.[2]

Naïve and folk artists are typically collapsed into a single classification (see Carraher 1970; Horwitz 1975; and Livingston and Beardsley 1982), although they share only minimal, superficial characteristics. As two chroniclers of idiosyncratic constructionists shrewdly note, "[F]olk art says 'We are,' but the works of the backyard builders cry 'I am'" (Crease and Mann 1983: 91). This observation underscores the collective nature of folk art, in contrast to the markedly individual character of the naïves.

The naïves capture the imagination of young artists more than do folk artists. In fact, it is unlikely that contemporary artists would feel very comfortable in a milieu where folk art predominates, and they would probably experience the constraints of such *Gemeinschaft*-like environments as repressive. They are attracted to the notion of a triumphant personal vision, not to traditional, normatively regulated production.

The symbolic appropriation of new artistic territories

The contribution of artists to the reappropriation of urban spaces has been widely credited. A similar process may colonize symbolic realms as well. Young artists often initiate a "symbolic gentrification," alerting collectors and others to interesting new territories through their explorations and active promotion. The interest young artists express in the naïves is triggered by sympathetic identification. Once activated, however, other motives replace this original impulse.

The manifest reason for this vicarious identification lies in the social structural situation commonly confronting unseasoned artists. It is well known that the market structure of all artistic disciplines demonstrates a severe inability to absorb more than a small proportion of qualified aspirants. In other words, many more individuals receive formal artistic training and desire to work in these fields than can ever successfully secure opportunities to do so. This produces the inevitable economic problems and also forecloses the opportunity to strengthen and confirm a sense of professionalism. Feelings of self-doubt and inadequacy are frequently the result.

In fields where formal training does not realistically provide a bridge between apprenticeship and professional status, individual travails must be assuaged in some manner. And in the plastic arts, the sense of a spiritual kinship with naïves probably provides a psychological safety net. An intuitively recognized set of affinities may boost those who have not as yet fared well in the conventional world, and may never do so. The work of naïves is symbolically appropriated long before it is ever physically acquired by the art establishment.

The social structural roots of this identification have now been proposed. But what specific characteristics of the naïves support this homologous association? If we examine the patterns of discovery and gradual renown of some naïve artists, three important sources of similarity emerge. First, the thematic nature of their work can touch sensitive and compassionate nerves in other artists. Second, the relationship of the naïve artist to his or her community as well as to the art world – be it adversarial, symbiotic, or some combination of mutual avoidance and attraction – often entails a mixture of insider and outsider statuses, in some respects being "in" but not "of" a social group (somewhat akin to Simmel's discussion of the stranger (1971) [1908]). This, too, is familiar territory for many other artists.

Finally, there can be a parallel between the "careers" of naïves and struggling artists: each frequently has to engage in work that is extrinsic to their artistic concerns and often menial in nature, in order to provide for sheer economic survival. Furthermore, naïves pursue an extremely idiosyncratic vision – often for a considerable part of their lives – before they are "discovered" and their worth is validated. Naïves may be viewed as a "farm team" of sorts, which may garner local honors and may also be called upon to revitalize play in the professional realm.

Adoration and the metaphorical displacement of authority

The discovery of the naïves and the homage paid to them inverts the status-conferring system that predominates in the arts. Those who are typically denied status in turn succeed in awarding status on their own terms. Supporters often become hagiographers; their expository, promotional and collecting activities take on some qualities of a reliquary. Every aspect of the naïves' lives is of interest: their origins, their everyday lives, their most mundane activities.

In fact, it becomes difficult to separate "what they do" from "who they are" when, as one enthusiast declares, "Their artistic production consists of almost everything they do . . . In a most unconventional and literal sense, they live their art" (Bonesteel 1985: 129). It therefore becomes easier to understand why a fan and supporter of

Chicago naïve artist Lee Godie cherishes a pair of toenail clippers she gave him: "'She has a lot of trouble with her feet,' he commented" (Bonesteel 1982: 22). We can also appreciate why the owner of the house where Chicagoan Henry Darger lived – a creative photographer in his own right – kept the man's room largely intact after this naïve died in 1972, in essence a shrine to his lifework.

Although this alternative recognition system is devised by those who are conventionally refused honors, they do not necessarily directly attain its rewards. Rather, they achieve reflected honor from their association with the naïves, maybe an artifact or two, sometimes a modest monetary gain. The bonanza typically goes to others who command reward systems, such as gallery owners who quickly step in and through their business acumen gain control over this property.

Naïve artist Minnie Evans was a gatekeeper in a North Carolina garden, doing work which stimulated her paintings of flowers (Slesin 1995). A more complex system of gatekeeping now works to locate and validate the work of Evans and others like her, similar to the systems which process and promote other cultural goods. In fact, a network of specialists who study and market this material has gradually emerged, from "pickers" who constantly roam back roads in search of fresh material, to consultants who work on retainer for corporations to enhance their collections (Draper 1991: 18), to the editors of publications such as *Raw Vision* which report discoveries and trends, to the massive "outsider art fairs" which are mounted annually in New York City, a grand emporium of this type of work. In addition, standard art historical tasks have been undertaken in relation to naïves, such as establishing "influences" and attribution, issuing monographs about an artist's life and production, and collecting and displaying works – museums are even opening in Baltimore and Chicago – thereby presenting and legitimating their work in a conventional manner.

One representative monograph fulfills the prerequisites of this genre of scholarly inquiry by relaying biographical information, exploring iconography, examining technique, and providing a catalog raisonné of the work of an individual named St. Eon (Patterson 1987). And finally, a core group of artists is now routinely cited in this field, in what has become a relatively stable canon (subject, of course, to future reappraisals and additions). It makes a great deal of sense to refer to "the world of naïve art and artists": although these practitioners are far-flung, often stubbornly individualistic, and display vastly different techniques and interests, they are increasingly managed by a cultural apparatus which is many times removed from their everyday experiences.

In the following examination of three naïve artists, the focus is as much on their supporters. The interaction between these otherwise different parties is as intriguing as the individuals themselves.

Jesse "Outlaw" Howard: the artist as contentious outsider

Jesse Howard (1885–1983) became well known through the hand-painted signs and idiosyncratic constructions that dotted his property (which he dubbed "Sorehead Hill") in Fulton, Missouri. While most people would probably recognize little of what he did as artistic, his work has been much sought-after by young artists and collectors,

Figure 5. Jesse Howard, *Brainwarsher* [sic] (enamel paint on wood) 8½×21 in, *c.* 1960. Courtesy of Mark Jackson, Chicago.

is commonly pictured and discussed in books (see Carraher 1970 and Hemphill 1974), and has been exhibited at such institutions as the Kansas City Art Institute (which has a collection of nearly one hundred pieces of his work) and the Walker Art Museum in Minneapolis.

One enthusiast proclaims him "the Grandma Moses of print culture. His seemingly pleasant retirement hobby has forced him to confront, painfully, the aesthetic, psychological, technical, and social realities of print culture" (Rhodes 1970: 43). This would be a heavy mantle for anyone to bear, but especially so for an elderly rural man who used planking from razed houses for his "canvasses," and such things as car doors, windows and discarded home appliances for his constructions.

Most of Howard's work recorded his personal philosophy or concerns. One of his signs announced:

> FOR THE PAST 24. YEARS
> I HAVE BEEN HARRASSED!
> HECKELED! BOYCOTTED!
> LIED TO! LIED, ABOUT! STOLE
> FROM! TOLD TO GET OFF
> THE STREET! ALL OF
> THIS BY "BOTH" WHITES
> AND BLACK'S! AND I AM "JUST
> STICKING AROUND TO SEE: WHAT THE
> >H" WILL HAPPEN NEXT (shown in Carraher 1970: 108)

Another brooded on the thought:

> 000.000
> NOTHING
> NO CONFIDENCE
> NO NOTHING
> NO: 0000 (shown in *St. Louis Post Dispatch*)

Howard began making his signs in approximately 1953, after laboring as an itinerant worker and farm hand. He attracted a supportive audience in the late 1960s, when he was an elderly man. He drew the ire of his own community, however, which was manifested in repeated badgering and the theft of his work, among other things.

Local disapproval even spawned a petition drive to have him committed to the nearby state mental hospital; it proved to be unsuccessful. The conflict has been explained in the following way: "Jesse Howard hasn't, to Fulton's way of thinking, the credentials to be an artist. He must therefore be a promoter, or simply a madman . . . Locals know he emerged from the same rural past as they, a way of life founded on a reserved, indirect verbal tradition. The public candor of his signs violates that reserve" (Rhodes 1970: 44–45).

Where his neighbors suspected disturbance and perceived nuisance, others found a creative force at work. In fact, key considerations are Howard's relationship to his community, and his connection with artists from outside that rural environment. His signs were simply the most tangible evidence of a fractious existence propagated by adverse reactions to his differentness.

Howard's defiance of his neighbors and his insistence on publicly displaying his thoughts probably explains a great deal of his appeal to artists. Howard exhibited an authenticity that many artists respect, and wish to encounter firsthand. In response, the School of the Art Institute of Chicago organized a summer course beginning in 1985 that tours the Midwest to observe artists like Howard working in their natural settings, a novelty that pointedly contradicts a formalist art historical approach.

Howard's signs required only a minimum of skill to execute, and do not reveal a complex philosophical mind at work. However, his tenaciousness in the face of opposition signaled a spirit that could serve as a role model for appreciative artists and other creative individuals. This was a life force to experience, and an example to draw from.

Accordingly, his admirer, Rhodes (a young writer at the time), walked with Howard through his property, sweated with him, explored his personal history, solicited explanations of the work, and examined how Howard defended himself against the reproaches of his neighbors. How Jesse Howard was treated and his stance towards the world assumed great importance, largely overriding the aesthetic value of what he produced.[3]

Howard's work seems more and more contemporary as time goes on. In a sense he predated what is now termed performance art. The artifacts Howard left behind somewhat incidentally validate that he in fact existed.

Henry Darger: the artist as ageless child

When an old man who had made his living primarily as a hospital janitor in Chicago died in 1973, an artist was revealed. A project that he began in 1916 by the title of *The Story of the Vivian Girls in What is Known as the Realms of the Unreal or the Glandelinian War Storm or the Glandico-Abbiennian Wars, as Caused by the Child Slave Rebellion* ceased to be only a private fantasy adventure, and instead became a widely publicized artistic vision.

The work is massive, consisting of thirteen volumes of narrative text and eighty-seven large watercolored murals. In 1977 this material merited its own show at the renowned Hyde Park Art Center in Chicago. Parts of it were included in a group show of outsider art in 1980 at the Museum of Contemporary Art in Chicago, and it has subsequently been featured in numerous other exhibits. Some of the artwork has been sold through commercial dealers. Darger's work is out of the closet and into the canon.

Although Darger obviously preferred to work in isolation, the dramatic contrast between his quotidian existence and what he transferred from his imagination onto paper only exaggerates the way many creative individuals are compelled to live and work. Further, the way in which Darger was "discovered" is noteworthy. Darger rented a small apartment in a house owned by an artist/photographer. Although this man was himself sixty years old when Darger died, and had impressive training and experience, he did not have his own one-person show of work until the following year.

While this might seem to contradict somewhat my earlier emphasis on young artists, it makes it clear that artistic recognition is often very slow in coming. Chronological age and professional status can diverge greatly. That Darger's work was saved instead of being discarded was largely due to serendipity. Many other landlords would have destroyed his entire output, rather than detect its artistic merit.

The thematic quality of Darger's work also elicits a sympathetic response. The story line of the Vivian girls' adventures includes catastrophic events, tortuous ordeals, and tales of heroism and salvation. As the catalog from the inaugural exhibition observed, "It is . . . significant that the Vivian princesses and most of the child slaves are female, and pretty, and that much of their suffering has to do with exposure and humiliation" (Morrison 1977). The motifs of abuse and fighting back from a relatively powerless position are once again central, metaphorically standing for the struggling artist's lot. There is a combination of childlike purity as well as the ever-present reality of feeling at the mercy of uncontrollable forces.

This innocent quality relates to another feature of this work, its technical execution. Darger's collages have a cartoon-like quality to them, largely because he incorporated material from children's books, comic strips and advertisements into his work. This evokes a sense of familiarity to which anyone can relate, while also raising the possibility that anyone would be capable of producing something comparable.

In actuality, Darger refined his own techniques: he ordered to size the photographic negatives of the images he wished to use, which he could then re-color, arrange and title to his liking (Bonesteel 1985: 132; Moseley 1977: 12). Because of these elaborations, no one else could have done the drawings in the same way. His unique aesthetic sense was indispensable to overseeing the project.

Lee Godie: not-so-naïve hustler

Lee Godie is the most complex of these naïves. While she certainly meets many of the criteria for inclusion into this category, her career rivaled carefully managed and successful ones in the art world. It is important, however, to look at the way in which

Figure 6. Henry Darger, *The Vivian Girls in the Snow* (watercolor on paper), 19×48in. From the Lerner collection, reproduced with the permission of the Darger Foundation and Nathan and Kiyoko Lerner, Chicago.

she became a local celebrity and achieved the rare distinction of being able to live from the sales of her creative work. Lee Godie was an enigmatic individual, but one whose experiences reveal a great deal about the workings of the contemporary art world.

Lee Godie was frequently mistaken for a baglady by those who didn't know her. Her eccentric, disheveled appearance and many aspects of her daily life conform to our notion of such individuals. Art students first noticed her hanging around the Art Institute of Chicago and its school in the late 1960s, then admired and purchased her paintings. She soon became a fixture thereabouts. Her reputation was initially established by those who were also peripheral to the art world, and only subsequently confirmed by a larger audience.

It cannot be accidental that Godie chose to base her operations where she did. She knew much more about the art world than most naïves, and actively utilized that understanding. She was able to locate a naturally compassionate audience around this art school, which led to an exhibit of her work in one of its own galleries, then to her inclusion in shows at countless other venues. She even acquired representation by a dealer in 1989 (Knight 1993: 7).

Godie was saluted as a celebrity by *People* magazine (Plummer 1985), and cited as a good investment by *The Wall Street Journal*. Lee Godie earned the oft- repeated appellation of "the most collected artist in Chicago." In 1993, when Godie was an eighty-five-year-old resident of a suburban Chicago nursing home, she was honored by a mayoral proclamation and feted by a major retrospective exhibit of her work at Chicago's Cultural Center. If she had looked out of the windows from her wheelchair on the night of the opening, Godie would have seen the grounds of the Art Institute and some of the other haunts on Michigan Avenue where she idled for so many years. Lee Godie died half a year later.

Artists and seasoned collectors both value her work. But these groups were attracted for different reasons. When she was alive, young artists were interested in the "whole person," not just her output. An admirer knowingly stated, "Godie's paintings are just the tip of an artistic iceberg known as the Lee Godie phenomenon. Her eccentric and unpredictable behavior, her bizarre habits and perceptions, her considerable charm and wit – all must be included in the oeuvre of this Outsider artist" (Bonesteel 1985: 131).

Godie's conduct directly challenged many sacralized notions in the art world. For example, it was she who decided to whom to sell her paintings, and when. Having money was not sufficient to make a purchase. The prospective buyer had to demonstrate the proper enthusiasm and a sense of "worthiness." She thereby bypassed the established system of critics and galleries. Godie was her own gatekeeper, par excellence.

Godie also blatantly incorporated the work of others into her paintings. It is not unusual, for example, to find tracings of paintings by Picasso – directly transferred from postcards purchased in the Art Institute gift shop – affixed to her work. She perfected this well before rappers began to sample musical passages, and Godie also anticipated the postmodernist penchant for appropriation which now pervades contemporary visual art.

Godie further challenged the established art historical canon by unabashedly declaring herself to be a "French Impressionist," and "much better than Cézanne" (Bonesteel 1982: 1). Someone with no formal training, but with this apparent level of success, turns the art world on its evaluative head.

Godie commonly painted on window shades, cardboard or even Styrofoam (anything can become a canvas), and typically did simple busts of wide-eyed individuals (anyone can become an artist, anyone a suitable model). She developed male and female archetypes over the years, including "Prince Charming/Prince of the City" and the "Gibson Girl." The unsullied, natural qualities of her work attracted her early supporters, but tend to confuse those who now know that her paintings are a good investment, without understanding why: "To my untrained eye, the painting [he was being offered] seems a long way from finished," puzzled the *Wall Street Journal* reporter. Nevertheless, he met her asking price of $95 (Freedman 1985: 25).[4]

Some might question how Lee Godie can be classified as a naïve artist, given her active commerce with the art world. In fact, Howard Becker argues that "To the degree that the artist begins to take account of what her new colleagues expect of her and are prepared to cooperate with, she has become an integrated professional, even though

Figure 7. Lee Godie, *Lady Love* (mixed media (pen and ink, watercolor, and candle wax) on canvas), 13½×19 in, *c.* 1968-69. Courtesy of Mark Jackson, Chicago.

she has been integrated into a world which has somewhat changed itself to accommodate the variations she has created " (1976: 714).

But just who has been manipulated? Who coöpted? Godie remained a determined iconoclast whom the label integrated professional scarcely fitted. She stretched the notion of naïve to the limit.

Sympathetic resistance and identity

Can larger lessons be drawn from this material? The interest in and promotion of naïve artists signifies a usurpation of authority by those who do not commonly possess it. This democratizes the making of aesthetic judgments about what should be considered interesting and important to the artistic world. The celebration of this type of work elevates it to a position from which it can stand in critique: for while the art world has become increasingly cerebral, the naïves signify untrammeled emotion. Their proponents therefore gain in proportion to how much acceptance they can garner for an alternative expressive approach.

Conventionally oriented artists who are themselves marginal project their own structural problems in a metaphorical way by their fascination and involvement with these alternative modes of expression. Their struggle is thereby acted out in the cultural sphere, not by directly attacking the social structural problems that profoundly affect their work lives, but by this symbolic act of discontent. This identification with the naïves therefore contributes to a heightened sense of importance for both parties, and provides some crucial social space. Think of it like releasing steam from a pressure cooker.

An important compensatory fantasy is enacted by lionizing marginal figures. This is, in effect, a rejection of one's rejecters. It reflects a powerful tension between the desire for acceptance, and repulsion at the thought of finally being granted membership in a club with which one can find much fault. But we should not be surprised by this ambivalence, grounded as it is in distinct social conditions (Merton and Barber 1976).

The attraction between struggling artists and the naïves is illuminated by Weber's concept of "elective affinities," the notion that there is a connection between ideas and social action, and ideas and social interests (see Weber 1958: 91–92, and Howe 1978). Although we are most accustomed to thinking in such terms in relation to the fit between Calvinism and the development of capitalism, or more recently in regard to those different doctrines either promoted by heretics or defended by orthodox believers (Kurtz 1983), the configuration here is much the same. While naïves don't explicitly espouse an ideological position themselves, their manner of working and what they produce implicitly establish a distinctive point of view.

Naïve works can be seen as a preserve or sanctuary for spontaneous feeling, of "pure," unconventionalized work. As one supporter rhetorically asks, "Academic artists 'know how', but do they *know*?" (Cardinal 1972: 10). This same commentator endorses an uneducated artist who can write only his own name: "His is the independence of the man who refuses to sign the socio-cultural contract, and any 'culture' he has is what he himself has elaborated by dint of mediating upon the circumstances of his life" (Cardinal 1972: 75). Such a position obviously places feelings above intellect, and intuition and freedom over conscious deliberation and operating within normative bounds.[5]

Those who endorse the work of naïve artists register a moment of resistance to the restrictions of conventionalized cultural production.[6] This can best be understood as an acute sensitivity to what Simmel characterized as "the conflict in modern culture," or how all culturally constructed phenomena are structured by basic forms of interaction, expression and sociability. Naïves are exalted as those who are the least affected by these seemingly inexorable laws. For those who have not yet secured their places within the artistic world, and who have not garnered its benefits, these Rousseau-like noble savages are an attractive contrast to what they might generally experience as an unyielding cultural establishment.

There may be a conservative element to this interpretation. The channeling off of tensions and the willingness of an artistic establishment to accommodate some naïve types of expression may simultaneously reduce the impetus for those who are disenfranchised to tackle more significant structural changes. It may dissipate the energy available for sustained struggle, while it allows those controlling the art world to appear responsive to different modes of expression.[7]

The promotion of naïve expression could preface more significant questioning, perhaps underwriting a direct assault upon the way the artistic world is structured. Or it might merely provide an interesting diversionary interlude for those who are continuing to orient their activities toward wresting rewards from professional art worlds as they are presently constructed.

Discussion

Naïves are successfully labeled as deviant artists. There exists a much larger pool of similar individuals who could be identified and promoted than ever comes to the public's attention. Further, naïves are relatively powerless to dispute this imputation because they generally don't know much about the artistic world. If the labeling process proceeds during a person's lifetime, there will probably be an amplification of this new identity and accompanying changes in his or her self-perception and associations. In some instances there may even be a degree of self-labeling (as in the case of Lee Godie), where individuals embrace these changed circumstances and actively promote themselves.

This process has an impact on others besides the naïve artists, however. Support for the naïves records in a shorthand manner the tension between cultural forms and the willingness to accede to them. It is a Polaroid shot of artistic creators being noncompliant – either reluctant to play by established rules, or bolstered by their knowledge of others who escape basic constraints. Young or otherwise marginal artists gain some measure of social-psychological support and a certain degree of relief through such surrogate heroes from the predictable stresses of their unsatisfactory situations. Furthermore, they can register their dissatisfaction with what one critic has called "the dealers' Great lie" (Goldin 1976: 51), the belief that by definition great art exhibits the acceptance of certain aesthetic, economic and cultural values.

The main conditions for the expression of this symbolic resistance are the following: (i) a population either undergoing professional training but/or presently excluded from professional success because of a market structure that is capable of absorbing only a portion of them; (ii) marginal practitioners onto whom the major tensions of a particular professional world can conveniently be displaced, and who will seem noble in their efforts; (iii) a marked ambivalence between compliance with conventions (with the possibility of future professional success), or resistance and the alternative of working on one's own terms (somewhat devaluing success); and (iv) a hesitation on withdrawing completely from these struggles.

In addition, these observations offer some insights into the process of building a reputation. Even the most carefully cultivated reputations are fragile at best, susceptible to many contingencies. Stylistic shifts can propel some fortunate individuals into stardom while simultaneously undermining support for the approach of others.

What this evidence suggests is that a reputation can be managed almost totally *for* someone. Naïve artists are generally reluctant beneficiaries of fame and success.[8] If it develops during their lifetimes, they frequently can't comprehend it. And if it happens posthumously, it only underscores the extent to which others project their own needs and interests onto these exceptional practitioners and their work.

As a final note, it has become a commonplace to examine how aesthetic judgments have class-based and political components, and to assume that such evaluations reinforce the social divisions of society. To some extent the arguments I'm putting forth highlight the need for a critical sociology "from below," examining how the activities of those on the margins may have some impact upon the canon.

There is merit to the notion that a style in the world of art roughly corresponds to a biological species (Goldin 1976: 50). In each circumstance agreed-upon characteristics permit observers to classify phenomena as belonging or not belonging. However, mutations are important in both realms as the source of change: as alternative forms are gradually assimilated, what was marginal can become central, expanding the orthodox array of categories.

Notes

I am grateful to Howard S Becker, Lester R. Kurtz, Barry Schwartz and Gary Schwartz for their comments and suggestions on earlier versions. One such version was presented at the twelfth Annual Social Theory, Politics and the Arts Conference, October, 1986, at the University of California–San Diego.

1 This definition is more restrictive than those commonly used or what's typically encountered in scholarly dialogue. Henri Rousseau, for example, known for his idyllic, dream-like scenes, is frequently labeled as a naïve. Yet his 1906 painting *Liberty Inviting Artists to Take Part in the Twenty-second Exhibition of the Société des Artistes Indépendants* demonstrates his awareness of a larger world beyond his own studio and imagination.

2 Over the past few years, "visionary" and "self-taught" have increasingly won favor as preferred terms for these individuals

3 Howard's work is usually represented by his distinctive signs. However, Rhodes reports that Howard's creative output also included several primitive paintings, some written manuscripts, and a type of manuscript illumination. Although these works conform more readily to what we typically think of as cultural products – and would make it easier for many people to understand the legitimacy of labeling Howard an artist – other references to these parts of Howard's oeuvre are rare.

4 I imagine that Godie sensed she had a sucker here. I bought a Prince Charming/Picasso knock-off from her in 1980 for $20. In 1990 a writer shared her delicately intricate negotiations with Godie in the delightful article "High Tea with Lee Godie" (see Shubart 1990); she paid $40. A person who has written extensively about this artist claims that she was getting from $50 to $200 per painting in the mid-1980s (Bonesteel 1993: 14). Godie had her own quirky sense of the art of the deal; there was probably no single, typical encounter with her.

5 Cawelti's study of the coalescence of literary genres and the concerns of particular social groups develops a similar argument (1976). See also Gans's 1974 discussion of "taste cultures." Marginality has frequently been a theme in painting. One thinks of Picasso's clowns or Manet's modern urban women (often "read" as prostitutes). The Impressionists – relatively unencumbered by the constraints of a patronage system – commonly took anonymity, marginality and shifting social roles as their themes (Clark 1985).

6 A number of British social scientists have noted how groups which are relatively powerless devise imaginary "solutions" to their concrete problems, thereby carving out additional "breathing space" for themselves (see Cohen 1980, Hall and Jefferson 1984, and Willis 1977).

7 This bears an obvious affinity to Marcuse's idea of repressive tolerance, and such issues of

containment and co-optation have been addressed by social theorists as diverse as Gramsci and Parsons.

8 A few naïve artists have caught onto the fact that this form of expression is now big business Howard Finster of Georgia is a prime example. A media darling, he has appeared on "The Tonight Show," his paintings have graced pop music album covers, and he has a toll-free sales number: 1–800–FINSTER (Brown 1995).

References

Becker, Howard S. 1976, "Art Worlds and Social Types," *American Behavioral Scientist* 19: 703–18.

1982, *Art Worlds*, University of California Press.

Blasdel, Gregg N. 1968, "The Grass-Roots Artist," *Art in America* 56: 24–41.

Bonesteel, Michael 1982, "The Mysterious Master of Michigan Ave.," *Chicago Reader*, January 8: 1, 20, 22–23, 26–28.

1985, "Chicago Originals," *Art in America* 73: 128–35.

1993, "Lee Godie: Art and Survival on the Streets of Chicago," *Artist–Lee Godie: A 20–Year Retrospective*, City of Chicago Department of Cultural Affairs, 8–26.

Brown, Patricia Leigh 1995, "Losing Paradise, Keeping His Faith," *New York Times*, June 29: C1, 6.

Cardinal, Roger 1972, *Outsider Art*, New York and Washington: Praeger Publishers.

Carraher, Ronald 1970, *Artists in Spite of Art*, New York: Van Nostrand Reinhold.

Cawelti, John 1976, *Adventure, Mystery, and Romance*, University of Chicago Press.

Clark, T. J. 1985, *The Painting of Modern Life: Paris in the Art of Manet and His Followers*, New York: Alfred A. Knopf.

Cohen, Stanley 1980, *Folk Devils and Moral Panics*, New York: St. Martin's Press.

Crease, Robert and Mann, Charles 1983, "Backyard creators of art that says: 'I did it, I'm here,'" *Smithsonian Magazine* 14: 82–91.

Dickie-Clark, H. F. 1966, *The Marginal Situation: A Sociological Study of a Coloured Group*, London: Routledge and Kegan Paul.

Draper, Robert 1991, "Plunder or Patronage?," *American Way*, May 15: 16–22.

Durkheim, Emile 1951, *Suicide* (translated by Spaulding, John A. and Simpson, George), New York: Free Press [originally 1897].

Freedman, Alix 1985, "Art Being Her Bag, This Bag Lady Wins Acclaim in Chicago," *Wall Street Journal*, March 27: 1,25.

Gans, Herbert F. 1974, *Popular Culture and High Culture*, New York: Basic.

Goldin, Amy 1976, "Problems in Folk Art," *Artforum* 14: 48–52.

Goodman, Walter 1987, "Art's Anguish Is a Constant Joy to Behold," *New York Times*, August 9: H19–20.

Hall, Stuart and Jefferson, Tony, eds. 1984, *Resistance Through Rituals: Youth Subcultures in Post-War Britain*, Dover, NH: Hutchinson Education.

Hemphill, Herbert 1974, *Twentieth Century American Folk Art and Artists*, New York: E. P. Dutton.

Horwitz, Elinor 1975, *Contemporary American Folk Artists*, Philadelphia: J.B. Lippincott.

Howe, Richard 1978, "Max Weber's Elective Affinities: Sociology within the Bounds of Pure Reason," *American Journal of Sociology* 84: 366–85.

Knight, Gregory G. 1993, Foreword and Acknowledgments, in *Artist–Lee Godie*, 6–7.

Kurtz, Lester R. 1983, "The Politics of Heresy," *American Journal of Sociology* 88: 1085–115.

Livingston, Jane and Beardsley, John 1982, *Black Folk Art in America,1930–1980*, University Press of Mississippi.

Merton, Robert K. and Barber, Elinor 1976, "Sociological Ambivalence," *Sociological Ambivalence and Other Essays*, ed. Robert K. Merton, New York: Free Press, 1–48.

Morrison, C. L. 1977, *Realms of the Unreal: The Work of Henry Darger*, Chicago: Hyde Park Art Center.

Moseley, Charlie 1977, "Glandelinians, Blengians, General Gingersnap,and the Vivian Girls Come to Hyde Park," *The Chicago Journal*, September 17: 12–13.

Park, Robert 1950, *Race and Culture*, Glencoe, IL: Free Press.

Patterson, Tom 1987, *St. Eon in the Land of Pasquan*, East Haven, CT: The Jargon Society.

Plummer, William 1985, "Baglady artist Lee Godie is a wacky success – her paintings are off the wall and in demand," *People Weekly* 23 (April 22): 50–52.

Rhodes, Richard 1970, *The Inland Ground: An Evocation of the American Middle West*, New York: Atheneum.

St. Louis Post Dispatch 1977, "Letters to the World from Sorehead Hill, Mo.," July 17: 5D.

Shubart, Margarita 1990, "High Tea with Lee Godie," *Chicago Reader*, January 5: 49– 50.

Simmel, Georg 1971, *On Individuality and Social Forms*, Levine, Donald N. (ed.), University of Chicago Press [originally 1908].

Slesin, Suzanne 1995, "Outsider Art Comes In," *The New York Times*, January 26: C1, 6.

Stonequist, Everett 1937, *The Marginal Man*, New York: Scribner's.

Weber, Max 1958, *The Protestant Ethic and the Spirit of Capitalism*, (translated by Talcott Parsons), New York: Scribner's [originally 1904–1905].

Willis, Paul 1977, *Learning to Labor: How Working Class Kids Get Working Class Jobs*, New York: Columbia University Press.

3

African legacies, American realities: art and artists on the edge

Vera L. Zolberg

Introduction

Within the space of less than a century, objects made by African carvers have passed through a career marked by striking mutations. Considered by Africans as religious or ancestral objects, and treated by Europeans as plunder, curiosities, artifacts or souvenirs, they were reclassified, by Europeans, first as magical emblems or functional artifacts; then, as primitive or tribal art and, subsequently, simply as art. By now, in the eyes of many, Westerners and Africans alike, they are aesthetic objects – oeuvres.

The redefinition of African objects as art by avant-garde artists nearly a century ago had become a recognized chapter of the art history of modernist aesthetics (Adams 1989). Recent scholarship has focused on the ideologies of appropriation by Western artists, collectors, and cultural institutions (Price 1990). Indeed, African art works have become some of their prized possessions. But this outcome was neither preordained nor immediate.[1]

The causes of aesthetic change are often attributed to macrotrends in society: global, political, and economic trends, and professional and academic developments. But macrosocietal forces alone do not account for the career trajectory of art – even African art – except at a general level (Halle 1993; Zolberg 1992). Although they provide the contexts within which genres that lie on the edge of conventional aesthetics may be redefined, I want to argue that it is the interplay of these forces with crucial actors, especially avant-garde artists, and the changing culture of art museums that account for the metamorphosis of African works into art.

As the most prestigious legitimating institutions for aesthetic culture, American art museums had been inhospitable to African art. Moreover, they were no more welcoming to works by living African American artists, nor did they draw in the small African American elite whose members might have wished to become museum patrons. Until recently, both artists and patrons were treated as outsiders as well. In the changing aesthetic and political context of the late twentieth century, however, both established and alternative museums have opened doors to African Americans, as artists and patrons. In this chapter I trace the trajectories of African works, African American artists, and patrons, as they relate to the most legitimating of institutions, the art museum, and their entry into it, and the consequences of acceptance for living African American artists.

The artistic discovery of African art

The discoverers of the primitive art of Africa were outsiders to Africa, with their own agendas and conceptions. Agents of the West or of Islam, explorers, conquerors, slavers and missionaries, they treated the works as booty, treasure, decorations, idols (Steiner 1994). Whatever their intentions, they opened the way for others. It was avant-garde artists who, by taking these works seriously, became key players in the redefinition of African works as art.[2]

In his book on primitive art, Robert Goldwater observed that as long ago as the 1889 Universal Exposition in Paris, Van Gogh and Gauguin were able to see "admired examples of the architecture and sculpture of 'primitive' peoples." In that time of "preparation," as Goldwater saw it, artists took from the works to which they had access the inspiration that suited ideas current during their time. From the mid-century onward, this consisted of an archaïcizing interest in the exotic, and aesthetic ideas that they associated with provincial regions distant from European art capitals, such as Brittany, or those in non-Western countries. Their preoccupation contained elements of nostalgia, as part of a Romantic search for the putative simplicity and harmony that seemed lost in the modern, urban, industrial condition. Incorporating exotic decorative stylistic ingredients into their own creations, some of these artists launched japonisme, symbolism, art nouveau and other fin-de-siècle styles. Later, the primitive was taken as a source of what Goldwater refers to as the "ferocious" rather than the nostalgic, serving as a key to unlock both the hypercivilized intellect and the repressed subconscious. In one way or another, these were concerns of Cubists, Expressionists and, later, Surrealists.[3]

Their ideas found support in Paris, Munich or New York, where opinion leaders and members of emergent elites were becoming a transnational set of supporters who shared an openness to new art forms (Zolberg 1983).[4] Some of them helped reorganize museum collections of colonialist states (Belgium, Germany, France, Great Britain) or of private collectors (Clifford 1988).

Art museums discover primitive art

As far as art museums were concerned, the attributes of African works were a mixed bag. Some lent themselves to art museum display, especially works from kingdoms, such as Ife (Nigeria), where durable metals or terra cotta were used in the representation of rulers.

Many objects for religious purposes, however, were made of relatively fragile materials that were permitted to molder and re-enter nature, eventually to be replaced by newly made works. But the bulk of objects were essentially tools or artifacts, intended to be used till worn out.

Within the dominant European art museum framework, objects are deemed valuable

Figure 8. Cast of the original Ife head, treasure of the Nigerian Government (half figure, bronze). Neg. 324342, courtesy of the Department of Library Services, American Museum of Natural History.

if they are authentic, rare, man-made, of valuable materials, associated with royalty, and have no mundane function. The history of collections exemplifies these criteria. Somewhat idiosyncratic in their origins, when private collections were opened to public viewing, and became a foundation for art museums, they were revalued – either to be displayed or stored away. Their chances of reaching public view were helped if they were old and rare: from the distant past – ancient Egypt, classical Greece and Rome – whether furniture, pottery, jewelry, architectural fragments or statuary (Alsop 1982). Age and preciousness are criteria that are especially salient in relation to curios, which cut across these categories.[5] Although curios now have denigrating connotations – as bric-a-brac or *bibelots*, with the taint of kitsch – such objects have a respectable ancestry. Depending upon the qualityof their fabrication and materials, completeness as a series, association with elites, they were esteemed in the eighteenth century as an expression of their owner's commitment to the scientific ordering of specimens. Nevertheless, unless they conformed to Kantian notions of artistic autonomy, the works came to be viewed as minor arts rather than high art. These factors impinge directly on African works, which tended to be assigned to the domain of curios.

In their trajectory, African objects were not helped in attaining aesthetic status by what became a dominant dimension of museum display: evolutionism. Following the publication of Darwin's theories, museum exhibits, whether of natural specimens or of objects made by humans, were reorganized along evolutionary lines. As the historian Alma Wittlin points out: "[A]ccording to the adherents of Museological Darwinism even specimens of archaeology or crafts were to be arranged as a consultative library of objects progressively subdivided into orders and genera . . ." (Wittlin 1970: 134–35).

This conflation of the cultural with the biological affected the way in which African objects were represented: as primitive predecessors to the arts of high civilization. By implication, not only were they inferior to European works, but the presumed makers of the works might be thought of as non-humans.

Even when the creators of the works were known, their creations were treated not as achievements by individual artists, but as the anonymous output of a folk (Adams 1989). Just as the supposedly unified, anonymous, communal, participants in medieval cathedral building, non-Western peoples were considered intrinsically different from – usually inferior to – those of European civilization.

Certain European artists and intellectuals, however, viewed this otherness in a positive light. The "Primitive" was more authentic because it embodied elemental human nature, as opposed to civilized artificiality (Goldwater 1986: 120). They saw it in a Romantic, *volkisch* light, similar to the *Gemeinschaft* delineated by Ferdinand Toennies (1963 [1887]).

Romanticism had another side that dominated art, that of the individual creative genius. But this aspect was not invoked for the primitive because only civilized Europeans were permitted individual singularity.[6] At its best, this more or less well meaning paternalism reduced them to the permanent status of minors rather than adults. Their works might be collected,[7] but only near the end of the nineteenth and beginning of the twentieth century did some of them start to be redefined as art.

Bolstered by the vision of avant-garde European artists, who became intrigued by exotic works, the market for these works grew. Scholars developed aesthetic concepts appropriate to their character (Adams 1989). Congruent with late nineteenth-century fine art and antiquities criteria, connoisseurs sought authenticity, purity and rarity in tribal arts. Preferring old to new, they often concealed the fact that many of them had been only recently created. Such assertions as authenticity were easier to uphold if the peoples to whom the works were attributed were dispersed, extinct, and if their culture had, for practical purposes, ceased to exist.[8]

New art is not always newly made, but may exist unrecognized as art until redefined. The museum history of African objects indicates the ambiguities of their standing. Because they often have practical functions, they were housed in ethnographic or history museums, or in historic houses, where such a rationale was appropriate. They were generally excluded from art museums, where valuation was pure aesthetic quality (Zolberg 1992: 14–16).

Thus whereas usefulness is not an absolute barrier to aesthetic legitimacy, it is a source of contamination that must be compensated for by other qualities, such as age. But by itself, age is not sufficient to lend legitimacy. It helps to have a connection with western European civilization. This may be why New World objects, regardless of age, complexity and sophistication, lagged in achieving high standing, and why many pre-Columbian works entered natural history or archaeological museums, rather than art museums.[9]

Still more difficult to assimilate as art are material products of peripheral subcultures of European or other countries. Lacking the prestige of court civilizations, their presence in museums is legitimated by an ethnographic rationale, as representatives of a *Gemeinschaft* or folk culture. Moreover, according to the customary division of labor of their societies, many of these works were made by women rather than men, an attribute even more denigrating (Adams 1989). With so much going against them, their qualities are reduced to "charm" and "craftsmanship," rather than "transcendance" or "universalism" in the Kantian sense (Bourdieu 1984).

Despite these ambiguities, African objects began to find their way into art museums. The details of this trajectory appear clearly in the case of the Art Institute of Chicago.

Slipping in through the side door

When the Art Institute of Chicago was founded (1879–82), it gained a reputation for daring receptiveness to new art, much of it by contemporary Europeans and some by Americans, but there were also some curiosities.[10] In 1889, the same year that the Paris Universal Exposition displayed Oceanic objects and Ashanti works from west Africa (Goldwater 1986: 317), the Art Institute acquired some "odd" objects of the primitive that "drifted in" (Zolberg 1974: 119). As in most art museums at the time, the works ended up in storage, even though some were fine, pre-Columbian gold objects.

This drifting in – entry by inadvertance – was typical of the way in which nearly anything offered to an American art museum, especially by socially prominent patrons, was accepted. But mere residence in a museum collection did not insure the work's artistic legitimacy. Lacking an aesthetic framework and intellectual rationale, the

Figure 9. View in African Hall. Photograph by J. Kirschner, 1910. Neg. 32926, courtesy of the Department of Library Services, American Museum of Natural History.

objects were doomed to obscurity. Although in many art museums obscurity is frequently the fate of many works, in this case, and for certain other genres, the entire category was relegated to the museum's reserves.

The redefining moment arrived at the turn of the century, as individual collectors, some of them European artists, such as Vlaminck, Matisse, Picasso, Derain, Pechner, and Barlach, acquired African or south Pacific sculpture, and incorporated certain primitive stylistic elements into their own creations (Goldwater 1986: 317). Even colonialist anthropological museums began to introduce an aestheticized rather than evolutionary arrangement. Some American collectors were drawn in as well. In 1909 Alfred Stieglitz exhibited African sculpture in his 291 Gallery in New York. By 1923 the first museum exhibition of African art ("Primitive Negro Sculpture") was held at the Brooklyn Museum (Goldwater 1986: 318). This exhibition toured the United States. The Art Institute of Chicago was on its itinerary (Zolberg 1974).

"Primitive Negro Sculpture" was followed to Chicago in 1927 by African carvings from the travelling exhibitions of New York's Harlem Museum, shown in the Art Institute's Children's Museum. Purchased by a Chicago patron, who subsequently donated them to the museum, they remained on display in the Children's Museum of the Art Institute until the 1950s.

The acceptance of the carvings as art at so early a date constitutes a step toward their legitimation, but this was undercut by being sited in the less prestigious department. It implied that these presumably anonymous pieces conveyed the charm of children's works, but lacked the gravitas of fine art. Still, the museum took it seriously in its annual report:

> In these days [referring to the late 1920s] when artists like Picasso, Friesz, Modigliani and Vlaminck are gaining permanent representation in those art museums where the authorities venture to exhibit what they consider great modern paintings, it seems most fitting to exhibit as well examples of those aesthetically signficant wood carvings of the African negroes [sic] which admittedly have had an influence on modern art. Few museums which do not pretend to be primarily ethnological in their interests seem to have felt sufficiently the sound artistic value of such carvings to place them side by side with the artistic creations of the civilized world [sic].
>
> (cited in Zolberg 1974: 224)

Occasionally the Art Institute acquired what was already considered important work: in 1933 a Benin plaque fragment was "fortuitously purchased." Collecting African works as art rather than artifacts was part of a new wave among other art museums. In New York's Museum of Modern Art, a major exhibition, *African Negro Art,* took place in 1935, including many works from European collections. Significantly, they had at first been refused duty free entry by United States Customs agents, who saw them not as art, but as dutiable goods: some looked like reproductions, none were signed or dated, and were more like jewelry and useful objects than art (Lynes 1973: 139).[11]

By the 1950s, once the Chicago Art Institute's holdings had become relatively substantial, it created a new Department of Primitive Art, supported by a special committee of museum patrons. In 1956 the museum exhibited the African sculpture collection of one of the committee's members "to encourage interest and indicate

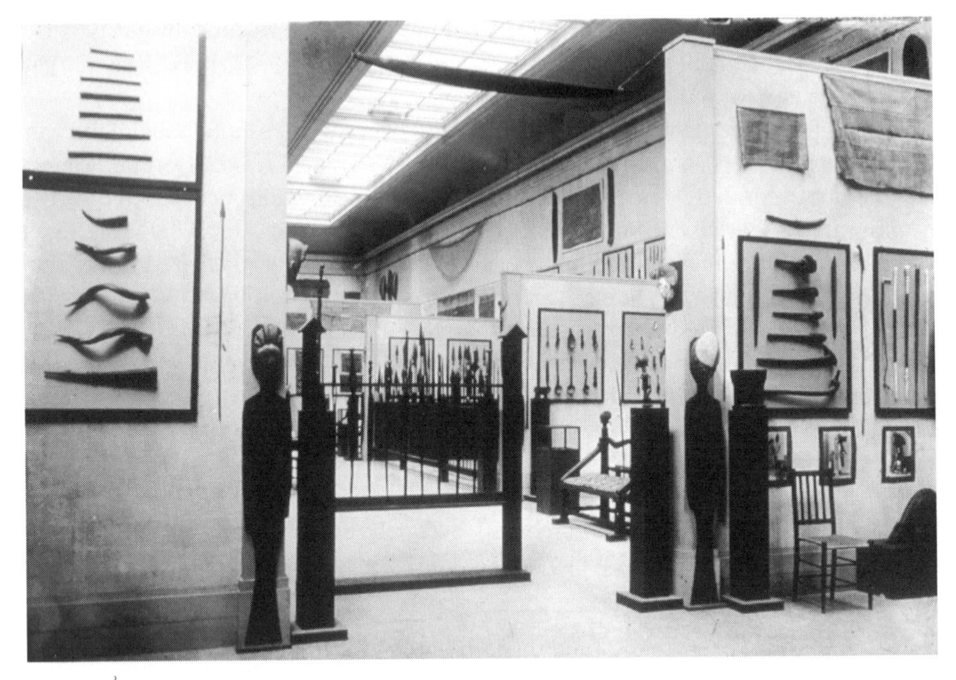

Figure 10. Entry to the 1923 Exhibition of African Negro Art at the Brooklyn Museum. Courtesy of the Brooklyn Museum.

directions in the Art Institute's expanding program of primitive art." A year later the assistant curator was made full curator of Primitive Art, and assigned an assistant. With the structure of staff and patronage in place, the museum organized several exhibitions, the most important of which was a collaborative effort with Chicago's Natural History Museum (the Field Museum) and forty private collectors. The event was hailed as a landmark:

> The collecting of primitive art has become increasingly important as connoisseurs have recognized the artistic validity of works which had previously been only of concern to anthropologists, and this exhibition will demonstrate the great interest Chicagoans have shown in these exotic arts. (cited in Zolberg 1974)

By the end of the 1950s, the relegation of primitive art to the children's department came to an end, and in 1965 a permanent Gallery for Primitive Art was established, and a catalog was published.

Making it official: African art in art museums

Robert Goldwater, who was then Chairman of the Administrative Committee of the Museum of Primitive Art, faulted art historians for still largely ignoring African art, and anthropologists for emphasizing its social functions rather than its aesthetic qualities (Goldwater 1986: xvi [1965]). As a champion of African art as fine art, Goldwater would have been gratified to read that the "discovery" of the Primitive was soon to be hailed by some recent critics as a corrective to the loss of "standards" that in their view had afflicted contemporary art after Abstract Expressionism (Canaday 1972: 29). In the art season of 1972, African statues and other art works, and a collection of nineteenth century Navajo blankets were simultaneously on view at three leading New York museums: the Metropolitan Museum of Art, the Museum of Modern Art, and the Brooklyn Museum. For John Canaday, they served as "a lovely sock in the teeth" for doubters (Canaday 1972).[12]

These events were crowned in rapid succession by four important institutional milestones: Nelson Rockefeller established the Museum of Primitive Art; the Smithsonian Institution created the new National Museum of African Art (1979–81); the Metropolitan Museum of Art added the Michael Rockefeller Wing, to which the Primitive Art Museum works were donated (1982); and a specialized institution, the Center (now, Museum) for African Art, was founded in New York (1983). With the institutional foundations in place, exhibits of African art became a regular feature of both the New York and the world scene.

But controversy over whether African art was art or non-art persisted. In 1984 in its Primitivism exhibition, the Museum of Modern Art linked primitive artistry to the artistry of the West. With its impeccable aesthetic credentials, the MoMA proclaimed that these worlds, seemingly divorced from one another, actually shared "affinities." This rationale implied that common roots bound together artists as diverse as European avant-gardists and the anonymously created, timeless-seeming works from distant places. The idea has been attacked as wrong-headed and dishonest because it is based on assumptions of a universalist, decontextualized aesthetic in which the art of the others is presented through the eyes of its appropriaters (Danto 1987).[13]

If the idea of affinities is taken as a self-serving device with no foundation, what is the connection, if any, between African art and the works of contemporary African American artists? And how does it relate to those artists and their African American patrons? We turn to this problem as we consider art that is newly made.

Through the front door: new art, new patrons

The American museum's dependence on donated works means that when the doors are opened to new types of art, they usually are opened to new patrons as well. The acquisition of wealth by particular social groups, and their concurrent moves to achieve status commensurate with their economic success, make prestigious museums a logical goal. Both museums and patrons gain from the arrangement: the museums provide a public arena for the display of their patrons' taste, and patrons bring the museums new works at little or no cost. But wealth and works alone may not be sufficient to open that door. Until the 1960s, most American museums tended to exclude individuals of certain religious, ethnic, or racial groups from important positions, especially on their boards of trustees. The Art Institute of Chicago provides an instance in which new art, new elites, and new money have converged virtually from its beginnings. Though initially held at arm's length, Jews, Catholics and members of the less prestigious

Protestant denominations eventually were solicited, both for financial donations and for their artworks. The last to be sought were African Americans.

When it came to art works by African Americans, the Art Institute was relatively open. Unlike some other art museums, the Art Institute had since the early 1900s collected a few of their works, such as those of the well known Henry Ossawa Tanner, for example. Several African Americans had had their works exhibited in group shows, especially under federally subsidized programs of the New Deal, during the Second World War, and under Great Society programs of President Lyndon Johnson. But not until 1971 did the museum host the first major one-person show of a black artist's work.[14]

Richard Hunt, an African American sculptor with a national and international reputation, had already exhibited in the Art Institute's popular Crossroads Gallery, had been invited to participate in the Meet-the-Artist Program (to introduce the work of American artists to museum members), and had served as a juror for the Art Institute's American Show of 1972. Under the sponsorship of one of the most prominent African American businessmen in the city (a publishing magnate), his one-person show was a gala affair. Shortly thereafter Hunt, who had already created outdoor sculpture for various private organizations, received a municipal commission for a major public work. The Art Institute soon invited his patron to a seat on the board of trustees. In so doing the museum was somewhat belatedly following the lead of the other cultural institutions of the city: the Civic Opera, the Chicago Symphony Orchestra, and the Museum of Contemporary Art, all of which had African American board members by the early 1970s.

Artists' choice: ethnic affinity as career strategy

What does a well-known sculptor who works within a Western aesthetic of abstraction, or of figurative surrealism have to do with a discussion of primitive or tribal art? African heritage does not seem to have salience here, since Hunt had not made his reputation purely as a "race" artist. Yet under the continuing American racial friction, African American artists such as he share commonalities with artists who explicitly incorporate their ethnic heritage into their art.

Some African American artists have emphasized their universalism, whereas others have stressed their essential "nature" – their descent from African roots. During their career, some have moved between, or combined these options. When the African American anthropologist and dancer, Kathryn Dunham, introduced an African idiom to a wide public in the United States and abroad in the 1940s, the dance critic, Anna Kisselgoff, noted that she was ahead of her time – before "negritude" and "Third World" came to intellectual light, Dunham was bringing to American blacks the heritage that for nearly three centuries had been denied them (Kisselgoff 1972). In combining art with anthropology Dunham created a niche for a new art form. For painters, the problem is far greater, since their work exists in relation to an already established field.[15]

As Wendy Griswold has pointed out, Third-World novelists are faced with similar aesthetic options: universalism (a "human" aesthetic), as opposed to an aesthetic particular to a certain country or region (a "social aesthetic"). Choosing the human, or universalistic, may enhance the creators' access to "insider" status in the realms where artistic power is currently concentrated because it appeals to gatekeepers. In the process, however, success is likely to make them outsiders to what they see as their own native communities (Griswold 1990).

But the options are rarely so starkly presented; nor are the artists' strategies mutually exclusive. The relationship of African American artists to African art is particularly ambiguous. Goldwater's advocacy of primitive art was founded on a certain essentialism. Although he wished African art to be incorporated into the universalistic tradition of the West, at the same time he saw it as imbued with the authenticity of Romanticist nostalgia. In that light he denigrated contemporary artists who work in primitive modes as "primitivistic," not authentically primitive. He had in mind principally Western artists, but his attitude excluded from consideration works by contemporary artists of the localities whence came traditional primitive works as well. To him their artistic practice was inauthentic because its purpose was different from the presumed goals of "authentic" artists. Instead of working with a religious purpose they worked for the market – "airport" art, a category for which critics such as himself had no use. Nor did he give consideration to art by African American artists, whether they were inspired by "tribal" or "primitive" art or not.[16]

On top of the racial discrimination that excluded them from full entry into the art world, African Americans faced a gallery-critic system that had become committed to an aesthetic inimical to their vision and, in many cases, their practice. The aesthetic of autonomous, abstract, modernist art, excluding narrative, reminiscence, or content-laden imagery, contributed to the difficulty African American artists had in breaking into the art market, in gaining funding and media attention, and in finding a public (Pindell 1989; 1990; Patton 1990: 77).

During the early 1970s, African American artists who carried their paintings to the Art Institute, thinking that this was the way to sell their work, were considered aesthetic "naïves" and gently told to go elsewhere (Zolberg 1974). But with the reemergence of the figurative, narrative, and political content in the mainstream art world, there are few intrinsically aesthetic barriers that can be invoked to keep such artists out. Since many white artists engage in similar aesthetic practices, it is not surprising that art museums are increasingly willing to consider the works of these outsiders as valid art forms. Artists of color who identify with Third-World origin are using their art to attain a degree of aesthetic and career empowerment that has long been denied them. Whether their aesthetic choice is spontaneous, or a strategic response to a rejecting art world, their options are more varied.

By the 1980s African American artists are more sophisticated and better educated than their predecessors. Many of them challenge the art worlds with which they are confronted, support the broadening of aesthetic possibilities, and seek alternative career ladders. Instead of approaching established art museums, they turn to experimental or alternative galleries, rely on sympathetic foundations, or corporate or government support, at municipal, state, or federal level.

An example of this process was the organization of a set of exhibits as a collaborative project of the Museum of Contemporary Hispanic Art (MoCHA), the New Museum of Contemporary Art, and the Studio Museum in Harlem in New York City. Under the heading of "The Decade Show," its sub-title, "Frameworks of Identity in the 1980s," opened it to subject-matter and artists of under-represented groups, welcoming socially conscious art, "border culture," multiculturalism.

Of the ninety-four artists invited to participate, twenty-six were African American, and most of the others emphasized identities centered on Hispanic or Asian origins, or gender themes. In a variety of ways they created art in which they explored these identities, in the process challenging "Western images and myths, politics and policy, hierarchical structure and social customs" (Patton 1990: 77–78).

In spite of the exhibitions' emphasis on race, gender or ethnicity, Africa itself was rarely an explicit presence in their works. Rather, most of the African American artists dealt with contemporary American discrimination and their exclusion from mainstream art worlds. Africa itself was treated as a spiritual realm of ritual and recollection, and rarely as a source of concrete forms to be appropriated.[17] This suggests that the choices put forth by Griswold are too sharply defined.

Robert Colescott, one of the most prominent artists in the Decade Show, transcends the dichotomous alternatives of the human or the social. Having studied in Paris with Léger, Colescott has since 1980 appropriated works of Western fine art by painting works in parallel with them, in which he substitutes one or more black personnages in order, so he says, to integrate blacks into white art history.Thus, he has featured blacks in Delacroix's *Liberté Guidant le Peuple*, and Van Eyck's *Arnolfini Betrothal*. One of his contributions to the Decade Show goes beyond his irony and parody by re-appropriating Picasso's *Demoiselles d'Avignon*, altering its composition and re-titling it *Les Demoiselles d'Alabama: Des Nudas* (1984). In his version "black and white women are shown in a Gauguinesque landscape *without* African mask faces (itself a critique of 'primitivism' in modern art)" [my emphasis]. As Sharon Patton, chief Curator of the Studio Museum comments, "No one can look at Picasso's *Les Demoiselles d'Avignon* without thinking of Colescott's painting" (Patton 1990: 84).

Although this is not an assessment with which everyone may necessarily agree, it highlights the difference between conquered colonial subjects, whose works were appropriated, and assertive African American artists who know the official scripts of the "canon" as well as their own experience, and can interpolate them to make their points.

Discussion

Formerly marginal to the mainstream, African art has gone through a career trajectory in which it is no longer relegated to ethnography (or natural history) museums, but is assigned domicile in art museums instead. In fact, aesthetic displays, with their spaciousness and highlighting of individual objects are increasingly found even in natural history museums when African works are featured.

In the course of appropriating it into the Western domain of aesthetic value,

Figure 11. Robert Colescott, *Les Demoiselles d'Alabama* (Des Nudas) (acrylic on canvas), 94×90 in, 1985. Courtesy of the Greenville County Museum of Art, South Carolina.

supporters of African art have developed concepts of formal values, expressive power, detailed examination of their social and psychological meanings (Goldwater 1986: 12–13). But its creators were rarely asked how they wanted them interpreted. The situation is quite different when it comes to their African American kin, who had also been excluded from mainstream art, but are now actively moving into it.

Artists are not obliged to choose between two paths only, that of universalism on the one hand, or ethnic solidarism on the other. Outsider art takes many different forms, of which the expression of ethnic or racial identity is only one. This becomes apparent when we consider the introduction to the joint catalog of The Decade Show, which presents a three-way taped conversation among the directors of the participating

Figure 12. Primitive art show, 1939, general view. Neg. 316091, courtesy of the Department of Library Services, American Museum of Natural History.

museums. Marcia Tucker of The New Museum points out that the idea of the "decade" would probably be very different if the curators had represented the homogeneous "white, very male, very mainstream view of what happened during the eighties . . . [M]y sense of it was a much more slippery, heterogeneous, complicated, and difficult one. My idea included work of people who were invisible in the mainstream but who seemed to be really critical to an understanding of the period." Nilda Peraza of the MoCHA agrees with her, adding that for her the decade "saw the move out of obscurity of what I call the 'parallel cultures' and 'parallel aesthetics.'" Coexisting with the mainstream, which continues to try to exclude it, Ms. Peraza wishes to create "a very generous and open art environment in this country, one that will allow and accept artists from all backgrounds, without stereotyping and pigeonholing."

But the third director, Kinshasha Conwill of the Studio Museum in Harlem, does not entirely concur. Even though her museum was established to serve the people of Harlem and African American artists, she finds a different value in the Decade Show. While she recognizes that its issue-oriented exhibits permit engagement with other cultures (*The Decade Show* 1990: 9–10), she is keenly aware of the project's ambiguities. These emerge when Marcia Tucker recalled Ms. Conwill's reaction to the aim of her

New Museum, which was to "break apart the 'canon,' so to speak, to position itself in opposition to or outside of the mainstream. At that time [Ms. Conwill] joked, 'Well you guys want to get rid of the canon just at the moment when we are about to enter it!'" (*The Decade Show* 1990: 11).

The dilemma presented confronts many other outsiders as well, whether they wish to express in their works ethnic or feminist or conceptual concerns or a combination of these. By now the absorptive capacity of mainstream art is sufficient to incorporate the artists individually, and ultimately weaken the cohesiveness on which much socially committed artistic expression is based. For some outsiders this is a desirable outcome, a form of appropriation in which artists themselves are active participants and beneficiaries. Most important to them is that their work be given serious public attention, and that they be permitted to engage in open discussion as to its merits. Under the condition of postmodernity, with its openness to a greater variety of styles and genres, and a multiplicity of entry points through alternative spaces and galleries, for better or for worse, the chances of this happening have rarely been so great.

Notes

1 An exception is James Clifford, whose analysis of the assumptions, procedures, and definitions of the primitive by anthropologists, and the struggle of subject peoples to create new identities for themselves, touches on many of these issues.

2 This trajectory has been analyzed by art historians (Goldwater 1939–1986; Adams 1989), anthropologists (Clifford 1988), critics (Kramer 1991; 1992) and museum professionals (Rubin 1984; Schildkrout and Keim 1990; Vogel 1988; Steiner 1994).

3 Goldwater's analysis of how the "primitive" came to be considered art has been criticized by, among others, Hal Foster, for a Whiggish aestheticism that ignores appropriation processes (1988). James Clifford is critical of his chronology, suggesting that it neglects the processes that culminated in Western hegemony over conquered peoples, with little regard to the meanings they assigned to certain works. The subject is revisited in the catalog for a major, controversial exhibition at the Museum of Modern Art (Rubin 1984), and in the catalog for an exhibition at the African Art Center, in which Susan Vogel raises questions about the validity of meanings attached to the idea of the primitive (1988). See also Schildkrout and Keim (1990) and Phillips (1995).

4 Among them were the English critics, Roger Fry and Clive Bell, the American photographer and arts publicist, Alfred Stieglitz, the French anthropologist, Marcel Griaule, Surrealist writer, Michel Leiris, and museum founder, Paul Rivet.

5 Clifford's analysis of museumification of tribal works stems from ideas of Jean Baudrillard as applied by A. J. Greimas. Conceptualizing it as an enclosed "semiotic square," Greimas divides art into zones of dominance in which uniqueness and authenticity are prized (Clifford 1988).

6 This idea underlies the Gothic revival in architecture in the 19th century and its appeal to intellectuals such as William Morris and his supporters. But as Sander Gilman warns, in spite of its seemingly positive features, such thinking is integral to the construction of a dehumanized other. As such it was used to justify European domination over the colonized (Gilman 1985), and thus the experience of the Pygmy, Ota Benga, who was for a time displayed in the Bronx Zoo in 1906 (Bradford and Blume 1992).

7 The low regard in which many were held is attested to by their treatment. Works made of precious metals, as from pre-Columbian civilizations, were frequently melted down. Until they realized that they had value on the curio or art market, Christian missionaries and Muslims alike burned what they considered religious fetishes (Torgovnick 1990: 19).
8 The elimination of numerous peoples on the African continent and of many of the native peoples of both American continents and the genocide perpetrated against the Jews of modern Europe made it relatively simple to appropriate their works and belongings. The Nazis' project to create a museum of an "extinct race" in Prague represents a highpoint of cynicism in this utter evil.
9 The Field Museum of Natural History in Chicago has collections of pre-Columbian works from Latin America, and objects from Tibet. Not till well into the twentieth century were similar works being collected by the Art Institute of Chicago.
10 The museum accepted early gifts of Impressionist and Post-Impressionist paintings, and despite opposition from certain quarters, welcomed temporary exhibits of controversial art, such as the Armory Show of 1913 (Zolberg 1974).
11 This was similar to the reception given by US Customs to abstractionist sculpture by Giacometti, Duchamp-Villon, Miró, Boccioni, Arp, and others less than a year later (ibid.).
12 Though it was not the first time that those museums had shown such works, rarely had there been such a density of African and Native American arts in so short a time. I have already referred to the Brooklyn Museum exhibit in the 1920s. The MoMA had exhibited "American Sources of Modern Art: Aztec, Mayan, Incan;" "African Sculpture" (this as early as 1933); "Prehistoric Rock Pictures in Europe and Africa." They launched a Harlem educational outreach program in 1935 (Lynes 1973: 441–2; 448; 450). At the Art Institute of Chicago, by the end of the 1970s, the department of Primitive Art had been replaced by a much enlarged department encompassing "Arts of Africa, the Americas and Oceania."
13 In 1996 the Guggenheim Museum opened its blockbuster exhibition "Africa: The Art of a Continent," which had first opened at London's Royal Academy (Phillips 1995).
14 An interesting sidelight on the Art Institute is that among its founders and patrons in the late nineteenth century were a number of devoted supporters of the Union during the Civil War. Black art students were admitted to its school as early as the turn of the century, and administrators and trustees defended them against objections by white students.
15 Kisselgoff is aware that Dunham was not the first to work as she did, but she makes no reference to the search for African essence as one of the strands in the work of African American intellectuals, such as Alain Locke, in the Harlem Renaissance.
16 Bennetta Jules-Rosette, an African American anthropologist, is one of the rare exceptions (1983: 443–66), as was Nelson Graburn (1976). More recently, Sally Price has shown that contemporary artists among the Maroons of Suriname have adapted to the demands of tourist buyers (Price 1990), as have those in Côte d'Ivoire, see Steiner (1994). Among the early American collectors of African works as art, in his idiosyncratic framework, was Albert Barnes (Zolberg 1995).
17 Emma Amos is one of the few exceptions, in that she incorporated African narrow-strip weavings into her collages.

References

Adams, Monni 1989, "African Visual Arts from an Art Historical Perspective," *African Studies Review*, vol. 32 no. 2: 55–103.

Alsop, Joseph 1982, *The Rare Art Traditions: The History of Art Collecting and Its Linked Phenomena Wherever They Have Appeared*, New York: Harper and Row.
Becker, Howard S. 1982, *Art Worlds*, Berkeley: University of California Press.
Bourdieu, Pierre 1984, *Distinction: A Social Critique of the Judgement of Taste* (translated by Richard Nice), Cambridge, MA: Harvard University Press.
Bradford, Phillips Verner and Blume, Harvey 1992, *Ota Benga: The Pygmy in the Zoo*, New York: St. Martin's Press.
Canaday, John 1972, "A Lovely Sock in the Teeth," *New York Times*, Oct. 22: 29.
Cinquina, M. 1989, "Art from the Margins: Far From Marginal," *The East Villager*, May: 17.
Clifford, James 1988, *The Predicament of Culture: Twentieth-Century Ethnography, Literature, and Art,* Cambridge, MA: Harvard University Press.
Danto, A. 1987, "'Primitivism' in 20th Century Art," in *The State of the Art*. New York: Prentice Hall Press, 23–27.
The Decade Show: Frameworks of Identity in the 1980s 1990, New York: MoCHA, NMCA, Studio Museum in Harlem.
Dubin, Steven C. 1989, "Impolitic Art and Uncivil Actors," unpublished paper.
Foster, Hal 1988, "The 'Primitive' Unconscious of Modern Art, or White Skin Black Masks," in *Recodings: Art, Spectacle, Cultural Politics*, Seattle: Bay Press, 157–80.
Geertz, Clifford 1983, "Art as a Social System," *Local Knowledge: Further Essays in Interpretive Anthropology*, ed. Geertz, New York: Basic Books, 94–120.
Gilman, Sander L. 1985, *Difference and Pathology: Stereotypes of Sexuality,Race, and Madness*, Ithaca: Cornell University Press.
Goldwater, Robert, 1986, *Primitivism in Modern Art* (enlarged edition), Cambridge: Harvard University Press [originally 1939].
Graburn, Nelson, ed., 1976, *Ethnic and Tourist Arts*, Berkeley: University of California Press.
Griswold, Wendy 1990, "The Importance of Being Marginal: Aesthetic Goals of Third World Writers," paper prepared for the World Congress of Sociology, Madrid, July 9–13.
Halle, David 1993, *Inside Culture: Art and Class in the Modern American Home,* University of Chicago Press.
Jules-Rosette, Bennetta 1983, "Tourist Art and Ethnic Identity in East Africa: New Dimensions in the Emergence of Popular Culture,"*Contribution to the Sociology of the Arts*, ed. E. Nikolov, Sofia: Research Institute for Culture, 443–66.
Kisselgoff, Anna 1972, "Dance: 'Choros,' Dunham Gem, Unveiled," *New York Times*, Nov. 27: 19.
Kramer, Hilton 1991, "'Africa Explores' Exhibit in City: Works Debasing Western Styles," *The New York Observer*, July 8–15: 1.
1992, "Met's Royal Art of Benin Elevates African Canon," *The New York Observer*, Feb. 24: 1.
Lynes, Russell 1973, *Good Old Modern: An Intimate Portrait of the Museum of Modern Art,* New York: Atheneum.
Patton, Sharon F. 1990, "The Agenda in the Eighties: Socially Conscious Art," *The Decade Show*, 77–91.
Phillips, Tom, ed., 1995, *Africa: The Art of a Continent*, London and Munich: Royal Academy of Arts and Prestel Verlag.
Pindell, Howardena 1989, "Art World Racism: A Documentation," *New Art Examiner*, March: 32–36.
1990, "Breaking the Silence: Art World Racism, the Glaring Omission," *New Art Examiner*, October: 18–23.

Price, Sally 1990, *Primitive Art in Civilized Places*, University of Chicago Press.
Rosenberg, Harold 1974, "The Art World: Peaceable Kingdom," *The New Yorker*, March 25: 128–34.
Rubin, William 1984, *"Primitivism" in 20th Century art: Affinity of the Tribal and the Modern*, New York: The Museum of Modern Art.
Schildkrout, Enid and Keim, Curtis A., eds., 1990, *African Reflections: Art from Northeastern Zaïre*, New York: American Museum of Natural History.
Steiner, Christopher B. 1994, *African Art in Transit*, Cambridge University Press.
Toennies, Ferdinand 1963, *Community and Society*, New York: Harper & Row [originally 1882].
Torgovnick, Marianna 1990, *Gone Primitive: Savage Intellects, Modern Lives*, University of Chicago Press.
Vogel, Susan, ed., 1988, *ART/artifact*, New York: The Center for African Art.
Wittlin, Alma 1970, *Museums: In Search of a Usable Future*, Cambridge, MA: MIT Press.
Zolberg, Vera L. 1974, "The Art Institute of Chicago: The Sociology of a Cultural Organization," Ph.D. thesis, University of Chicago.
1983, "New Art – New Patrons: Coincidence or Causality in the 20th-century Avant-Garde?," *Contribution to the Sociology of the Arts*, ed. E. Nikolov, Sofia: Research Institute for Culture, 309–35.
1992. "Art on the Edge: Political Aspects of Aestheticizing the Primitive," *Boekmancahier* 4/14, Dec. 1992: 413–25.
1995, "The Collection Despite Barnes: From Private Preserve to Blockbuster," *Art in Museums,* ed. Susan Pearce, Vol.V [New Research in Museum Studies] London: 94–108.

PART II

Career strategies of outsiders

Artistic success does not happen spontaneously. Success must be desired, constructed and maintained. This requires knowledge of, and attention to, the practices and mores of a given art world. This part contains essays that attempt to make manifest those activities and processes that are necessary (though not always sufficient) to achieve contemporary artistic recognition.

Henry Finney discusses a number of factors that affect success in today's visual arts world: biographical and career development, art training, stylistic affinities, race, gender, location, developing a persona, gallery selection, marketing strategies, networking, sponsorship, social visibility, and artistic friendship circles. Finney contends that great artistic talent alone is not sufficient for artistic success, but depends on an array of sociological considerations which can enhance or minimize the possibility thereof.

Strategic behaviors played a significant role in Pop Art's ascendance in the 1960s. Its practitioners went far beyond previous efforts to break the barrier between high and low art, and in the process ended the universal commitment to establishing theoretical guidelines for artistic practice. Joni Cherbo identifies important social conditions and strategies that facilitated Pop Art's meteoric rise: a booming art market; the natural affiliation/coalition among Pop artists, new patrons, and entrepreneurial gallery owners; the artistic social scene in New York City where art had achieved international recognition and exhaustive media attention.

Mark Kostabi's aggressive strategy for recognition in the art world elaborated and extended the trend set by Pop Art, mixing commercial and entrepreneurial activities and attitudes with fine art practices. András Szántó describes the factory-like practices of Kostabi World in producing, selecting, and marketing pictures. Kostabi World was subjected to invective primarily because it desecrated the sanctity of artistic creativity. Whether or not Kostabi's strategy ultimately succeeds will, according to Szántó, depend on a number of factors, not the least of which will be his ability simply to keep his gallery open, and thus confidence in his operation alive, during austerity in the art market.

While artists and art world practitioners are central to building success, all works which aspire to be art must eventually enter the public domain, and public reception of new art can have a daunting effect on its career. Nathalie Heinich compares public reactions to the Robert Mapplethorpe exhibition in Cincinnati, and to Daniel Buren's installation in the courtyard of the Palais-Royal and Christo's wrapping of the Pont-Neuf in Paris, contrasting the "scandals" produced by Mapplethorpe and Buren with the quietude that greeted Christo. She addresses notions of public perception of artistic authenticity, whether the work was accomplished with public or private monies, and whether it was intended to be permanent or temporary, and its sexual and moral character. These value domains, she contends, form the basis of the frame analysis for understanding public acceptance or rejection of art works, in the United States, in France, or elsewhere.

4

Art production and artists' careers: the transition from "outside" to "inside"

Henry C. Finney

For purposes of discussing the art-world transition from "outside" to "inside," it will be convenient – even if also somewhat misleading – to think of the inside as "The Art Establishment" (Rosenberg 1965). It is convenient because there are hierarchies, dominant academic perspectives and art world centers that shape existing patterns of prestige, reputation and income among artists.[1] It is misleading because there are not one but many art worlds, some of them overlapping, and each with its own hierarchy; and there are not one but many dimensions of inclusion or standing within each.

The simplest way to understand the status of being "inside" or "outside" – and the one adopted here – is in terms of a particular operating art world (Becker 1982), such as the one described by the author in previous research (Finney 1993).[2] But art worlds vary enormously, some being local or regional, others comprising major urban art scenes. Furthermore, major centers, like New York, are themselves split into multiple hierarchies that vary in terms of art style (e.g. traditional vs. modern vs. postmodern), commercial orientation (e.g. "graphic design" vs. "fine arts") and utilitarianism (e.g. "craft" vs. "art"). Each particular art world, then, has a hierarchy (or hierarchies) of success or reputation, with those participants suffering marginal or unrecognized status being "outsiders," those enjoying high reputation being "insiders," and "young" or "emerging" artists standing in between.

How, then, do artists cross the zone from "outside" to "inside" in one of these particular scenes? What are the art-world barriers to recognition and how are they overcome? Because the process actually starts quite early for some artists, it is helpful to imagine the typical life-cycle of a professional fine artist.[3] For instance, what social patterns typify the family origins of artists, their socialization and training, their adaptation to the adult art world, their success or failure, and their eventual reputation? In particular, is there evidence to suppose – as would seem reasonable – that "insiders" enjoy an advantage because of early formative experiences?

Surprisingly little research deals with the social origins of modern fine artists. Do they come from privileged backgrounds, like Cézanne or Degas? Or do they conform better to the poverty-stricken image of the *peintres maudits*, like Utrillo and Modigliani? Do artists differ psychologically in important ways from non-artists? What early experiences are especially formative? As summarized by Zolberg (1990:

107–35), studies by psychologists indicate that artists by no means conform to the popular stereotype of being maladjusted, withdrawn, unpredictable or socially alienated. Indeed, one rare study of the same artists over time found that, while talent and certain personality traits are germane, various socially potent factors, such as gender and ability to adapt to social pressures, are equally important for predicting the success of an artist (Getzels and Csikszentmihalyi 1976).

A few sociological studies do give hints of artists' social backgrounds, however, suggesting early advantage for many. While all social classes are represented among modern artists, Simpson's very small sample of SoHo artists (1981) suggested a preponderance of higher-status backgrounds – 75 percent of his artists came from comfortable or affluent middle-, upper-middle or upper-class families. Another more indirect study (Blau, Blau & Golden 1985) found that artists are relatively more numerous in predominantly white-collar cities.

Minority group experience is particularly relevant to current discussions of outsiders. While the number of minority-group artists in America's urban visual art scene is probably increasing (Failing 1989), African and Hispanic Americans are underrepresented. Although African Americans account for about 12 percent of the total population, they made up only 3.6 percent of visual artists in 1988 (US Bureau of the Census 1990: 389); and this reality is echoed in their comparatively much lower levels of participation generally in the visual arts (DiMaggio and Ostrower 1990). The early 1990s, however, saw many exhibitions by minority-group artists in the New York scene, as well as the establishment of specialized minority-oriented centers like the Museum for African Art in SoHo and, earlier, the Studio Museum in Harlem.[4]

Minorities and women are both under-represented in America's important urban galleries and museums, but the dynamics giving rise to the imbalance may differ for the two groups. Both have undoubtedly experienced discrimination in the art-world's upper reaches; but unlike the situation for African-Americans, whose under-representation evidently partly reflects their lower levels of interest as a group to begin with (DiMaggio and Ostrower 1990), the lower visibility of women appears to be mainly due to some process of selection or discrimination. At least one must surmise that this is the cause of the great discrepancy between women's documented under-representation at the "top," as opposed to their equal or even majority representation among artists generally (US Bureau of the Census 1990: 389), among artists in local art worlds (Finney 1993), and among art students in particular (Getzels and Csikszentmihalyi 1976; Strauss 1970). As suggested by one pair of researchers (Getzels and Csikszentmihalyi 1976), who found that women art students were much less likely than men to continue their commitment to art in later life, part of the "discrimination" may work through self-selection. But gender discrimination at the top, as various commentators, such as Lippard (1976) have so often reminded us, as have the posters and performances of the Guerrilla Girls, is undoubtedly also a significant contributor to women's outsider status in the big city art world.

Crossing the insider/outsider boundary may also be seen as a long-term process of artistic career development. For instance, certain early formative experiences generate what several researchers describe as the first stage of a developing artist's typical career

(Simpson 1981: Chapter 4; Moulin 1987: Chapter 6; Manfredi 1982: Chapter 5). Simpson describes it as the stage of developing "motivation" (1981). As shown by two studies of early formative influences (Griff 1964; Strauss 1970), many artists cite such experiences as "Saturday morning art classes" during childhood; being treated by primary and high school teachers and fellow students as the "class artist"; recognition and encouragement by particular early art teachers; and art-related work experiences. Some also mention parental encouragement; but just as common, however, are reports of parental discouragement, due evidently to parental fears that pursuing careers in art will lower their children's subsequent socio-economic status.

Through the 1980s the proportion of artists for whom early art schooling was a major formative experience increased.[5] Art educators have long bewailed public school neglect of art, noting, for example, that as of the early 1980s, the number of contact hours in art was fewer than one per week in nearly two-thirds of all primary schools (Chapman 1982: 54). Nevertheless, over half (57 percent) of all primary schools in one study were "served" by a visual art teacher, and this percentage increased by one-third during the 1980s (Moorman 1989). At the high school level during the same period, 85 percent of schools offered visual art education, although only 35 percent of students took it up (Moorman 1989), and in almost no schools was it required (Chapman 1982: 75).

The 1980s growth pattern is even clearer at the college level, especially in programs specifically for training artists. This is one of the starting points, indeed, of transition from "outside" to "inside." The field of potential recruits narrows as some students move to what Simpson (1981) identifies as the second career stage of the emerging artist. At this stage the artist typically declares independence from parental control, begins to embrace the social role of the "artist" (Simpson 1981: Chapter 4), and starts to learn the myriad art "conventions" (Becker 1982) that must be mastered to become a professional (Manfredi 1982: Chapter 5). Commenting on a particularly critical step in this transition, several studies of college art training (Griff 1964; Strauss 1970) indicate that the process of self-sorting into different majors – fine art, commercial art or art education – is highly formative. Gender figures significantly in the process; more women students are likely to favor art education, a factor that may help account for their higher subsequent drop-out rate in fine art and their under-representation in major galleries and museums.

As shown in a recent study (Finney 1995), the learning of existing art-world styles and conventions during the course of acquiring an advanced degree in fine arts is a much more dynamic process than is often supposed in the standard sociological approach (Becker 1982). At their least creative, aspiring artists merely play an existing art-style "game" – that is, they imitate, or even copy, some favorite historical or contemporary style. Indeed, this "strategy" is the norm among hobby and amateur artists.[6] Such imitative strategies are not respected among professional big-city artists, however. Accordingly, especially among students committed to modern or postmodern styles, mastery of convention is often coupled with a highly innovative process of game invention in which an established game (e.g. abstract expressionism) is combined with elements of other stylistic games (e.g. appropriationism, or "word" art), or on occasion, an entirely new game is invented. Indeed, this "burden of ... an independent vision" (Simpson 1981: 77) is one of the most conspicuous norms of the contemporary big-city art world.[7] Consequently, stylistic inventiveness is a central barrier in the transition from outsider to insider status. This is not to say that students adopting modern or postmodern styles do not also imitate or copy; but at their best, the mastery and use of stylistic conventions are more dynamic and innovative than is often recognized by sociologists.

More broadly, the growing significance of college art education must be understood as part of the phenomenal growth of the art world during the 1970s and 1980s, including a dramatic increase in the number of artists – that is, of academically trained "insiders."[8] For instance, the number of painters, sculptors and artist-printmakers in the country increased by 76 percent between 1970 and 1980 – about two-and-a-half times the increase for the labor force as a whole – and some increase continued through the 1980s, although at a lower rate (Bradshaw 1989; Robinson 1989). Thus, even though art school admissions are highly selective, the number of art students has increased dramatically. More generally, one late-1980s estimate put the number of art professionals graduating per year at 40,000, an increase of nearly 50 percent since 1970 (Brown 1989: 19). By 1980 the total number of studio graduates, in particular, was about 15,000 per year (Tompkins 1988: 74). However, paralleling the more recent decline of the art world in terms of sales, prices and gallery closings, these rates of increase have probably slowed or even reversed in the mid-1990s.

In addition, during the 1980s the percentage of nationally known successful artists with an advanced degree (MFA or PhD) has increased dramatically (Larson 1983). As one study reported (Crane 1987: 9–10), in the 1940s and 1950s only 10 percent of prominent artists (the abstract expressionists) had an advanced art degree, while in the 1980s 51 percent of one prominent group (pattern-and-decoration painters) had such a credential. Even with the dramatic growth in the number of galleries over the same period, the county's art schools and programs were turning out more trained artists than the art world could absorb (Larson 1983). The result for artists was illustrated by Ivan Karp's experience at SoHo's OK Harris Gallery:

> Karp . . . claims that he looks at the work of a hundred and fifty or two hundred artists a week, without appointment. About a third of the artists he sees are fully professional, he says, and out of that number maybe twenty deserve to be shown in a New York Gallery.
>
> He has taken on only two new artists in the last year . . . (Tompkins 1988: 72)

Thus, the problem of post-graduate survival is aggravated for many artists who, in terms of the current discussion, remain "outside" the system despite their "insider" training to enter it.

Simpson identifies this period after graduation as the typical artist's third career stage (1981: Chapter 4). It is a period of "prolonged incubation" in which the young artist struggles, often against great odds, to gain recognition. It is a time of fateful decisions, such as whether one will enter the "New York scene," with which circles of young artists one will associate, how to develop a style that is simultaneously innovative and marketable, what new styles or media one will embrace, what shows or galleries one will approach, how one will support oneself in the absence of sufficient income from art, and how to promote one's work. As many art students have complained, these are the things art schools don't teach.

Specifically, the artists' resulting adaptation to their immediate art world, its institutions and its networks largely determines – along with a lot of good luck – their status as insiders or outsiders. As the author's study of a local art world illustrates (Finney 1993), a large number of artists of widely differing styles compete for recognition by a few art-world gatekeepers, and the result is an artists' stratification system in which certain types of art and artists are accorded more of an insider status than others. Ranging from lowest (outsider) to highest (insider) status, the primary artists' status groups in this community were naïves, hobbyists, serious amateurs, aspiring pre-professionals and professionals.

The naïves tended to produce the types of art associated with "grass roots" art, with its well-known primitive style, lacking as it usually does much command of illusionist technique or of materials. Generally, the naïves' work was excluded from the community's more prestigious galleries and show spaces, with the important exception of several shows and one gallery shop featuring their work as part of the recent urban art-world "rediscovery" of naïve art. Also, the naïves did not participate in any of the area's many artist organizations or events, nor did they think of themselves as "artists."

The hobbyists and amateurs tended to embrace traditional, representational styles in watercolor or pastel. Although the hobbyists still saw themselves as outsiders in terms of technical mastery, they demonstrated aspirations for improvement through attending numerous workshops and classes. The more accomplished "serious amateurs" consequently succeeded in achieving local insider status through their frequent sales and inclusion in local shows and competitions. Especially among the amateurs, the level of art-world participation was high. Theirs was a local insider status, however, for these artists generally showed little interest, knowledge or mastery of modernist, abstract or postmodern styles. Accordingly, except among the most accomplished amateurs, these artists were profoundly ambivalent as to whether to call themselves "artists."

The pre-professionals, by contrast, had crossed the line of self-identification and commitment. They were also more centrally visible in local art-world networks, better trained, more technically competent, more likely to work in oils or acrylics on canvas, more likely to be accepted in the local area's most prestigious show spaces, and much more likely to embrace modernist styles, including abstraction. In short, they were definitely the insiders of the local scene. Although most were not art-school graduates, they generally thought of themselves as "artists" and harbored aspirations for eventual full-time, professional status. Like the naïves, hobbyists and amateurs, the pre-professionals were overwhelmingly women.

The professionals, finally, differed significantly from most of the others. They tended to be the area's art teachers, working part- or full-time in local school or college art departments; to have completed the MFA; to have shown in more prestigious distant urban settings; both to identify themselves and to be seen by others as "professional artists"; to work in multiple and major media; and to work in both modern and postmodern styles. Significantly, a majority of the professionals were men, although the sex ratio had recently become more balanced. The professionals were active participants in more distant networks, but they either avoided involvement in the local art-world hierarchy, or participated "downwards" as invited urban art-world insiders.

The dynamics of the local scene revealed primary mechanisms that differentiate outsiders from insiders in most visual art worlds. Many artists moved upwards through the various levels as their local art careers unfolded. As they moved upward, their level of professional commitment, art-world involvement, knowledge of art, skill, and artistic style tended to change also. The most important selective mechanisms for insider status were formal art education, acquiring professional attitudes, artistic style, network centrality, jurying, and sales – factors bearing a close similarity to those reported in other studies.[9] Except as noted earlier, truly naïve and imitative traditional styles were excluded from the upper levels in favor of modernist abstraction, innovative figuration and sophisticated forms of *art brut*.

In both local and big-city art worlds (except for the naïves), artists at various levels often function within a more-or-less cohesive "status community" (Simpson 1981). Small groups or social circles (Kadushin 1976) of artists whose art-world status and artistic style are similar, associate closely as friends, supporting each other with companionship, encouragement, and information about jobs and show opportunities (Simpson 1981; Moulin 1987; Finney 1993). Strong norms against harsh artistic criticism operate within these groups, protecting participants from stigmatization as "outsiders." So supportive and formative are these communities or "movement circles" (Ridgeway 1989) that new styles sometimes originate there, illustrating that group-formation can be one of the mechanisms for making the transition from outside to inside. Important examples include the Batignolles group of Impressionists in the late nineteenth century (Rogers 1970) and the circle of abstract expressionists who congregated at Greenwich Village's Cedar Tavern in the 1950s. Styles have differed greatly, however, in the degree to which their artists have been closely associated in a status community (Crane 1987; 1989).

Some artists are eventually recognized, however, and move on to a fourth stage of career success as art world insiders (Simpson 1981: Chapter 5). Just how to define "success" (i.e. truly "inside" status) is debatable, however. According to one very strict definition, "successful" artists are those who support themselves entirely from art sales. By this definition, only 1–5 percent of SoHo artists are successful (Simpson 1981). By extension, if one accepts the subsequent 1988 US Census enumeration of 215,000 visual artists, simple arithmetic extrapolation from this strict definition suggests there are from 2,150 to 10,750 successful artists in the entire country (US Bureau of the Census 1988). Although nobody knows the precise figure, nor how it varies from one art world to another, curiously, the 1–5 percent figure is close to the 8 percent of student artists who were found in one longitudinal study still to be pursuing art careers at mid-life (Csikszentmihalyi, Getzels and Kahn 1984). This low success rate is also reflected in lower-than-average artist incomes, according to one large study of painters and sculptors.[10]

A more forgiving definition is defensible, however, for many thousands of artists are supported by art-related institutional salaries or stipends, rather than through sales.

The most significant of these institutions are the nation's colleges and universities, whose art faculties are expected to make art and who have extended periods (summers, sabbaticals) in which to do so. Noting the existence in 1988 of some 1,600 schools and departments of art and design in higher education, one recent estimate put the level of support for college and university art programs at $2 billion annually (Lyons 1990). Up to two-thirds of this amount is probably accounted for in faculty salaries. By contrast, the National Endowment for the Arts allocated only $6 million for its visual art programs in the same year.

Whatever definition one prefers – whether "strict" or "forgiving" – the severe downturn of the art market in the early 1990s, the subsequent closing of many galleries, and the drastic mid-1990s reductions in congressional funding of arts organizations through the National Endowments for the Arts and for the Humanities undoubtedly require some reduction in estimates for the rate of "success" among artists.

However the concept is defined, "successful" or "inside" artists achieve recognition as much by effectively finding their way in the complex institutional and economic world of art as through artistic talent and the aesthetic quality of their work – as sociologists have argued at length (Becker 1982; Moulin 1987; Zolberg 1990; Finney 1993). As just noted, one successful social adaptation is college or university employment. The minimal prerequisite for that is an MFA and, increasingly, some prior success in the world of big-city exhibitions.

In larger metropolitan art worlds, however, recognition by respected galleries and museums leading to sales is more central to achieving insider status, and is undoubtedly the criterion that guides most aspiring and professional artists. The standard is sometimes rather crassly formulated, as in successful artist Jeff Koons' remark that "I want to be as big an art star as possible . . . I like the idea of my work selling for a lot of money. That's very sexual to me" (Cox 1989: A1). John Alexander, a successful artist who lectures widely to art-school students, reports their extremely high hopes in this regard (Gardner 1990: 135):

> The students say, "Jeff Koons did it – how can I succeed?" They all want to be art stars. If they haven't made it by the age of 35, they feel that opportunity has passed them by . . . The kids come to New York, see what's trendy – and then make art to fit the trend and the collectors who are buying *into* that trend.

Increasingly, it would seem that artists are coming to appreciate that recognition as an insider requires "hustle" as well as talent and productivity. Some strategies are relatively ineffective, including uninvited approaches to prestigious galleries. More promising are a range of individual, group and marketplace tactics (Rosenblum 1985; Gardner 1990). Some individual assets cited by observers, such as being young, male and handsome cannot always be so easily acquired. Others can, including cultivation of a personal image or "persona," becoming known as an arts writer, and systematic socializing. The payoffs from aggressive "networking" were cynically described by Andy Warhol:

> Here's how it works. You meet rich people and you hang around with them and one night they've had a few drinks and they say, "I'll buy it!" Then they tell their friends . . ., and that's all you need. That's all it takes. Get it? (Gardner 1990: 134)

Or, as one artist said to a friend at a New York opening, "I'd love to talk, but I've only got forty minutes to work the room" (Gardner 1990: 137). These reports of mercenary expediency may not describe the typical artist; but there is no doubt that visibility through informal contact and acquaintance is an important dimension in artist recognition (Finney 1993).

Also effective are various forms of sponsorship and group association. These include working in a well-known atelier, such as Tyler Graphics (in Bedford, NY) or Universal Limited Art Editions (Long Island); being a relative, friend or studio assistant of an established artist; founding an artists' group that is subsequently labeled by the art world; association with a "hot" alternative space or artists' cooperative gallery; and active social and market promotion by your gallery if you are already associated with one. In particular, sponsorship by senior, established artists is an especially effective route to recognition (Ridgeway 1989). Well-known artists often act, in effect, as intermediaries between unknown artists and the commercial galleries that serve as primary gatekeepers to recognition.

Development of a conscious "marketing" strategy can also help. Artist Jeff Koons, again, forthrightly counsels that "you have to understand the market you want. You have to realize your audience. Then, direct your work to that economy" (Gardner 1990). Also, many successful artists' careers have begun through recognition by a well-known regional art critic or museum curator. Whatever the tactic, it is safe to say that recognition requires good luck and often lots of hustle.

However, the quest for insider status is complicated by artists' ambivalence and even strain in their orientation to their various "publics," such as buyers, collectors, viewers and critics (Rosenberg and Fliegel 1965). One study (Simpson 1981) scrutinized how SoHo artists adapted to such conflicts. For instance, the process of jockeying for gallery recognition – required for success in New York City – involves intense competition with other artists, including friends, and is beset by such dangers as confusing "sales" with "reputation" (some galleries are best avoided). Once a dealer connection has been made, new strains arise, for the artist must place considerable "situational trust" in the dealer. This can be tricky, for the dealer is likely to make decisions affecting the artist as much out of consideration for gallery status or the gallery's other artists as for the artist in question.

There is also the challenge of balancing galleries' conflicting expectations for innovativeness with maintenance of a consistently recognizable style. Rosenberg's "tradition of the new" (1961) and Poggioli's "error of traditionalism" (1971) must be balanced against the gallery's need, as a marketing strategy, for long-term stylistic recognizability and consistency. Another possible ball in the artist's juggling act is somehow to remain true to one's deeper aesthetic concerns and original idealism, while still responding to gallery pressures and the art world's changing media or styles. Success also forces changes in the artist's relationship to less successful friends and status-group associates. Two patterns are common – sponsorship and avoidance, both based on the fact that the successful artist has less need of status-group supports. Other concerns increasingly take precedence, such as developing disciplined work habits (Simpson 1981).

Short-term success, of course, does not guarantee enduring "insider" reputation. To what extent do various "social" factors, such as the tactics of art-world recognition, contribute to long-term as well as more immediate success? To answer that question, what Becker (1982: Chapter 11) calls the "conventional theory of reputation" must be contrasted against the more mundane "institutional" or sociological explanation. The "conventional" theory, with its emphasis on artistic talent and universal aesthetics, argues that long-term artistic reputation stems essentially from the exceptional talents of great creators. Such artists create works that are exceptional because they articulate universal aesthetic qualities and universal human and cultural values. Their reputation is ensured, according to the conventional theory, when other qualified observers, such as art historians, great collectors or art connoisseurs, recognize these artists' exceptional gifts. According to this view, any great art will eventually be recognized.

The weakness of the conventional view is not that it is all wrong, necessarily. Even Becker, who strongly opposes it, grants that it can be neither proved nor disproved (1982: Chapter 11); and Zolberg (1990) urges consideration of both the conventional and the sociological perspectives. What is wrong with the traditional view is that it seriously exaggerates its case and severely underestimates the role of social processes. It ignores the relevance of all of the promotional activities described earlier; and it ignores the vagaries of the history of taste, with the consequent very loose fit between quality and reputation, as illustrated by the esteemed artists of times past who are now forgotten. A more balanced approach must take both social and aesthetic factors into account.

Recent research by the Langs does just that (1988; 1990) by formulating and actually testing a sociological theory of reputation. It focuses on the artist-etching movement in France, Britain and the United States from the mid-nineteenth century until 1930. Although all of their sample of 336 artist-etchers were well known in their day, the reputations of a large proportion of them did not survive. Thus, we have a study of the historical failure of insider status among some artists who were all successful contemporaries.

The sociological question is: why did some reputations "fail"? In a painstaking effort, the Langs looked for various strictly social (as opposed to aesthetic) factors that were actually correlated with the survival of reputation among the etchers. Various social factors that emerged included the following: the sheer volume of work produced by the artist; good catalog records by the artist of his oeuvre; self-conscious efforts by artist and friends to arrange for "custodianship" of works by museums and galleries; having friends or relatives who survived the artist who would promote their work posthumously; having created some news or sensation regarding one's work that was picked up by journals of the day; "ideological congruence" of the work with dominant cultural and political themes of the time; and association with some other famous artist or artist's group. Talent may be necessary for enduring reputation; but alone it is often not enough.

We have seen, then, that the determinants of "insider" status among artists are complex. There is a deconstructionist tendency today to oversimplify the process of "admission" to the inside by reducing it to an outcome of a power struggle between the powerful and the powerless (e.g. Bourdieu 1984). And as we noted especially when commenting on the role of gender and race, power and prejudice certainly play a role. But the process is more complex than simple exclusion by the powerful. It is also a process involving marketplace, local communities, art worlds, status groups, stylistic or cultural trends, promotional strategies, stylistic game playing and invention, and biographical career development. And it is a process that is highly unstable and relativistic: what may seem "inside" to some (such as unrecognized fine arts graduates in their period of "protracted incubation") is "outside" to others (such as established artists and institutional gate-keepers); what is "inside" now may not be in years hence, as shown by the Langs; and what was rejected once by the art "establishment," such as naïve art, later becomes all the rage, as grass roots art is now. Indeed, so long as what is "in" today can be redefined almost arbitrarily through art-world trends and collective behavior as "out" tomorrow, the structural basis of the insider/outsider distinction will remain unstable. As Andy Warhol noted, we each get only fifteen minutes of fame.

Notes

1 Sociologically, Rosenberg (1965) did not get this far; but he did recognize something of the complexity or elusiveness of his concept by noting at one point that the "art establishment" consists mostly of "talk."
2 That study, and a more recent one (Finney 1995), were based on the author's dual status and experience as a professional painter (MFA) and sociologist. He now maintains studios in New York City and Los Alamos, New Mexico.
3 Many outsiders, of course, have no professional aspirations. We shall return to their circumstances, especially in local art worlds.
4 Exhibitions, galleries and public spaces devoted to art by Asian Americans, Eastern Europeans, Hispanic Americans, artists from Latin America and grassroots artists were also much in evidence in New York during the early 1990s.
5 School budget retrenchments during the early 1990s have undoubtedly reduced or even reversed this trend, however.
6 This strategy of "traditional reproduction" encompasses a wide range of different stylistic games, such as "impressionism," "classic figure" and "cowboy" (Finney 1995).
7 This is the norm of what Harold Rosenberg called "The Tradition of the New" (1961), and Poggioli called the "... irremediable and absolute esthetic error ... [of] ... a traditional artistic creation, an art that imitates and repeats itself" (1971: 82).
8 For those in the insider/outsider debate who see the glass as half empty, this means an increase in "credentialization" at the expense of outsider artists; for those who see the glass half full, it means a great increase in mobility from outside to inside.
9 Namely, Anheier and Gerhards (1991), Frey and Pommerehne (1989), Greenfeld (1989), McCall (1978) and Levine (1972).
10 Lower, that is, than other types of artists and the workforce generally (Frey and Pommerehne 1989: 153). While the workforce earned an average salary of $12,200 in the year of the study, painters and sculptors earned an average of only $10,300 – substantially less than all other artists, including art teachers, with the exception of dancers and choreographers.

References

Anheier, Helmut K. and Gerhards, Jurgen 1991, "Literary Myths and Social Structure," *Social Forces* 69: 811–30.
Becker, Howard S. 1982, *Art Worlds*, Berkeley: University of California Press.
Blau, Judith R., Blau, Peter M. and Golden, Reid M. 1985, "Social Inequality and the Arts," *American Journal of Sociology* 91: 309–31.
Bourdieu, Pierre 1984, *Distinction*, Cambridge, MA: Harvard University Press.
Bradshaw, Tom 1989, "Forecasting Artist Employment to the Year 2000," *The Modern Muse: The Support and Condition of Artists*, ed. C. R. Swaim, New York: American Council for the Arts, 47–54.
Brown, Richard Harvey 1989, "Art as a Commodity," in C.R. Swaim (ed.), *The Modern Muse: The Support and Condition of Artists*, New York: American Council for the Arts, 13–26.
Chapman, Laura H. 1982, *Instant Art, Instant Culture*, New York: Teachers College Press of Columbia University.
Cox, Meg 1989, "Feeling Victimized? Then Strike Back: Become an Artist," *Wall Street Journal* Feb. 13: A1, A8.
Crane, Diana 1987, *The Transformation of the Avant-garde*, University of Chicago Press.
1989, "Reward Systems in Avant-Garde Art: Social Networks and Stylistic Change," *Art and Society*, eds. Foster, A. W. and Blau, J. R., State University of New York Press, 261–78.
Csikszentmihalyi, Mihalyi, Getzels, Jacob W., and Kahn, Stephen 1984, "Talent and Achievement: A Longitudinal Study of Artists," *Report to the Spencer and MacArthur Foundations*, University of Chicago Press.
DiMaggio, Paul and Ostrower, Francie 1990, "Participation in the Arts by Black and White Americans," *Social Forces* 68: 753–78.
Failing, Patricia 1989, "Black Artists Today: A Case of Exclusion," *Art News*: March: 124–31.
Finney, Henry C. 1993, "Mediating Claims to Artistry: Social Stratification in a Local Visual Arts Community," *Sociological Forum* 8: 403–31.
1995, "The Stylistic Games that Visual Artists Play," *Boekmancahier* 23: 23–4.
Frey, Bruno S., and Pommerehne, Werner W. 1989, *Muses and Markets*, Oxford: Basil Blackwell Publishers.
Gardner, Paul 1990, "How to Succeed (By Really Trying)," *Art News*: February: 134–37.
Getzels, Jacob W., and Csikszentmihalyi, Mihali 1976, *The Creative Vision: A Longitudinal Study of Problem Finding in Art*, New York: Wiley Publishers.
Greenfeld, Liah 1989, *Different Worlds: A Sociological Study of Taste, Choice and Success in Art*, Cambridge University Press.
Griff, Mason 1964, "The Recruitment of the Artist," *The Arts in Society*, ed. Wilson, R. N., Prentice Hall Publishers, 63–91.
Kadushin, Charles 1976, "Networks and Circles in the Production of Culture," *The Production of Culture*, ed. Peterson, R. A., Sage Press, 107–22.
Lang, Gladys Engel, and Lang, Kurt 1988, "Recognition and Renown: The Survival of Artistic Reputation," *American Journal of Sociology* 94: 79–109.
1990, *Etched in Memory: The Building and Survival of Artistic Reputation*, University of North Carolina Press.
Larson, Kay 1983, "How Should Artists be Educated?" *Art News* November: 85–91.
Levine, Edward M. 1972, "Chicago's Art World: The Influence of Status Interests on its Social and Distribution Systems," *Urban Life and Culture* 1: 293–322.
Lippard, Lucy R. 1976, "Sexual Politics: Art Style," *From the Center*, Dutton Publishers, 28–37.

Lyons, Beauvais 1990, "Public Support for Artists," *New Art Examiner* January: 13–14.
McCall, Michal 1978, "The Sociology of Female Artists," *Studies in Symbolic Interaction: An Annual Compilation of Research*, ed. Denzin, Norman K., Vol. 1, JAI Press, 289–318.
Manfredi, John 1982, *The Social Limits of Art*, University of Massachusetts Press.
Moorman, Margaret 1989, "The Great Art Education Debate," *Art News* Summer; 124–30.
Moulin, Raymonde 1987, *The French Art Market*, Rutgers University Press [originally 1967].
Poggioli, Renato 1971, *The Theory of the Avant-Garde*, Harper & Row [Icon Editions].
Ridgeway, Sally 1989, "Artist Groups: Patrons and Gate-Keepers," *Art and Society*, eds. Foster, A. W. and Blau, J. R., Albany: State University of New York Press, 205–20.
Robinson, John P. 1989, "Assessing the Artist's Condition," *The Modern Muse: The Support and Condition of Artists*, ed. Swaim, C. R., American Council for the Arts, 29–34.
Rogers, Maria 1970, "The Batignolles Group: Creators of Impressionism," *The Sociology of Art and Literature,* eds. Albrecht, M. C., Barnett, J. H., and Griff, M., New York: Praeger Publishers, 1970, 194–220 [originally 1959].
Rosenberg, Harold 1961, *The Tradition of the New*, Grove Press.
1965, "The Art Establishment," *Esquire* LXIII January–June: 388–95.
Rosenberg, Bernard and Fliegel, Norris 1965, "The Artist and His Publics: The Ambiguity of Success," *The Vanguard Artist: Portrait and Self-Portrait*, Quadrangle Books, 191–214.
Rosenblum, Barbara 1985, "The Artist as Economic Actor in the Art Market," *Art, Ideology, and Politics*, eds. Balfe, J. H., and Wyszomirski, M. J., New York: Praeger Publishers, 63–79.
Simpson, Charles R. 1981, *SoHo: The Artist in the City*, University of Chicago Press.
Strauss, Anselm 1970, "The Art School and its Students," *The Sociology of Art and Literature: A Reader*, eds. Albrecht, M. C., Barnett, J. H. and Griff, M., New York: Praeger Publishers, 159–75.
Tompkins, Calvin 1988, *Post- to Neo-: The Art World of the 1980s*, Penguin.
US Bureau of the Census 1988, 1990, *Statistical Abstracts of the US*, US Government Printing Office.
Zolberg, Vera L. 1990, *Constructing a Sociology of the Arts*, Cambridge University Press.

5

Pop Art: ugly duckling to swan

Joni Maya Cherbo

It does not take a trained eye to note that historically it is the fluctuation of styles not their stability that is the rule, though some styles experience longer periods of stability than others. New visions, techniques, patrons, categories of painters – outsiders to reigning artistic practices and sensibilities – inevitably knock on the door of the establishment asking for inclusion. Some succeed, others do not (Becker 1982; Kubler 1962; Zolberg 1990; Wolff 1983).

The trademark of twentieth century art is its rapid succession of "isms" with its insistence on change and experimentation as a mark of creativity. Pop Art holds a meteoric and distinct record in this history. It was the first American movement that did not struggle for recognition, but found its glory with unparalled swiftness. Pop Art made its debut in the late 1950s. In six years it had become a recognized art movement enjoying popular acclaim, financial recognition and a place in the annals of American art. Furthermore, in its wake the movement shattered the semblance of an artistic canon and diminished the power of the critical community.

Pop was jolting to most of the existing establishment. Its philosophy inverted the beliefs of its renowned predecessors, the Abstract Expressionists. They were a high-minded group who practiced art as an ongoing existential involvement between the individual and reality. Art to them was a lofty engagement, moral and humanistic. They stood apart from the mainstream, fearful that incorporation would diminish their creative and critical faculties.

Pop Art embraced the artist as a common man and art as simply another of life's activities. Its subject matter, inspired by popular culture, defied the accepted topicality of respectable high art. Its use of commercial techniques such as ben-day dots (a screen of minute dots used to achieve color shadings in a comic strip), silk screens, stencils, and billboard painting were an affront to established painterly techniques. And it questioned whether art was a calling, or whether art must display a conscience. As such, Pop Artists levelled the heightened sense of purpose that had marked the Abstract Expressionists.

In return, Pop Art was derided and demeaned by most of the artistic community. At its onset, it was an outsider – an ugly duckling that was later acclaimed a swan.

What accounted for the success of these outsiders? What impelled these painters – their stylistic sensibilities and aesthetics – and accounted for their reception?

Pop Art's recognition was due in the main to a set of social factors characteristic of mid-century America, which was highly receptive to the arts, and a new constellation of painters, dealers and patrons who expropriated the recognition process.

Prior to the advent of Pop Art the recognition process was marked by a defined trajectory and established coalition of art-world persons. Select galleries promoted new art. Patrons were introduced to aspiring artists and new trends. Art critics attended to new works and acted as evaluators and gatekeepers of quality. Gallery representation, critical acceptance and patronage usually secured a market for the new art. Finally, the museums, by including new works in their exhibitions and collections, bestowed legitimacy.

Pop Art altered this trajectory and coalition. It ushered in a new constellation of artists/dealers/patrons and went directly to the marketplace for approval, bypassing the critics and museums, who were forced to acknowledge the movement after it become popular and financially sucessful. As such, Pop Art serves as a distinct chapter in the history of contemporary taste-making.

Pop Art germinated in the 1950s, a period characterized by the hegemony of Abstract Expressionism, which had by then attained international repute. In the middle of the century, modernism in America was supported by a mere handful of galleries, critics, patrons and museums. It was a small elite enclave open only to the committed and informed (Crane 1987; Kadushin 1976: 107).

Though Abstract Expressionism reigned supreme, mid-century American art was in fact pluralistic, with a number of styles vying for attention. A second generation of Abstract Expressionists was coming into focus, with such painters as Joan Mitchell, Milton Resnick and Sam Francis. Figurative Expressionist artists such as Larry Rivers, Richard Diebenkorn, Leon Golub and Nathan Oliveria were in evidence, as were distinct regional forms such as the works of Thomas Hart Benton. Many painters and sculptors were beginning to concentrate on formal properties such as line, color fields and form – experiments that eventually resulted in the minimalist works of Ellsworth Kelly, Frank Stella, Keneth Noland, Morris Louis and Donald Judd. Robert Rauschenberg was developing his "combines" – a melange of sculptural objects and traditional canvas painting – and Jasper Johns was painting his targets and flags, experimenting with the intersection between the object and art.

Within this New York-based community of new artists, a number were experimenting with ideas, images and practices closely allied with everyday life. Their core consisted of Claes Oldenberg, Jim Dine, Tom Wesselman, James Rosenquist, Roy Lichtenstein and Andy Warhol. Many were influenced by Allen Kaprow, art historian and director of the Hansa Cooperative, and the musician John Cage, then at the New School for Social Research.

Pop Art was, however, neither new, nor an exclusively New York phenomenon. The history of contemporary art is peppered with artists appropriating commercial, media and popular imagery, but in a far more limited manner. Pop Art harks back to Dada and to Zen with its unquestioning acceptance of life. Duchamp, Braque and Picasso had included everyday objects in their art. Furthermore, artists in Britain and Los Angeles were also using popular imagery. It was in New York, however, that the movement blossomed and gained its reputation.

The biographies and generational experiences of the Pop Artists also contrasted significantly with their successful predecessors. Many of the New York School of Abstract Expressionists were of European descent. A large number were Jewish. Most had experienced the Second World War and the Depression. They had acquired their art training in the studios of established painters. Few had college degrees. They felt alien to middle-class existence and popular culture. They were humanists who tended to be remote and lead bohemian lives.

In contrast, most of the Pop-ists were native-born and well assimilated in the American mainstream. They came from middle-class families. They matured in the 1950s and did not experience the war or the Depression. Many had college degrees and worked in commercial art or as art instructors prior to recognition – a means of providing a semblance of financial security that eluded their immediate forebears. They grew up in an era more sympathetic to and supportive of fine art than did their predecessors.

To the Pop-ists, the second generation of Abstract Expressionist painters looked old and worn out, and the social and aesthetic issues that had inspired these seminal painters, failed to resonate. The Pop Artists were of another era.

Gradually a cohesive practice and agenda evolved among the Pop artists. They became deeply involved in creating an art that simulated and emphasized the immediate and commonplace aspects of everyday life. Their art plagiarized the pervasive images of the mass media and commercial world, using these images sometimes with wit or as parody, but mostly in a deadpan manner without overt comment. They often used found as opposed to created images, and applied commercial techniques to their canvas paintings.

Their program was to re-knit the ties between art and life, to put art and artists back into life rather than apart from it. They attempted to demote art from its elevated status and to reduce the artist to an ordinary person. As Lichtenstein said:

> I think art since Cézanne has become extremely romantic and unreal, feeding on art: it is utopian. It looks inward . . . outside is the world, it's there. Pop art looks out into the world: it appears to accept its environment, which is not good or bad, just different – another state of mind. (Cited in Coplans 1972: 52)

Oldenberg's often quoted missive became almost an official statement for the new art.

> I am for an art that does something other than sit on its ass in a museum. I am for an art that grows up not knowing it is art at all, an art given the chance of having a starting point of zero. I am for an art that involves itself with the everyday crap and still comes out on top. I am for an art that takes its form from the lines of life, that twists and extends impossibly and accumulates and spits and drips, and is sweet and stupid as life itself. I am for an artist who vanishes, turning up in a white cap, painting signs or hallways. (Cited in Johnson 1971: 17)

Rosenquist saw his art as an indistinguishable part of the present. Commenting on the fifty-one panels of his *F-111*, a 10 ft by 85 ft 3 in mural painting that depicts the

Figure 13. Installation shot of Roy Lichtenstein exhibition at the Leo Castelli Gallery, 4 E.77th Street, NYC, Feb.10–March 3, 1962. Photograph by Rudolph Burckhart, courtesy of the Leo Castelli Photo Archives.

fuselage of the F-111 airplane, obscured by a huge tire, a scuba-diver, angel-food cake, a bowl of spaghetti, light bulbs and a little girl under a hair dryer, he stated:

> And then anyone interested in buying a blank part of this knowingly or unknowingly – that's the joke – he would think he is buying art and, after all he would be buying a thing that paralled part of the life he lives. (Cited in Archives of American Art E)

Despite their rejection of their immediate predecessors, the Pop Artists remained committed to modernism's essential belief in individualized self-expression, that one must innovate and redefine the artistic endeavor. All were actively looking for ways out of Abstract Expressionism on the road to finding their own unique identity.

Though they claimed that artistic notoriety, including their own, was transitory, they were not adverse to recognition. Some, such as Warhol, pursued it obsessively. The pursuit of success was the American way.

Artists have taken on many guises throughout history. They have been intellectuals, workers, recorders of religious, heroic and moral convictions, social critics, beatniks and isolated geniuses. In the 1960s they became bourgeois – chroniclers of the mainstream.

In the hands of these creators, art was grounded as a common denominator to which anyone could relate. It was an accessible, recognizable, unthreatening, undemanding art, which paved the way for a groundswell of new participants.

Figure 14. Installation shot of James Rosenquist's *F-111*, 1965, shown at the Leo Castelli Gallery, 4 E.77th Street, NYC, April 17–May 13, 1965. Photograph by Rudolph Burckhart, courtesy of the Leo Castelli Gallery.

And to whom did this new art appeal? Not the critics.

The majority of popular art journals such as *Art Forum*, *Art International*, *Art in America*, were focused primariy on the new Abstract Expressionists and figurative painters. Though they all covered the avant-garde galleries that showed experimental work, they were late in picking up on the momentum of the Pop Art movement.

Irving Sandler's article in *Art International*, October, 1960, "Ash Can Revisited," was an oddball, a positive, early detection of the new art (Sandler 1960: 28). Dorothy Gees Seckler in 1961 noted the "New Dada" in her "Gallery Notes" in *Art in America* (Seckler 1961: 85–134). The first article devoted to Pop Art in *Art Forum* was in 1963, a brief two-pager (Karp 1963: 26). An uninformed reader relying on *Art News* for coverage of the contemporary art scene would hardly have been aware of the existence of Pop Art.

A few serious scholars and critics such as Gene Swenson, Lawrence Alloway, Henry Geldzahler, Alan Solomon, and Leo Steinberg, gave the movement some serious attention and thus a touch of respectability, but they were the exception. The majority of art historians and art critics, in particular the luminaries of the time, either ignored Pop Art or found it fraudulent.

Critical onslaughts against Pop Art were often ferocious. Max Kozloff writing in 1962 tersely dismissed Pop artists as, ". . . vulgarians, kitchniks, impoverished, repulsive, pinheads, gum chewers, bobby socksers, delinquents using hard sell to hard sell" (Kozloff 1962: 34). John Canaday's *Embattled Critic,* a compilation of his commentary written between 1959 and 196l, speaks of the visual arts as descending to objects of

Figure 15. Andy Warhol, *Campbell's Soup Cans* (acrylic and silkscreen), each 35×24 in, 1965. Courtesy of the Leo Castelli Photo Archives and the Andy Warhol Foundation for the Visual Arts.

stimulation, bent on amusing and being chic (Canaday 1962). Hilton Kramer lamented that the art world had lost its capacity to distinguish an authentic artistic vision from a vulgar counterfeit (Kramer 1973). Clement Greenberg and Harold Rosenberg valorized Abstract Expressionism. Both remained attached to pet artistic theories and artists, and never opened their eyes to the new art with any sympathy. Greenberg dismissed Pop Art as degenerate, as fashion not art. Rosenberg, as early as 1960, announced that Pop Art had run its course (Greenberg 1961; Rosenberg 1965).

After Pop Art became successful, a handful of "Cassandra critics" remained bitter and disillusioned at the decline of the art world they had known. Many lamented that the art world had become a mecca for promotional dealers, advertising hype, ambitious, socially driven collectors, and artists who were driven by the desire for popularity and success, not the inspirational muse. Art had lapsed into consumer culture.

Critical hindsight, however, acknowledged that, given the ebb and flow of twentieth-century art, any artistic work, however repugnant at first glance, stood a chance of becoming heralded as a masterpiece. Later, many came to see the Pop Art movement as a logical stylistic outcome of its day and age. As Alan Solomon said:

in retrospect, the way the present group emerged has not only an air of undeniable consistency but also a distinct flavor of historical inevitability. The new style could neither have been encour-

Denied Duty-Free Status

National Gallery Refuses to Pass Pop Art, Dealer Says

What is art?

The question has been raised again by the alleged refusal of the National Gallery of Canada to classify creations by the noted U.S. pop artist Andy Warhol as art, in order for them to qualify for duty-free entry into the country.

The case could become an international cause celebre in the art world, according to Toronto art dealer Jerrold Morris.

An exhibition of Warhol's work will open March 18 at the Jerrold Morris International Gallery on Bloor Street. The artist himself will come from New York for the opening.

A scheduled part of the show was an exhibition of 80 of Warhol's facsimiles of Campbell Soup and Brillo soap-pad cartons, 40 of each.

Works of art may be imported into the country without duty. In the case of sculpture, a tariff item requires that the National Gallery of Canada issue a certificate to the effect that it is a work of art.

The Warhol cartons must be imported as sculpture. But Dr. Charles F. Comfort, director of the National Gallery, has refused to issue the required certificate, Mr. Morris said.

"What the National Gallery is doing is refusing to recognize these as art," he said. "The rest of the world has recognized pop art as art—but our National Gallery seems to be afraid of the boxes."

Mr. Morris, who manages the Bloor Street gallery, said an exhibition of sculpture by Manolo that ran there until Feb. 4 was imported under precisely the same regulation and there was no hitch of any kind.

This time, however, despite last-minute telephone appeals Wednesday to Dr. Comfort in Ottawa, no certificate was issued classifying Warhol's work as art, Mr. Morris said.

"The National Gallery is discriminating between Manolo, which is classic art, and a bunch of pop-art boxes, which they are frightened of."

Without Dr. Comfort's certificate, the Warhol cartons would have had to be imported into Canada as ordinary merchandise. ("The sculptured boxes . . . are dutiable according to their composition," says a letter written March 2 to Mr. Morris' broker from the Department of National Revenue, Customs and Excise Division.)

Each of the 80 cartons, worth an estimated $300, would have been dutiable at 20 per cent, according to Mr. Morris.

"This we could not afford," he said. "I had to telephone New York and cancel shipment of the boxes."

The National Gallery's inaction may make it the laughingstock of the art world, Mr. Morris said.

"In refusing a certificate for Warhol's works they have set up a situation which exactly duplicates the Brancusi scandal of the 1920s, when a U.S. customs inspector refused to allow the famous sculptor's Bird of Flight into the country as a work of art and assessed it as a hunk of metal by weight."

"It's a disgrace to Canada to be confronted with this," Emilio del Junco, president of the Jerrold Morris International Gallery, said.

National Gallery officials in Ottawa would not discuss Mr. Morris' allegations last night.

Dr. Comfort was unable to come to the telephone, a caller to his home was told.

J. R. Viet, Dr. Comfort's administrative assistant, would not comment. Dr. William S. A. Dale, assistant director of the National Gallery, said it was not true the Gallery had branded the Warhol works as not being art, but would not elaborate.

The artist was reached in his studio in New York. "It's really true, eh — I though they were kidding me," he said.

He said his works had previously been imported into England, France and Germany without holdups.

He was apathetic to the Canadian action. "It really doesn't matter much to me — I don't care much," he said several times.

The issue marks Dr. Comfort's second involvement in an art controversy since he took over directorship of the Gallery in 1960. In November, 1962, he became the focal point in a scandal that has since been called one of the greatest art hoaxes perpetrated in this century.

The scandal centred on a major exhibition of works drawn from the collection of Walter P. Chrysler, son of the U.S. automotive giant. Soon after the exhibition opened at the Gallery more than half the paintings were judged to be either fakes or work of doubtful attribution.

The controversy raised a storm in the House of Commons when it was alleged Dr. Comfort had been warned of the exhibition's contents several months before the paintings reached Ottawa. The Gallery director denied he had received any warnings and at the time stated he had complete faith in Mr. Chrysler's integrity.

Figure 16. "National Gallery Refuses to Pass Pop Art, Dealer Says," *The Globe and Mail*, Toronto, Canada, March 5, 1965. Courtesy of *The Globe and Mail*.

aged nor prevented, nor could it have been contrived; it has followed an organic course which makes it an absolute product of its time. (Solomon 1968: 52)

The museums as well were inconsequential in Pop's ascent. A few museums, responding to pressures to be contemporary and relevant, collected and exhibited some of the new art during its early years; the Pasadena Art Museum, the Los Angeles County Museum and the Oakland Museum along with the Museum of Modern Art and the Whitney showed some of the new art in group shows in the early 1960s. Yet these exhibitions were infrequent, and most museums remained hesitant towards being on the front line with work fresh out of the studio.

Attention to the new art came initially from a select handful of dealers involved with new, experimental art. Richard Bellamy was the first dealer to exhibit the Pop artists. He was the talent scout of the 1950s, but a poor businessman. It took the reputation and experience of dealers Eleanor Ward, Martha Jackson, and Sidney Janis to bring Pop Art to the public eye. Leo Castelli, however, became the master builder of Pop Art's success.

Exhibitions at Eleanor Ward and Martha Jackson's well-known galleries provided an impetus for the vanguard art. Sidney Janis's exhibition, "New Realists," in the Fall of 1962 is credited as being a turning point for Pop Art. It was a comprehensive showing of Pop Art by a person respected in the contemporary art field. Janis had supported Abstract Expressionism and was affiliated with the Museum of Modern Art for a number of years prior to opening his gallery in 1948. His opinions were germane.

Knowledge of Castelli's entrepreneurship is essential for understanding Pop Art's success. It was Castelli's acknowledged ambition to become a central figure in the making of art history,

. . . like the patrons used to do in the time of the Renaissance or the Baroque period and then later during the age of Louis XIX [sic] . . . and then in the nineteenth century . . . I mean there

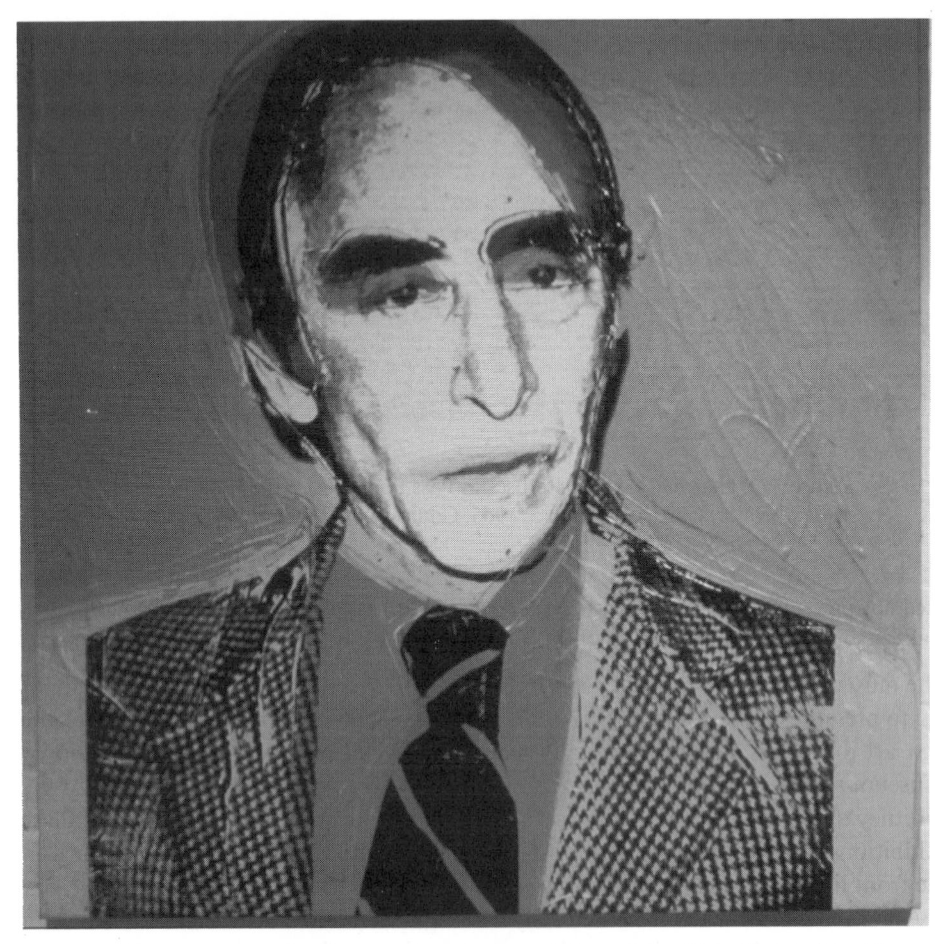

Figure 17. Andy Warhol, *Portrait of Leo* (painting of Leo Castelli, acrylic and silkscreen on canvas), 40×40 in, 1975. Thanks to Leo Castelli Photo Archives and the Andy Warhol Foundation for the Visual Arts.

was that sense of history that always felt in connection with which I was doing although things have changed so much, I still feel that there is some kind of mission that I have.
(Archives of American Art B)

Castelli did not approach art with preconceived ideas of aesthetic worth or have definitive aesthetic preferences:

Painting is what it is, what artists make of it. One has to accept what painters do. One does not have to like it, but one cannot discard it; one can lament a certain fashion, but one can't do anything about it. One cannot say "This is not art, it will go away." Who decides what is art: Who is responsible for the decision? Not I. Certainly not I. (Archives of American Art B)

He also knew that movements were made, not born:

Why should anyone want to buy a Cézanne for $800,000? What's a little Cézanne, a house in the middle of a landscape? Why should it have value? Because it's a myth. We make myths about politics, we make myths about everything . . . My responsibility is the myth making of myth making material – which handled properly and imaginatively is the job of a dealer – and I have to go at it completely. (Archives of American Art C)

Castelli hired Ivan Karp in 1959. Karp had worked with Richard Bellamy and had spent a year as a talent scout for Martha Jackson. The Castelli-Karp union lasted ten years. Together they frequented artists' studios, searching for new talent and trends.

Finding a handful of painters working in everyday, commercial imagery, Castelli promoted the trend with the acumen of an astute businessman in a world still dominated primarily by subjective passions. When Castelli showed Roy Lichtenstein in February–March, 1962, he persuaded the Green Gallery to show Rosenquist simultaneously, to create the sense of a movement. He supported his artists financially in order that they could produce full-time and he could maintain a ready inventory and monopoly of Pop works. He placed his artists' works carefully, selling the better pieces to more influential clients and often giving them discounts. The gallery would on occasion donate or loan a piece to a museum with the presumption that it would be shown.

Castelli managed the price structure of his artists by selling selectively and keeping the better pieces in storage until an artist's prices rose. He cultivated critics and on occasion financed an article favorable to an artist in his stable. Such actions led to the accusation that he was buying critics. Castelli advertised regularly in art magazines and popular periodicals. The atmosphere in his gallery was clubby, with open spaces where people could mingle, linger and interact. As the movement took hold, Castelli and his ex-wife, Ileana Sonnabend, opened a gallery in Paris where they had a monopoly in Europe on the new art for many years. Recognizing that an event of historical importance required documentation, Castelli, with foresight, maintained systematic records.

Collectors came from many sources, though most were newly monied, professional or business persons. Philip Johnson and Burton Tremain were among Pop Art's early collectors. Robert and Ethel Scull were the first to concentrate exclusively on Pop Art. Other collectors such as Richard Brown Baker, Muriel Newman, Al Ordover, Myron Orlofsky, Leon Krauschar, Robert Manuchin, Eugene and Barbara Schwartz, Harry Abrams and David Hayes followed as the movement gained attention.

Their attraction to Pop was multifaceted. Art collecting was a means of attaining social recognition. It was also a form of financial speculation. Pop Art was relatively inexpensive in comparison with older art and Abstract Expressionism, which had by that time become prohibitive. Furthermore, Pop Art's identifiable images and democratic program were familiar and comprehensible to these patrons. As Robert Scull explained:

Pop was not an isolated art. It came with an entire Pop scene in which everything was Pop. In other words, what happened is that it was truly an expression of its moment; the clothes, people, vinyl, movies, fads . . . it was so new that it took our breath away. The high luster of it was the way we were living; the parties we were giving, the good times, the Pop scene, the whole crack out of breaking the old mores, traditions; and living was swinging; and it was exemplified by the fact that an artist can do it on canvas or do it with his work. There were no more restrictions. Everything is possible. Everything was possible. And that's what we learned from Pop.

(Archives of American Art G)

Leon Krauschar justified his attraction to Pop in a similar fashion:

It was when I discovered pop art that I became really involved. Here was a timely and aggressive image that spoke directly to me about things I understood. The paintings from this school are today. The expression is completely American, with no apologies to the European past. This is my art, the only work being done today that has meaning for me.

(Cited in Rublowsky 1965: 157)

The real thrill for these collectors, however, came from collecting unknown artists to speculate on their future. If the artists became successful, their collectors would become central persons in the history of taste-making. As Castelli said:

My collectors do not come to my gallery to find paintings to hang on their walls. They come to be part of an historic venture, to be part of a great period of art.

(Archives of American Art G: 208–9)

A new coalition was formed: the rise of media and commercially based images, along with a more democratic artistic agenda among a handful of younger artists, attracted entrepreneurial dealers eager to create art history and newly monied collectors eager to realize varied ambitions through participation in the arts. It was a compatible alliance.

The success of this new coalition was set against the political and economic prosperity of the 1950s (Guilbaut 1983). Abstract Expressionism's international stature had relocated the center of modernism from Paris to New York. A wave of enthusiasm and support for the arts spread through America like an epidemic whose epicenter was New York City. America was undergoing what Alvin Toffler called "a mania for pigment" (Toffler 1964: 20).

Federal involvement in the arts was in the wings. The National Endowment for the Arts was established in 1965, and soon thereafter each state established an arts council. Corporate art collections were budding. Universities were extending their art programs, establishing galleries and employing artists. New markets for art and art-related products, in particular for glossy, exquisitely printed art books, increased. Museum and gallery openings were becoming social events attended by art persons and celebrities alike and were widely covered by the entire roster of newspapers and popular publications.

The small, intimate art world of the 1950s and earlier had exploded into a hustling maze of ever-increasing numbers of newcomers. Art had become an American industry and a national preoccupation.

Those involved in Pop Art did not relate to the arts as a quiet retreat, forming an elite involvement, as did their forebears. Their attraction to Pop was also an attraction to the social scene with its attendant celebrity. Pop Art became consecrated by and within popular culture.

Terrific! said the smiling young man backed up against the wall by a mounting crush of people. The young man was artist Andy Warhol, and the crush was a tidal wave of guests at a party given to celebrate the opening of his latest showing in New York last week. The wave grew to fantastic proportions. The dancing guests jammed together in the big West Side apartment, frugging in place, like a mob of bears back-scratching against the trees of a thick forest. A *New York Times* photographer retrieved a coat from a pile of overware. The pile grew so surrealistically high that Norman Mailer, who arrived late, was led solicitously aside by the host to park his vestments in private. Such is success in New York's Babel of art . . . (Archives of American Art D)

The Pop Art movement had at least three significant consequences. First, it grounded a once lofty art world. It marked the end of art's previous estrangement from everyday life. Art became accessible and easy to understand, and audience participation swelled.

Secondly, the Pop Art movement institutionalized artistic experimentation, the search for new visions. The perennial question, "What is art?," became permanently open-ended. Since Pop Art, outsider art – regardless of the artists' credentials or the artistic form – has entered an art world where new visions are welcomed as prospective insider art. The shock of the new has become the search for the new. In Leo Steinberg's words: ". . . the rapid domestication of the outrageous is the most characteristic feature of our artistic life, and the time lag between shock received and thanks returned gets progressively shorter" (Battcock 1966: 31).

Thirdly, the Pop Art movement reordered the recognition process. It by-passed the official bodies once invested with conferring legitimation – critics and museums – and went straight to the marketplace and media for recognition. After Pop Art, art criticism suffered a significant loss of confidence. Criticism became a troubled and risky business, with some predicting the demise of aesthetics. Most museums relinquished any interest in being on the front line with new art. Today, it is those art world agents involved in constructing a marketplace for new art who have become central players in determining the success of a new art form. It is what Robert Hughes has called "supply-side aesthetics" (Hughes 1982: 6).

If one of the cornerstones of the postmodern world was the end of overarching ideologies, then Pop Art's triumph of media popularity and commercialism over a formal artistic canon mirrored larger trends. We have come to accept Rosenberg's "anxious object" as the common condition for aspiring outsiders, and the devaluation of an artistic canon as the normal state of affairs (Rosenberg 1964). In the absence of standards and standard bearers, artistic success becomes multi-dimensional – measured by popularity, critical acclaim, financial success, visual appeal, insiders' valuation. And the processes by which various types and degrees of success occur become a complicated social construction of art world personages.

References

Archives of American Art A, 1969, *Ivan Karp Interviewed by Paul Cummings.*
Archives of American Art B, 1969–1973, *Leo Castelli Interviewed by Paul Cummings.*
Archives of American Art C, 1958–1968, *Leo Castelli Papers: General Introduction and Jasper Johns.*
Archives of American Art D,1964–1968, *Leo Castelli Papers: Group V Andy Warhol.*

Archives of American Art E, 1961–1968, *Leo Castelli Papers: Group III James Rosenquist.*
Archives of American Art F, 1963, *Richard Brown Baker interview.*
Archives of American Art G, 1972, *Robert Scull interviewed by Paul Cummings.*
Archives of American Art H, 1965, *Roy Lichenstein interviewed by John Jones.*
Archives of American Art I, 1962–1968, *Leo Castelli Papers: Group III Roy Lichtenstein.*
Battcock, Gregory 1966, *The New Art – A Critical Anthology,* New York: E.P. Dutton and Co.
Becker, Howard 1982, *Art Worlds*, University of California Press.
Canaday, John 1962, *Embattled Critic*, New York: Noonday Press.
Cherbo, Joni 1985, "Critically Thinking: Art Criticism in the 1960s," Unpublished manuscript.
Coplans, John, ed., 1972, *Roy Lichtenstein*, New York: Praeger Publishers.
Crane, Diana 1987, *The Transformation of the Avant-Garde: The New York Art World 1940–85*, University of Chicago Press.
Gablik, Suzi 1977, *Progress in Art*, New York: Rizzoli.
Glazer, Bruce 1966, "Interview with Claes Oldenberg, Roy Lichtenstein and Andy Warhol," *Art Forum* February: 21–24.
Greenberg, Clement 1961, *Art and Culture*, Boston: Beacon Press.
Greenfeld, Liah 1984, "The Role of the Public in the Success of Artistic Styles," *Archives of European Sociology*, XXV: 83–98.
Guilbaut, Serge 1983, *How New York Stole the Idea of Modern Art*, University of Chicago Press.
Haskell, Barbara 1984, *BLAM! The Explosion of Pop, Minimalism and Performance, 1958–64*, Whitney Museum of American Art and W. W. Norton and Co.
Hauser, Arnold 1951, *The Social History of Art* (four vols.), New York: Vintage Books.
Hughes, Robert 1982, "The Rise of Andy Warhol," *New York Review of Books*, 18 February: 6–10.
Johnson, Ellen 1971, *Claes Oldenberg*, Baltimore, Maryland: Penguin Books.
Kadushin, Charles 1976, "Networks and Circles in the Production of Culture," in Peterson (ed.), 107–22.
Karp, Ivan 1963, "Anti-sensibility Painting," *Art Forum*, Vol. 2 September: 26–27.
Kozloff, Max 1962, "Pop Culture, Metaphysical Disgust, and the New Vulgarians," *Art International*, Vol. 6: 34–36.
Kramer, Hilton 1973, *The Age of the Avant-Garde*, New York: Farrar, Strauss, Giroux.
Kubler, George 1962, *The Shape of Time*, Yale University Press.
Lippard, Lucy, ed., 1966, *Pop Art*, Oxford University Press.
Mahsum, Carol Anne, ed., 1989, *Pop Art: the critical dialogue*, Ann Arbor, Michigan: UMI Press.
Peterson, Richard A., ed., 1976, *The Production of Culture*, Berkeley, California: Sage Publications.
Pierre, Jose 1977, *An Illustrated Dictionary of Pop Art*, London: Eyre Methuen.
Rosenberg, Harold 1964, *The Anxious Object*, New York: Horizon.
1965, "The Art Establishment," *Esquire,* LX111: 43, 46, 114.
Rublowsky, John 1965, *Pop Art*, New York: Basic Books.
Russell, John and Gablik, Suzi 1969, *Pop Art Redefined*, New York: Praeger Publishers.
Sandler, Irving 1960, "Ash Can Revisited," *Art International*, Vol. IV: 28–30.
1978, *The New York School: The Painters and Sculptors of the Fifties*, New York: Harper and Row.
Seckler, Dorothy Gees 1961, "Gallery Notes," *Art in America*, Vol. 49 No. 3: 85–134.
Secrest, Meryle 1982, "Leo Castelli Dealing In Myths," *Art News*, Vol. 81 (Summer): 66–72.

Solomon, Alan 1968, "The New Art," *Pop Art: the critical dialogue,* ed. Mahsum, Carol Anne, Ann Arbor, Michigan: UMI Press, Ann Arbor, Michigan, 35–61.
Steinberg, Leo 1966, "Contemporary Art and the Plight of Its Public," *The New Art: A Critical Anthology*, ed. Battcock, Gregory, New York: E. P. Dutton and Co., 27–37.
Swenson, Gene 1963–1964, "What is Pop Art? Interview with Roy Lichtenstein, Jim Dine, Robert Indiana, Andy Warhol," *Art News*, LXIII (February and November).
Toffler, Alvin 1964, *The Culture Consumers: A Study of Art and Affluence in America*, New York: St. Martin's.
Varnedoe, Kirk and Gopnik, Adam 1990, *High and Low: Modern Art and Popular Culture*, New York: The Museum of Modern Art.
Warhol, Andy 1975, *The Philosophy of Andy Warhol From A to B and Back Again*, New York: Harcourt, Brace, Janovich.
Wolff, Janet 1983, *Aesthetics and the Sociology of Art*, London: Allen and Unwin.
Zolberg, Vera 1990, *Constructing a Sociology of Art*, Cambridge University Press.

6

Playing with fire: institutionalizing the artist at Kostabi World

András Szántó

The artist as institution

Kostabi World is a three-story warehouse on Manhattan's West Side, at Eleventh Avenue and 38th Street. This neighborhood, named "Hell's Kitchen" after the reeking horse stables and the huge slaughterhouses that once sent torrents of blood down these tenement-lined streets, is not known as a haven of the arts. Since 1989, Kostabi World's spiffy red awning and the proud sign at the door, "Art Gallery, Open 10–6, Seven Days A Week," have posed a startling contrast to the adjacent buildings, which contain a carriage house, a car body shop, the Macro Remy Alarm Company, and the Basic Warewashing Corporation.[1]

The visitor arrives through a glass door to a reception area tended by a secretary. To the rear some workers congregate around a pool table inside a sprawling gallery lined with Mark Kostabi paintings, which exude the pungent aroma of fresh paint. Someone is playing the black baby-grand piano, Kostabi's favorite instrument. The maintenance man guides the large freight elevator up to the increasingly intimate levels of the building. The second floor houses management, administration, and various support functions, such as the archive, canvas stretching, and the library. The top floor of the 15,000 sq ft warehouse is the painting studio. This is where each of the eighteen artists whom Kostabi employs to paint his pictures for him complete two to four canvases a week, or roughly a combined 150 artworks per month.

Kostabi, whose name appears on all the artworks, participates in the production process not as an artist or craftsman, but as an entrepreneur. He has developed an idea – a style of painting – and now runs a company which manufactures his product in the framework of a modern capitalist enterprise. His brush will touch the canvas only once: when the time comes to sign it. As one of his workers says: "He is very smart in that he has hired a lot of good people to help him handle the responsibility of generating so much work . . . He saw that they could paint for him, and he didn't have to paint. He could spend all his time dealing with clients, museums, galleries, the media."

The routinization of painting is the modus operandi of Kostabi World. This involves divesting the artist even of his most elemental function: the formulation of ideas. The main source of creative ideas at Kostabi World is not Kostabi himself but two hired employees, working under his supervision, who constitute the "Think Tank." It is their job to lay out the basic structure of the pictures, often using photocopies or clippings of other existing images, and occasionally putting to paper rudimentary themes outlined by Kostabi. "Sometimes Mark would come with an idea," says one Think Tank person. "He might say, 'I need two Kostabi figures, lying down,' or something – but I only really saw him draw once."

From the Think Tank, every new idea makes its way upstairs to the artists. One of them explains her task: "They give us a sketch and we project it onto a canvas, and then it's painted. Sometimes we decide the colors and sometimes it's already written on the painting . . . When you run out of ideas, you run down there and pick one . . . You take a pencil, you follow the outlines, and then you have a contour drawing. And then you bring it up here to the studio and start painting."

The painters usually choose an idea they prefer and execute the painting alone. As some painters are better at certain skills than others, specific pieces may be assigned to the specialists of a particular technique or subject matter. Collaboration exists, but it has not evolved into a production-line-like division of labor in the studio. Each artist toils individually over his or her "own" canvas.

Once finished, paintings are signed by Kostabi. There was a time when even signatures were delegated to a hired specialist and taken downstairs to the photography department. The photographers make four prints and twelve slides of every painting. They also make images for the self-published Kostabi books, catalogs and invitation cards. Their most important function, however, is to update the Kostabi archive. Archiving is the life-blood of Kostabi's operations, since it is the only way to prevent forgery (which is all too likely, as the attribution of a Kostabi picture is by definition impossible). Photographs also ease the communication with galleries and collectors: works are so abundant, in the absence of the duplicates nobody would remember them.

Paintings leave Kostabi World in sales, consignments, or an occasional exchange. Prices, an assistant reveals, are determined by size: "A smaller one would be $6,000; a 24in by 24in would be $30,000. This is how it goes up: seven, eight, twelve, fifteen thousand." Depending on their size, paintings range from $6,000 to $45,000. Sculptures are assigned higher values, while cheaper prints and miniature paintings – "bread-and-butter pieces," as they are affectionately called – come at affordable prices so as to offer something for the general public.

The employee hierarchy is capped by Kostabi's brother, who is responsible for running the organization in Mark's absence. The two brothers form the pinnacle of the chain of command. Co-ordination of day-to-day affairs is the task of the studio manager. She shares her time and space with the accountant, whose desk in the center of the second floor occupies the physical axis-point of the building. To the back, a door opens into to the plush office of the public relations officer. Impeccably decked out in a Chanel suit, Kostabi's one-time dealer from Los Angeles is here to provide a Madison Avenue look to make collectors feel at home.

Many other people cooperate with Kostabi as part-timers or outsiders. Among them are a fast-handed billboard painter who does rush-jobs, a sculptor who makes the Kostabi bronzes, Russian painters who fax ideas across the Atlantic, and a scion of the

Rockefeller and Stillman families whose signature adds luster to the Kostabi product. A small army of individuals and organizations do business with Kostabi: the dealers, the collectors, the art consultants; the galleries and the museums; the bankers, the landlords, and the art lawyers; the newspapers, the art journals, the tabloids and the TV shows; purveyors of paint, canvas, brushes, and food; producers of books, stationery, business cards, and promotion films; designers of exhibition catalogs, Kostabi memorabilia, and, not the least, a trendy line of "Kostabi Gear" leisure- wear.

It is impossible to pin down who sees, even less, who likes Kostabi's works. It's more appropriate to ask who buys them. According to Kostabi, that depends on what one means by buying: "The fact that you are taking me seriously as an artist and a social phenomenon, that is your form of buying me, if I look at buying and selling more universally." But, he adds, "as for people who pay money, even there it's pretty all-encompassing – I have something for everybody."

Ronald Feldman, a dealer who has exhibited Kostabi in his respected SoHo gallery, is more to the point. "He sells an incredible volume of art, a probably unheard of volume of art. It's all over. One place it is not going is the more rarified area that I would call the 'real fine art area' of better galleries and museums. They really are staying away from Mark Kostabi."

The art establishment's distrust of Kostabi cannot be overstated, but some prestigious institutions (including the Guggenheim Museum) have acquired his works. Token Kostabis are probably hidden in the vaults of some serious collectors. But most of the people who acquire Kostabi paintings are occasional buyers of art who patronize "commercial" galleries which lie outside the boundaries of the legitimate art world. In the booming 1980s, when the scale of contemporary art acquisition outdistanced any comparable period in history, they matched Kostabi's profuse supply of art with an apparently bottomless demand. Japanese collectors and secondary dealers often bought Kostabi paintings en masse. Japanese clients once acquired 97 canvases (at about $15,000 each) in a single afternoon.

What are these people buying? What kind of art does the vast machine of Kostabi World churn out? What makes a Kostabi a "Kostabi"? The answers given by Kostabi's associates always come back to the theme of standardization. "A lot of the imagery is simpler figures," says one painter. "A Kostabi painting has to have some basic elements that all paintings have to have: balance, composition, sometimes color (not necessarily) . . . It is quick; it is easy."

As a rule, the elements of a Kostabi painting tend to be relatively simple (thus reducing the amount of time it takes to paint in the canvas), and devoid of personal gestures and textures (this allows executors to be interchangeable). Figuration is a thread that runs through virtually all Kostabi paintings (a wise choice for works destined for a market segment where abstraction is unpopular). Such strategies of pictorial standardization are vital to the routinized, mass-market operations of Kostabi World.

The other predominant feature of Kostabi's paintings is their instant recognizability, a factor that helps to unite the vast oeuvre into a seeming whole. The trademark of almost every Kostabi painting are the faceless, androgenous, dummy-like characters

Figure 18. *Backlash* (oil on canvas) 48×90 in, Oct. 28, 1991. Photograph by courtesy of Mark Kostabi.

Figure 19. *Modern Times* (oil on canvas) 46×84 in, 1990. Photograph by courtesy of Mark Kostabi.

rendered in a style suggestive of de Chirico's surrealist compositions. Devoid of personality, age and gender, these everyman figures tend to find themselves in haunting, grotesque or amusing contemporary situations. "I think they are expressive, but I don't think they are very deep," remarks a painter. "And I think that is the whole thing – mass production of images without too much depth, maybe even reflecting the whole modern world."

Kostabi's career has been brief and explosive. A first-generation Estonian, he got his first show on South Rodeo Drive in his native Los Angeles in 1980, at the age of twenty. The move to New York shortly thereafter provided excellent opportunities for exposure. Kostabi's drawings appeared in the *New York Times* and on Bloomingdale's shopping bags. He was fortunate to arrive in New York at the peak of the East Village art gallery scene. Shows were opening in scores, often several a night, allowing newcomers to build reputations. Immensely prolific, Kostabi exhibited in many galleries (his forty-five shows in 1983 even won him the *Village Voice* Proliferation Award). His goal, not fashioned yet into an ideology, was to put out a huge amount of work and infiltrate the established gallery system.

"At that time he made the statement that every artist needs a stable of galleries," the dealer that eventually took him on remembers. "I said that I wasn't interested in his having a stable of galleries, but that someone had to oversee all this and keep track of what was going on, otherwise it was just total chaos . . . But it was impossible to keep up. We would have had to stop what we were doing and become Kostabi World itself in order to keep up with him."

Painters who are much in demand often engage assistants who do more than just stretch canvas or mix paint, but this is rarely acknowledged publicly. Assistants belong to the backstage of the art world, a hidden resource that contradicts the myth of the painter as solitary fount of creativity. The event that gave rise to Kostabi's notoriety was his publication of three advertisements in the *Village Voice*, in 1987, inviting artists to paint his pictures for a minimum wage. The *Voice* advertisements, which elicited 300 applications, amounted to an open polemic with art-world norms. Kostabi, the mass producing artist, became "Kostabi World" – a performance piece commenting on hypocrisy in contemporary art, molded into a commercial enterprise.

Kostabi World was a public relations hit and a lucrative business. In 1988, the organization climbed into the big time, financially, bucking the bullish art market. Controversy and hype were now essential to Kostabi's operations. The formula was simple: outrageous appearances in the media would garner name recognition and money, while allowing Kostabi to vent his acerbic criticism of the art world. "He wanted to make statements that were provocative," says an assistant. "The statements are horrifying in terms of what we consider art to be: 'Take the R out of FREE' – everything having to do with merchandizing and making money – 'Take the L out of PLAY.' I guess he just wanted to make statements that were provocative and that would get him talked about more."

In "a deliberate attempt to mislead the public" about himself, Kostabi's media escapades ranged from sophomoric pranks, like shredding $100 bills on the Oprah

Winfrey Show, to tasteless and disturbing homophobic quips about AIDS, which earned him lasting scorn. Obnoxious or funny, clever or quaint, the statements always attempted to combine shrewd marketing with incisive commentary. They enveloped the enterprise in a cloak of discourse, mostly about the untrammeled commercialization of the art world, for which Kostabi World was to be the most poignant, if caricature-like, example.

Kostabi World was gradually tailored to the satirical notions that buttressed the art factory's reputation. The way in which the paintings were made became Kostabi's message, and Kostabi, a gifted farceur, took every opportunity to extrapolate his message to its most absurd, and to many, incensing conclusion. But the art world failed to accept the conceptual agenda of Kostabi World. For many artists, critics, curators and dealers, Kostabi was no cultural critic. In their eyes, he appeared as the apotheosis of bad taste, bad art, and bad politics, as just another money-hungry young painter riding the wave of the art boom.

Ironically, Kostabi saw himself disenfranchised in the art world at the same time as the demand for his work skyrocketed and the number of his assistants multiplied. After the move to the 38th Street warehouse, Kostabi World shifted into full gear, producing art on a gargantuan scale. By the end of the 1980s the factory could yield up to two thousand finished, signed, and inventoried artworks per year.

Procurement statistics, quoted by the studio manager, indicate the operation's scale at its peak: "When I order paint I usually have to order at least 20 or 30 tubes of each paint, large tubes. I have to do that once a month, and the order is about $2,500. Canvas we order usually once every month or two months; that's about a $1,000 for a huge, long roll, about 2 feet thick and about 10 feet wide. Paintbrushes? Painters go through paintbrushes pretty quickly because they are painting constantly. I would say each month we spend about $1–2,000 on paintbrushes. And then there is the turpentine which we have to buy; the rubber gloves we have to buy; we have to buy stretchers . . . The expenses at Kostabi World are incredible."

At Kostabi World routine duties are ascribed to contractually obligated, specialized employees. The enterprise is designed to carry out the large-scale production of art in the most effective manner possible. The company accumulates profit and makes a rational accounting of its finances. What may be the final stage of this routinization emerges from Kostabi's musings about the future: "I haven't put it in writing yet, but I have toyed with the idea of having my assistants continue painting when I die, and sign my name: 'Kostabi' . . . In some press interviews I have announced that Kostabis will continue to be made after my death."

Perhaps. For the moment let us conclude that Kostabi World is none other than this: Mark Kostabi, institutionalized. A simple question remains. Is this "art"?

The artist as innovator

The definition of what legitimately passes for art is subject to constant negotiation in the art world, and this debate intensifies when it comes to artists who openly challenge conventions. Innovators question the traditional boundaries of the art world. If they

Figure 20. *Rhythm of Inspiration* (oil on canvas) 7×12 ft, 1995. Photograph by Hiromi Nakano, courtesy of Mark Kostabi.

succeed, they are lauded for expanding the definition of art; if they fail, they can find themselves excluded from the art world and its unique rewards. For entrepreneurial innovators, like Kostabi, the question comes down to this: *Is it possible to challenge the structures and norms encompassing the creation of art while holding at bay the impending threats to quality and legitimacy?*

Two misunderstandings must first be laid to rest. First, that Kostabi shamelessly exploits his painters. Wages at Kostabi World are comparable to what's offered at typical places of employment for young New York artists, and it is counterbalanced by flexible hours, a casual atmosphere, and the opportunity to practice one's craft. The artists themselves are not too bellicose about the pay. "If I was working anywhere it would be the same shit; I'd be sick of doing the same job every day," says one. "Yes, he's selling our souls, but this happens every day; this is nothing compared to the oppression that goes on in other aspects of this world." Another painter appreciates that she can work in "any state of mind." "Even though Mark is hated all over America," she notes, "it's better than working in a restaurant." Some have more complex rationalizations: "The artists that are willing to work here are making a statement by making stuff that has got to sell as a Kostabi. They don't have to sell it to anybody," argues one member of the studio. "When that guy or girl starts getting known better, people are going to say, 'Oh, that's a Kostabi, and James did that one.'"

Another misunderstanding concerns assistants. There is nothing deviant about hired help. Living artists and old masters[2] have long used them. One of Kostabi's employees once worked for Jenny Holzer, whose credentials are beyond question, and found obvious parallels between the two artists. "It's a process: she writes something on a piece of paper; she sends it off to an architect who will do a blueprint . . . then she sends that to a sandblaster . . . but she signs them, she says 'I did this.' And she did. Without her it wouldn't exist – and the same goes here."[3] The true hazards of Kostabi's innovations have nothing to do with the banality of exploitation or apprenticeship.

Challenging structures: from artisan to entrepreneur

"Everyone in society works with other people. There's no escaping that. All I've done is embrace that reality and taken it to an extreme." Kostabi's portrayal of his undertaking suggests the essence of what might be called his structural innovation. Bureaucracy, legalism, and formal organizations have so far left only a faint mark on the landscape of visual art. One could argue, with a touch of elitism, that this splendid isolation from modern institutions has been crucial in upholding art's critical distance and edge. But large-scale social transformations are bound to be reflected in the architecture of the art world. Kostabi World is the most eccentric proof of such changes.

The adaptation to modern forms of behavior and organization which Mark Kostabi exemplifies can be described in terms of a shift from the artisan to the entrepreneur. These two ideal-typifications of the artist are distinguished by their inverse relation to the fabrication and the dissemination of art. The artisan concentrates most of his or her efforts on the execution of the work while delegating market activities to another party, usually a gallery. Conversely, the entrepreneurial artist entrusts part or most of the manual execution of the artworks to someone else in order to concentrate on management and controlling the market.

Crucial to this distinction, which is never absolute, is the shift in emphasis within the broad cycle of art production. One need not build Kostabi World to be entrepreneurial. It is enough to reorganize priorities to the point where the aesthetics of creation become subordinate to the logistics of production. When an artist forsakes the isolation of the studio, abjures the intimacy of manual labor, and is consumed by the calculated professionalism entailed by the management of a collectively organized creative process, he or she can rightly be labelled entrepreneurial.

Why does the image of the entrepreneur painter appear somehow improper? It is better to turn this question around. Why should painting be immune to the emergence of the entrepreneur creator? This figure has long been commonplace in other cultural fields. Film, theatre, architecture or academic research would be unimaginable without a rational coordination of resources and the corresponding figures of the producer, the company director, the studio manager and the head researcher, none of whom pose a threat to the validity of their undertaking. Logistical needs predisposed these fields to routinize, to be sure, but what ultimately stimulated their evolution toward complex organizations was mass demand. Creative professions routinize if their markets reward such adaptations. But while mass interest has long blessed film, theatre, architecture and science, in the case of visual art the pressure of large-scale demand is relatively recent. The brief history of routinization, above all, makes the entrepreneurial stance controversial.

A predominant sociological trait of modernity has been the expansion of art patronage. Once the playpen of a narrow elite, the art market is now a dense field populated by upper-middle- and middle-class collectors as well as an abundance of institutional buyers, including museums, corporate collections and investment funds. The 1980s gave rise to a luxury mass market for painting. Collectors of blue-chip art remained relatively few in number, but thousands of buyers appeared on the second tier of the art market, where paintings sell for lower prices. This segment of the art market can absorb a large scale of output from an individual painter that would be impossible to match without hired assistants and a formally organized studio.[4]

With its industrial-scale production of paintings, Kostabi World was an organizational solution to a structural dilemma posed by the expansion of the art market. This adaptation is embodied in Mark Kostabi, the entrepreneur artist.

Challenging norms: from autonomous genius to integrated professional

To focus simply on "the way things are working," as Kostabi himself warns, "is only to look at the surface." Change in cultural fields is conditioned by norms as much as by structures. Such norms raise expectations about the content of art and about the way in which artists should go about doing their work. Norms have been Kostabi's main weapon in forging his reputation. His caricature of art-world hypocrisy is a scathing performance piece about the dark side of contemporary art in the 1980s. The myopic pursuit of money and fame is unmistakably captured in the fun-house mirror of Kostabi World. But taunting norms in the art world can be as dangerous as playing with fire.

Kostabi portrays his actions as an attempt to redefine the norms of art production. In private, he appears deeply concerned about the exploitation of artists in the marketplace, principally by art dealers. He draws attention to all the rampant exploitation and hype, he contends, by advancing a preposterous example of these very phenomena. But what he is really trying to promote, he contends, is the need for artists to change their values in order to flourish.

In his view, present-day conditions are due in part to an outdated role pattern and ideology that entraps visual artists. An inheritance of the nineteenth century, this Romantic set of practices and beliefs – embodied in the ideal of the artist as autonomous genius – is characterized by a resentment of commercialism and mainstream organizations. As a result, it helps to exclude artists from the material rewards of their calling, largely to the benefit of dealers and speculators. Hence the need for a new normative role pattern to complement the structural shift to entrepreneurialism. This shift can be described as the evolution into the integrated professional.[5]

Part-hero and part-bohemian, aloof from production and business, the autonomous genius is a newcomer to the stage of art history. The gallery-critic system that postdated the academies (White and White 1965) and the internalist perspective of arts discourse[6] perpetuate the myth of the autonomous genius, even though artists stand to gain economically from embracing the marketplace and are often kept from doing so only by convention.[7]

In contrast, the integrated professional whom Kostabi personifies adapts to the commercial environment by assuming the *habitus* of a businessman. The symbolic repertoire of professionalism may appear gauche in the light of prevailing norms, but the adoption of such norms is hardly an irrational strategy to achieve recognition and reward. It is a pragmatic response to the prevailing milieu of art.

Will entrepreneurialism and professionalism allow Kostabi (and others like him) to maintain a steady success and respect in the art world? Innovators like Kostabi must reckon with traditional constraints. Any challenge to structures and norms in the contemporary fine-art field must take into account the looming threats to quality and legitimacy to which I now turn.

Threatened quality: from entrepreneur to artisan

Once the decisive step is taken toward the routinization of painting, dilemmas of creativity become entwined with dilemmas of production. The first complications to arise are organizational frictions and coordination breakdowns. Like any other work place, Kostabi World has its share of disputes and squabbling, firings and walkouts, rate-busting controversies, sabotage and theft. Peculiar disruptions result from painters' anguish over their lack of autonomy. A veteran employee complains that he no longer has a say in what gets made: "[Kostabi] would ask if we liked an idea and we would say 'yes' or 'no' . . . but now it's not like that at all. . . You can't say 'no, I don't like this idea' because it's so much removed from him. The ideas come from downstairs, and we don't really like doing something we're not interested in."

Another hazard of cooperation is the threat to the integrity of the product. Kostabi World, as mentioned, is structured by a workshop-style division of labor. The risk incurred when each painter toils over a single canvas (instead of performing an isolated sequence of the process, as on a production line) is that hired artists will impose their personal styles over Kostabi's. By the late 1980s the consistency of Kostabi's art did begin to dissolve; individualized styles emerged in the studio. Whether the market accepts this fragmentation is debatable. If Kostabi's signature is established as a brand name on a familiar product, new "lines" of Kostabi art are theoretically possible.[8] However, if Kostabi World turns out paintings executed in a myriad individualized styles, all marketed under the Kostabi logo, the original purpose of Kostabi World will be called into question. Instead of multiplying Kostabi's art, the organization will eclipse and exclude Kostabi, and the appropriation of the painters' work will appear flagrantly exploitative.

Such worries are compelling, but towering above the aforementioned dilemmas, incorporating them all, is the threat to quality. I use the term quality in its most basic connotation, namely, as a certain level of precision and sophistication brought to bear on the conceptualization and execution of art. All complex enterprises must deal with quality control, but it is acutely salient when the product, so to speak, is art. When the manufacturing process accelerates and is disengaged from individual workers as well as the manager-creator, quality is likely to deteriorate. As a supporter of Kostabi put it, "the dangers are inherent in the production itself: the larger you get the less control you have over what it is that is being produced and what it looks like . . . Rather than being idea driven, painting-by-painting and subject-by-subject, which was the original reason that Mark founded Kostabi World, now there is a shortage of ideas and more emphasis on . . . putting out a product."

The greater the complexity and sophistication of the work, the more difficult standards are to impose. The more fragmented the creative process, the more likely that the hired painters will lose sight of the way in which portions of the whole procedure contribute to the art work, and the less likely that they can end up with a piece that is visually and intellectually compelling. Ultimately, the deterioration of quality can be attributed to the lack of dedication to the picture on the part of the person whose paintbrush touches the canvas. As a mere wage laborer, estranged from the product of his or her work (to use a standard argument), the immediate creator of the painting will not muster the requisite commitment to make a high quality work of art.

In his defense of the quality issue, Kostabi, likes to compare his factory process to watercolor painting. A watercolorist works with diluted pigment on saturated paper, manipulating the unpredictable chemistry of his medium. The result will not wholly conform to the watercolorist's vision; it will only be molded, as it were, by the painter's intentions. In his studio, Kostabi argues, hired men and women play the role of randomly flowing and mingling paint; they become the erratic agents of the artist's will. And if the watercolorist's art can yield paintings of high quality, why shouldn't Kostabi World?

This reasoning has its merits, but it skims over the crucial detail that when humans take the place of chemical substances, an assembly of wills is brought to bear on the creative process. Assistants do not conform to unbendable laws of nature. Their morale might act as a positive stimulus, even enhancing the quality of the work in ways that its "director" would not have imagined. But they can equally undermine Kostabi's intentions, in subtle acts of subterfuge, or out of sheer boredom and lackluster interest in the finished product.

Who is this alienated and disenchanted person who thus threatens the routinized art enterprise? It is the artisan whom Kostabi abandoned during his metamorphosis into the entrepreneur.

The entrepreneur artist leaves behind him a creative void, a lack of motivation that can only formally be offset by contractually hired hands.[9] In practice, the responsibility that underlies the artisan's relation to the artwork cannot be enforced by contract. The only conceivable remedy to the deterioration in quality is to somehow revive artisanship within the framework of routinized production. The latter, however, invigorates the evolution of individual styles, which, as shown, likewise threaten the ultimate aims of the organization.

The entrepreneurial redefinition of artisanship thus opens up unique opportunities (for increasing output and augmenting revenues), but it can also be expected to pose severe structural obstacles to the realization of the entrepreneurial artist's intentions. Routinization carries a price tag. How much the innovative artist will be able to reap its rewards will depend on his or her ability to negotiate the logic of entrepreneurialism in a field that continues to hinge critically on the hand of the artisan.

Threat to legitimacy: from integrated professional to autonomous genius

Norms associated with how art is made today were earlier examined in the context of roles. The metamorphosis from an autonomous genius (who decries commerce and its ethos) into an integrated professional (who disdains the culture of the marketplace), helps an artist like Kostabi exploit the rewards of entrepreneurialism and achieve, as he has, a commercial triumph of enviable proportions. Merit in the art world, however, is rarely gauged by wealth. It depends on legitimacy, which is the art world's principal measure of respect.

Legitimacy refers to rules and dispositions that make for a hierarchy of value among cultural artifacts.[10] What distinguishes a legitimate artwork from one that is not legitimate is its entitlement to be seen in the light of such rules and dispositions. A legitimate artifact claiming the title of "artwork" is valued on the basis of a finite set of aesthetic attributes. These attributes place the artwork in a referential relationship with other legitimate works and forms of art. It is not the positive or negative judgment along these attributes that make an object "art," but the sheer fact that it is fit to be appraised by the prevailing aesthetic. Legitimacy, in short, is the privilege to be judged. Shared rules of distinction place the artwork in the league of other legitimate cultural artifacts, and its maker in the league of other legitimate cultural actors.

The rules underlying legitimacy are arbitrated by institutions. While the supreme arbiter is the educational system, when it comes to visual art – a self-contained and self-referential cultural field – the institution in charge is the art world. Norms generated in the art world license the distinction between "high culture" and "popular culture," as well as verdicts on what separates "works of art" from consumer products, or "mere ordinary things." In the art market the latter distinction between "art" and "ordinary thing" is essential. Legitimacy is here translated into exaggerated disparities in price. The entitlement to be judged aesthetically leads to exorbitant pricing, because the object in question is deemed by those in the art world to possess the necessary attributes. Market price, as such, is an indirect consequence of legitimacy.

In shedding the role of the autonomous genius, the integrated-professional artist runs the risk of displacement from the symbolic boundaries of the art world. The rejection of the art world's shared behavioral repertoires can jeopardize membership of the group that determines the legitimacy of his or her work. Such symbolic estrangement from the art world can result in nothing short of the loss of the right to be judged aesthetically. After a given point in the alienation from the community of other artists and art professionals, the work of the integrated-professional – even if it is successful in broad commercial distribution – might no longer claim the label of legitimate "art."

The fickle nature of legitimacy poses a tangible threat to Kostabi and his enterprise. Kostabi World was designed, originally, as a mockery of the art world. Today it is more likely to be seen as a manifestation of the very symptoms – greed, hype, plagiarism – Kostabi once aimed to parody. What could have been a legitimate artistic performance piece on the social realities of culture-making is now prone to be construed as an exercise in self-promotion. Kostabi's paintings are disparaged by art-world members as mass consumer products that deserve no place in a legitimate art gallery. For the most part, these opinions are not based on a proper analysis of the quality of Kostabi's works (those who hate Kostabi rarely look at his pictures), but on preconceptions about his intentions. The problem that fellow artists have with Kostabi is not that he has routinized his operation, but the way in which he has gone about doing so. More than the structure of his activities, it is the values he appears to stand for that incense many of them.

Kostabi's claim to recognition and financial independence is thus threatened by the eradication of the credentials that, in the long run, stimulate critical validation and market demand for his art. He must walk a fine line. His particular claim to legitimacy, involving the questioning of the art world's norms, has caused him to burn his symbolic bridges to those who are supposed to accredit legitimacy to him.

Aware that he is becoming an outcast, Kostabi makes an unusual bid for legitimacy. By switching to the role of the integrated professional and rejecting prevailing art-world norms, he stubbornly believes he deserves to recapture the mantle of the autonomous genius. Historically, the ideology of genius has insisted on autonomy from society at large. Kostabi's autonomy, in contrast, takes aim at the art world. Ostracized by the art community, separated from traditional avenues of legitimation, reliant on his own gallery distribution, he hopes to claim legitimacy not by demonizing mainstream social arrangements but by attacking the norms of the art world.[11] In his own, admittedly self-serving words, Mark Kostabi "may indeed be the ultimate lone visionary." "I am the new kind of Van Gogh," he rhapsodizes. "I feel like I'm a loner. Like I am battling a one-man war against the art establishment."

No matter how resourcefully Kostabi discourses about his entitlement to be accepted, the forces involved in his legitimation are beyond his control. The most important lesson Kostabi World offers is that the artist who wants to change his universe cannot tailor his actions solely to practical imperatives. His every move must take account of the particular norms that govern the field of art. Here, the legitimacy of the entrepreneurial artist will ultimately depend on his ability to negotiate the logic of integrated professionalism in a field that critically hinges on the respect for the *autonomous genius*.

The artist as opportunist

It would be pointless to talk about cultural innovation in the absence of the goals that any such innovation professes to serve. It may come as a surprise that Mark Kostabi harbors many idealistic sentiments. For him, Kostabi World's purpose is to diffuse art on an unprecedented scale to enrich the lives of a countless number of people. The studio provides for scores of young artists employment and a chance to practice one's craft (he calls Kostabi World an "art school where you get paid to learn"). Kostabi feels he is embroiled in a quixotic challenge to a harsh and monolithic art world.

Kostabi also believes that he has demonstrated how artists can emancipate themselves from the yoke of the art establishment. But he aims higher. The goal is not money, he asserts, but the command of the resources that are required to manipulate the world, so as to make it a more dignified and beautiful place. In his vision of society, artists would take their place next to politicians and businessmen at the table of influential people who can alter the course of history. In order to do this, however, they must learn to play the game of society at large.

The dilemma in this strategy resides in the tension between ends and means. Kostabi's innovations call for the abandonment of the structural and normative conventions surrounding art-making today. Such an abjuration of principles in the service of avowedly positive goals has an analogy in the political life, a field similarly marred by deep ambiguities between ends and means. In the vocabulary of politics this dilemma is called "opportunism."

In its analytical, non-pejorative sense, opportunism means the attainment of goals through the temporary suspension of principles. At Kostabi World, the principles on hold are those which traditionally prevent the artist from embracing the market and its institutions. Kostabi believes that integration in the market is only a means by which to attain virtuous ends, ends that transcend, even contradict, the marketplace. But opportunism as a strategy for action, in art as in politics, can easily backfire.

Opportunist practices become self-defeating and limited in their rationality, Claus Offe points out, when they "cease to be justifiable by standards of either survival or goal attainment" (1985: 219–220). For the entrepreneurial artist operating in the spirit of integrated professionalism, like Kostabi, this dangerous moment sets in when his practical and symbolic behavior raises doubts about quality and legitimacy. The danger is increased if market orientation is perceived to become an end in itself.

At the time of writing (1990) there is evidence that Kostabi World may be approaching such a crossroads. Challenges to quality and legitimacy threaten the organization's survival. The predominance of market motivations is eclipsing Kostabi's goals. Kostabi, the innovator artist, must now seek an answer to a new dilemma. Should he redesign his strategy the better to serve his goals, or should he forsake his goals to justify his strategy? Whatever his decision, one conclusion is certain. The acceptance of the "transitory rationality of opportunism" may emancipate an artist from one set of historical constraints, but it also presents him with new ones. These should form the crux of Mark Kostabi's future innovations.

Postscript

Kostabi World as I saw it in 1989–1990 no longer exists. In May 1993 it moved to Broadway and Houston Streets on the edge of SoHo, Manhattan's contemporary art district. The new loft is adjacent to the studio of Jeff Koons, an artist who has captured and maintained the confidence of many serious critics, despite his controversial tactics which suggest a kinship with Mark Kostabi. An East Village graduate, like Kostabi, Koons tested the art world's limits by commissioning ceramic sculptures based on appropriated images that were made entirely by hired craftsmen. Obsessed with media exposure, Koons made himself the talk of the town when he exhibited explicit images of himself engaged in sexual acts with his wife, the Italian porn actress, Cicciolina. Koons' show, however, was organized by Sonnabend, one of Manhattan's premier art galleries. Under such auspices, the whole art world flocked to the event.

The same did not happen when Kostabi World reopened in 1993. Kostabi did put on a good show. The walls of the sprawling front gallery were lined with familiar-looking Kostabi paintings. There was a coin-operated peep-show slot through which guests could observe the infamous back-room, all but empty now, since Kostabi had dismissed most of his painters to focus on the sale of his gigantic inventory of finished artworks. Next to a table laden with gourmet delicacies and refreshments, young Japanese women lined up to have their pictures taken with the artist, who remains popular in their country. But the regular art-world crowd was conspicuously absent. Scorn and outrage, it appeared, had given way to indifference.

The lack of interest in Kostabi World was not the result of a stubborn denial of the practices its founder had set out to parody. In the wake of the art-market collapse of 1990–1992, an atmosphere of self-doubt and self-scrutiny had descended upon the art world. Many old myths were discarded; eighties euphemisms ceded to a nineties-style of matter-of-fact pragmatism. Among other realities, the art world came to terms with the fact that some artists operate studios with many assistants. And, to survive in a harsh art market, many must work in a calculated, professional manner. The feature article of the January 1993 issue of *Art in America* was dedicated – favorably – to the theme of "Artists and Assistants."[12]

My impression at the reopening was that Kostabi had indeed managed to achieve banishment from the legitimate art world, as I had predicted earlier. Nothing appeared to testify to this more poignantly than the decision by art dealer Ronald Feldman, Kostabi's last remaining link to "high art", to drop him from his gallery roster. My impression was that Kostabi would never make art again, either with assistants or without; that he would eke out an existence as a resale dealer of his own oeuvre in the lower echelons of the international art trade. With a copy of his huge vanity book, *Kostabi: The Early Years*, under my arm, I left the reopening thinking that the attempt to rationalize and routinize art-making at Kostabi World had reached a dubious conclusion – it had eliminated all remnants of creative activity. Not only was Kostabi outside the legitimate art world, but he appeared to be existing even beyond the periphery of art making.

I returned to Kostabi World in 1995, and found many of my earlier impressions disproved. Kostabi looked older and more mature, but as confident as ever. All around him were signs of the activity of the years that passed since the reopening.

Large and elaborate new paintings adorned the front gallery, executed with painstaking precision – a tangible improvement over the earlier work. Twelve employees, including seven painters, were now active in the studio. A glass vitrine in Kostabi's office contained various artifacts bearing his recent designs: a Kostabi Swatch; a copy of Jack D. Schwager's book, *Marketing Wizards*, with a Kostabi jacket cover; a bottle of Label Twist soda, a line of cosmetics, and a restaurant menu, all designed by Kostabi; and the most widely distributed Kostabi image to date, the jacket design for "Use Your Illusion," the platinum-selling double CD set by the hard rock band Guns 'n' Roses.

The walls of the loft were lined with posters advertising recent Kostabi shows around the world and the front pages of international magazines and art journals featuring photographs of Kostabi or his work.[13] Kostabi is proud of this attention, especially of his appearance, in September 1990, on the front cover of *Flash Art*, a leading international art magazine. Such attention is the most obvious proof, he boasts, that while the recession set him back, now he is "doing better than ever."

Kostabi is in great demand in Japan, Italy and the booming Germany. Italians especially love his work ("it goes well with Italian design"). One Italian dealer buys paintings by the dozen, like the Japanese in the eighties. Kostabi has started a cable television show in New York and he regularly hosts fund-raising events in his studio. He has rekindled his interest in the piano, having recorded a cycle of serious compositions that he performed to an enthusiastic audience in his native Estonia. His goal is to have a major orchestra perform his compositions one day, perhaps at Carnegie Hall, while he creates paintings on the stage. The art would be auctioned for a good cause after the final item.

Kostabi has yet to regain the confidence of the art world, but there are signs that his seclusion might be ending. He talks about reputable artists dropping by his studio, and of negotiations with established dealers who might show his work. He believes that the art world will come around and notice that he has persevered in times when so many visual artists turned to other interests, such as film, and that he kept his gallery afloat when scores of dealers closed.

The time might even come of a nostalgia for the 1980s. If and when that happens, Mark Kostabi, the quintessential boom-time artist, will be ready and waiting, ripe for "rediscovery."

Figure 21. *Concentration* (oil on canvas) 54×44 in, 1994. Photograph by Hiromi Nakano, courtesy of Mark Kostabi.

Notes

1 The original (much longer) version of this essay was written in 1990, based on research conducted in 1989–1990. With the exception of the postscript, this text reflects conditions at Kostabi World at the time of research.

2 Sculpture has a long history of routinization. Auguste Rodin never cast a work himself. Among painters, Rembrandt's studio is a subject of great scholarly and public interest. Though such analogies are often invoked with respect to Kostabi, their applicability is limited. Identical artistic practices have diverse meanings in varied socio-historical contexts (Horkheimer 1978 [1935]).

3 Many artists commit their work to subordinates, Kostabi's associates point out. "This is a general practice but people don't usually talk about it because it is considered to lower the price," says Kostabi's public relations representative. "Michelangelo did it, Da Vinci did it, the Renaissance painters did it, all the Romantics did it. Today other artists don't have other people thinking up their ideas, but they have other people executing their work – even Roy Lichtenstein has people doing his dots – but they just don't advertise it." Kostabi's painters are just as equivocal. Says one: "Robert Longo doesn't do his stuff at all. A friend of mine works for Frank Stella, and Frank would come in and say, 'I want this color, and this color, and this.' He pretty much lets them do it all."

4 Painters routinely satisfied large-scale demand by creating simpler works and multiples. Such efforts, however, can prove damaging to reputations, as the examples of Pablo Picasso and Salvador Dali show (both artists exposed themselves to the threat of forgery, and criticism about the quality of multiples). Style can be simplified, but this option is limited by the taste of patrons.

5 "Autonomous genius" is from Pierre Bourdieu, who applied it to intellectuals in "Intellectual Field and Creative Project," (1969: 89–119). "Integrated professional" was used by Howard S. Becker in *Art Worlds* (1982: 228–33). Becker's definition focuses on norms, but he sees integration as assimilation into the "shared history of problems and solutions" of the art world, not of mainstream society. My use assumes adaptation to commercial society, in defiance of art-world norms. This approximates what Raymond Williams in *The Sociology of Culture* calls "instituted artists," who are "officially recognized as part of the central social organization itself" (1981: 36).

6 For a comparison of the internalist perspective of aesthetics and criticism and the externalist approach of socially oriented art history and sociology, see Vera Zolberg (1990).

7 This is how Kostabi describes the problem: "After Van Gogh there was this short-term myth of the artist as lone visionary, or as a hero battling the forces of society. But this is not an epic chapter in history . . . The idea that the artist is a transmitter without an audience, a lone unrecognized visionary, is absurd." Van Gogh remains the archetype of the autonomous genius, even though medical research has attributed the artist's peculiar behavior and suicide to Ménière's syndrome, an inner ear disorder that causes audial hallucinations and excruciating pain (the likely reason for the famous excised ear) (*New York Times*, July 25, 1990: C17).

8 Such arrangements are common in large, commercial design industries (such as the creative franchise – "Lagerfeld for Chanel" – in haute couture fashion).

9 This may be the key difference between the seemingly analogous structure of the old master's studio and Kostabi World. Their internal networks are similar, but the content of the relationships vary. A contract is not a substitute for the bonds of loyalty and duty that bind apprentice to master.

10 The idea of legitimacy was adapted for cultural analysis by Pierre Bourdieu, who derived it

from Max Weber's theory of authority (1969: 106–07; 1984: 28–29). A similar argument is made by Arthur C. Danto (1981), who speaks, instead of legitimacy, of a "discourse of reasons" in which art is enveloped.

11 This claim is in some respects more adequate in the self-referential field of visual art. If art tends toward an internalist dialogue among theoretical viewpoints, irrespective of the social world, why should the role of the artist depend on opposition to a realm outside the art world?

12 The special section (advertised on the front cover) included descriptions of elaborate support operations in the studios of Henry Moore, Richard Serra, Ann Hamilton, Peter Halley, Robert Longo, Vito Acconci, and others.

13 *Sunstorm*, December 1988; *Magneet* (Sweden) July 1993; *New York* January 24, 1994; *Artnotes* Fall 1990; *ArtWord* April/May, 1994; *Chess Life* July 1994; *New York, NY* (Japan) 1995: 8–9.

References

Becker, Howard S. 1982, *Art Worlds*, University of California Press.

Bourdieu, Pierre 1969, "Intellectual Field and Creative Project," *Social Science Information* 8: 89–119.

1984, *Distinction: A Social Critique of the Judgement of Taste*, Harvard University Press.

Danto, Arthur C. 1981, *The Transfiguration of the Commonplace*, Harvard University Press.

Horkheimer Max 1978, "On the Problem of Truth," *The Essential Frankfurt School Reader*, eds. A. Arato and E. Gebhardt, New York: Urizen Books [originally 1935].

Offe, Claus 1985, "Two Logics of Collective Action," *Disorganized Capitalism*, M. I. T. Press: 170–220.

White, Harrison and White, Cynthia 1965, *Canvases and Careers: Institutional Change in the French Painting World*, New York: John Wiley.

Williams, Raymond 1981, *The Sociology of Culture*, New York: Schocken.

Zolberg, Vera L. 1990, *Constructing a Sociology of the Arts*, Cambridge University Press.

7

Outside art and insider artists: gauging public reactions to contemporary public art

Nathalie Heinich

The idea of insider or outsider artists has different meanings. First, at its simplest level, it refers to a geographical opposition, such as that between artists living in big cities or in small towns. This is the heart of the center/periphery scheme formulated by Enrico Castelnuovo and Carlo Ginsburg (1979) to conceptualize the process whereby Florence gained artistic dominance over other cities during the early Renaissance. Secondly, it may refer to a sociological opposition between legitimate (or dominant) and illegitimate (or dominated) positions in the artistic field, as adumbrated by Pierre Bourdieu in his theory of how cultural domination is perpetuated (1992). Thirdly, it encapsulates the cognitive (or mental) structuring of what is inside or outside the boundary definition of art as opposed to non-art, of who is or is not an artist (Heinich 1992). Finally, it may be a mere physical opposition between art shown inside or outside the walls of museums and galleries.

In terms of these meanings an artist may be a complete insider if he lives in a big city in the West, becomes famous with a solid position in the international art world, and produces a kind of art that does not transgress the usual aesthetic expectations and can take its place in a museum. At the opposite extreme, the complete outsider is le Facteur Cheval, a French postman who devoted much of his life to building a fantastic world of bizarre sculptures made of found objects, in his own garden. A good many amateurs or local artists today, who practice classical styles of painting, are cognitive and physical insiders, but hopeless outsiders according to geographical and sociological meanings. There is a small number of artists who systematically practice as outsiders according to the cognitive and physical boundaries of accepted art, yet succeed in belonging to the small elite of the internationally recognized avant-garde. They contribute to redefining what an insider should be, and what constitutes insider art.

It is in accord with this categorization of outsider-insider artist that I analyze in this essay the work of three famous artists. My focus is the reception of their works by non-specialists – the lay public – focusing on two examples in France and one in the United States. These cases gave rise to widely publicized scandals. The first involved a photographer, the second scandal centered on a conceptual artist, and the third centered on a land artist. Whereas the first may be considered a cognitive outsider, as photography still remains on the boundary of inclusion, the last two are outsiders in both the cognitive and physical senses.[1]

The first two scandals (or "affaires") concerning contemporary art were the Robert Mapplethorpe exhibition in the Contemporary Art Center in Cincinnati in 1990, and the awarding of a commission to the artist, Daniel Buren, for a site-specific work in the courtyard of the Palais-Royal in Paris in 1986. In both cases the works gave rise to a mobilization against them of viewers who had not previously been part of a formally constituted group. They joined forces temporarily in order to protest against an art exhibition and an artistic installation organized by public institutions and supported by agencies of the state.

In both cases the events included public protests, articles in national newspapers and magazines, the organization of voluntary associations, petitions and letters to the authorities, political debates, and, finally, legal proceedings in the form of trials. And in both cases the conclusion was the same: the court found in favor of contemporary art supporters against their opponents.

In the case of Dennis Barrie, director of the the Cincinnati gallery, who had organized the Mapplethorpe exhibition (supported in part by a grant from the National Endowment for the Arts), he was acquitted of the charge of obscenity by a jury of laymen. In the Buren case, François Léotard (who had succeeded Jack Lang as Minister of Culture, and whose political party had been critical of many of his predecessor's policies) ended up allowing Buren's "Les deux plateaux" to be completed, almost exactly as the artist had proposed initially. Parisians can now see it whenever they like, and even if they don't like.

Beyond these similarities, there were obvious differences in the content of the arguments raised against the Mapplethorpe photographs exhibited by the Cincinnati gallery and the Buren installation, commissioned by the French Minister of Culture. Mapplethorpe's photographs were contested, mainly on moral and sexual grounds, as obscene. A large number of art specialists, however, consider Robert Mapplethorpe to be one of the major contemporary art photographers. In the Buren case, the main argument focused on the defense of public heritage, because of the siting of the work in the courtyard of the Palais-Royal, a historic public building. Buren's project consisted of a complex of permanent stony columns striped in black and white, and was considered to be seriously damaging to the Palais-Royal site. In this case too, art specialists regard Daniel Buren as one of the major contemporary conceptual artists.

Sexual morals as opposed to public heritage, obscenity as opposed to vandalism, disrespect of decency as opposed to disrespect of the past, the human body as opposed to urban architecture: herein lie the differences between two of the most famous cases in the last few years in which contemporary art was rejected. Understanding the deep, commonly held public values and mores provides a clue to understanding the acceptance/rejection of these public art projects.

The Buren case might be compared with the controversy over Richard Serra's publicly commissioned "Tilted Arc" in New York City, for aesthetic and functional, rather than for ethical reasons. The difference here is that the American artist failed in his struggle to keep his site-specific work in place, whereas Buren finally succeeded. We should note, however, that the Serra case is quite exceptional for the United States, and stands in sharp contrast to the many rejections of contemporary art in which ethical values are paramount. In France most negative reactions appear to be grounded on artistic authenticity rather than on moral or political claims. The Mapplethorpe case is but the most scandalous of a large number of similar cases occurring in the United States, whereas in France it would be impossible to find a comparable scandal at the national level. This sort of chiasm between the United States and France – frequency as opposed to rarity of ethical or political controversies, rarity as opposed to frequency of aesthetic or cognitive polemics dominate – offers a good illustration of the deep differences between the French and American situations and their attitudes to the problems raised nowadays by contemporary art.

Let us now compare the Buren scandal with another French case: the Christo[2] wrapping of the Pont-Neuf in Paris, carried out in autumn 1985, only a few months before Buren's columns were installed. The work did not elicit strong protests – at least not strong enough to provoke any actual mobilization of public objections. Only a few letters were sent to the newspapers and were printed. Some of the people I interviewed in the streets showed reluctance, incomprehension and, sometimes, hostility to this unusual event. But there were neither petitions nor associations created to protest against it, and, of course, no judicial proceeding – except for the one that came about when the Christo and Jeanne-Claude Corporation brought a law suit against a photographic agency that sold postcards of the wrapped Pont-Neuf without authorisation. The agency tried to defend itself before the court by arguing that the wrapping of a bridge could not be considered a work of art, and thus was not covered by the 1957 law protecting artists' moral rights. The Corporation was the winner: the judgment recognized the artistic nature of the installation, the moral right to the wrapped Pont-Neuf and, as such, the commercial copyright of any reproduction of it.

Why was there such a difference in the public reception of these two contemporary public art installations, occurring at the same time and in the same city? Why was there relative indulgence in the Christo case and such massive opposition in that of Buren?

There are various possible answers. First, the Christo Corporation had organized a very professional and efficient information campaign before beginning the project, so that resistance or misunderstanding might be avoided. It offered two rationales for allowing this project to go forward: one was that the scheme involved only private funds. Actually, there was some mystery for the general public surrounding the exact financial circumstances of the operation. Some respondents speculated that the project was a huge publicity stunt for the nearby department store La Samaritaine, or the backdrop scenery for a film shoot, or perhaps an advertising commercial sponsored by Japanese tour operators. Nevertheless, it appears that as soon as people understood that the installation did not benefit financially from any state or public funding, they considered the whole event as an individual and private matter: the silly caprice of an American [sic] artist, or the fantastic invention of a universal genius.

The second part of the rationale that had been provided was that the wrapping was not permanent, and would be in place for a mere two weeks. As such the public could be at ease about protecting the Pont-Neuf, a major landmark of Parisian historical

Figure 22. Pont-Neuf, Paris, wrapped by Christo, 1985. Courtesy of Christo and Jeanne-Claude Corporation, Photograph by Nathalie Heinich.

heritage: the wrapping would cause no damage, no disrespect. But the fact that it was temporary brought more suspicion as to the artistic nature of the undertaking: the ordinary public considers a work of art – such as the *Mona Lisa* – to be something that remains for centuries to be admired in a museum, is made out of canvas and colors or out of marble or clay and, preferably, represents a recognizeable image.

Contrary to the Christo case, Buren's project was neither temporary nor private. It was, indeed, the very opposite. Buren's installation was intended to share a site with an historical monument; and it was commissioned by the Minister of Culture himself, Jack Lang, who represented both a left-wing government and an avant-gardist culture. Morever, Jack Lang had authorized the installation of Buren's zebra striped columns against the advice of the specialized state committee for historical monuments. The art was predicated on a state decision (coming from a contested government) and would irreversibly transform a public historical monument. The conjunction of these two factors account for the strength of public mobilization of protest, and the scope of the Buren scandal.

We should also note that the form of mobilization of public opinion is closely connected with the content of the arguments evoked. The wrapping of the Pont-Neuf did not provoke strong protests because the project avoided the two main issues that fueled the case for Buren's opponents: the public ownership of civil, historical monuments, and commissioning of art works with tax monies. The way in which public architecture is treated and the use of taxpayer's funds appear to be two very grave public concerns.

"How shall we pay for that?," and "Does this so-called work of art deserve to deface such a jewel of classic architecture?" were the two principal arguments used against the Buren work, but rarely against the Christo work. Still, the latter could not escape some other negative arguments, which are recurrent in most of the protests against contemporary public art. Let us now summarize them.

When economics intersect with the general or public interest, rejection is often expressed in the name of civic values. The objection – "How much does it cost?" – indicates that the price of a work is resented as too expensive in terms of the benefit expected by the public. In such cases, respondents tend to see art in contrast to health or social welfare, which appear as more general public values. Skepticism about art is almost unavoidable in the case of works commissoned by the state, but can also be encountered by certain privately financed artistic operations, especially when they take a very public form. For example, people interviewed near the Pont-Neuf were indignant because so much money was "wasted" for a completely useless thing, when it could have been given to hospitals or to the unemployed.

Rejection may also focus on values related to the quantity and quality of the work and the effort expended or talent embodied in making the object. This is expressed in the often heard comment: "A child could do the same . . . Anybody could do the same." This reaction seems to be as recurrent a remark criticizing art as "How much does it cost?" The price of the so-called work of art is considered out of scale, based on the amount of work or the ability perceived necessary for its fabrication. If there is a discrepancy, it is quite contrary to ordinary morality: what is given should be proportion-

Figure 23. Daniel Buren, *Les Deux Plateaux*. Palais Royal, Paris, 1986. Photograph by Vera L. Zolberg (1992).

ate to what is deserved, and what is deserved should be proportionate to the amount of work going into it. When the effort that has gone into creating the art work is not evident to the lay public, then a feeling of injustice or deception takes hold – a sense of being had!

Paradoxically, the public interest and the quality and quantity of work seem to be much more often invoked as arguments for or against art than considerations of an aesthetic nature, about beauty. The aesthetic argument is far from being as omnipresent as one might imagine. People do not systematically argue aesthetically against art works – at least in formal and written forms. They rarely speak of their ugliness, and do not address the concept of beauty at all. This rather amazing fact has two explanations. First, the aesthetic argument is probably more relevant in face-to-face interactions, that is, in private discussions which do not require universal and objective arguments. When more general public values are involved, the rejection is more formal and official (as in petitions, letters, and so on). Arguments relating to beauty may seem too subjective, too particular, too determined by personal taste to justify any reference to the general interest and public action.

A second reason why beauty or ugliness are invoked so rarely in these arguments lies in the very heart of contemporary art, which often questions what constitutes aesthetic quality, and on what grounds an art work may be considered a genuine work of art. That is why, besides the general public interest and the amount of work involved, the main argument surrounding an artistic piece still concerns artistic authenticity: art itself is the most central value invoked in rejections of contemporary creations. This is what is being expressed in the common protest, "This is not art!," or better, "This is not art! A child could do it. On top of that, look how much it costs!"

The question of what is genuine art may arise in local or regional settings when people criticize official policies which tend to privilege national or international artists rather than regional ones. This does not contradict a widely shared idea that great art is universal and that it should be understood immediately by anybody, instead of requiring interpretation by learned specialists, who are often criticized for representing nothing but "snobbism" and "elitism." Local art, because it is embedded in a particular culture, is assumed to be genuine, understandable by anyone, because it is related to deep universal qualities.

This attachment to universal standards helps to explain the continued support usually associated with tradition in art: genuine art is part of tradition and universality, in that tradition testifies to and proves its universality, simply by existing as such and lasting over several generations. But genuine art may also be associated with modernity, provided that the work has undergone a selection process in which discernment has been exercised to valorize "good" and reject "bad" art, and that it is a "real" work and not a fraud. The intention is to reward genuine talent and to reject poseurs engaged in a confidence trick, who appear to be invading everything, like weeds.

So the demand for artistic authenticity may be associated with, first, the defense of territorial integrity, as demonstrated when public works are rejected in the name of preserving part of the public heritage (the Buren case); second, with the defense of sexual morals, as demonstrated when an exhibited work shows naked bodies in obviously sexualized situations, and many people are unable to maintain sufficient emotional distance to allow the moral neutrality commonly associated with other art works (the Mapplethorpe case).

Artistic authenticity, the integrity of heritage, sexual morality: these are three categories of values that share the common imperatives of respect for established boundaries, discrimination between good and bad, and the avoidance of commingling objects and behavior which are not considered to belong together. These include intimacy and public space; nakedness and public gaze; avant-garde art and classical aesthetics; creative innovation and preservation of national heritage; the inventions of "zanies" in search of sensation, and the efforts of true, dedicated artists; hoax and serious craft; confidence tricks and genuine creations.

Selecting "true" artists, protecting heritage and preserving morals have in common a concern for purity, for separation, for defending good against evil, the authentic against the inauthentic, old against new, order against disorder. These juxtapositions are closely akin to the taboo against the stain, the concern with purity that Mary Douglas has located in several civilizations (1966).

The main arguments invoked against contemporary public art are also related to the values or "worlds" evidenced by Luc Boltanski and Laurent Thévenot in their analysis of the various modes of justification (1991). Thus, the domestic world of tradition and the civic world of the general interest are particularly relevant in protests against contemporary art. Structural pairings are also likely to occur, such as domestic/inspired, when defending local artists; domestic/civic, when defending public heritage; or civic opinion, when defending the consensus of sensible people.

Rejecting, protesting, arguing against – these are the principal actions I have considered. Any action involves three dimensions of experience: first, the subject who produces the action; second, the object produced or considered for action; third, the situation in which the subject produces or considers the object. This action, indeed any rejection of contemporary art, involves the following three elements: a situation (i.e. an exhibition, a public commission etc.), a subject (i.e. a person able to develop an opinion), and an object (i.e. Mapplethorpe's photographs exhibited by a museum's curator in Cincinnati, Buren's installation in the Palais-Royal commissioned by the Ministry of Culture, the Christos' wrapping of the Pont-Neuf, authorized by the mayor of Paris). When opponents of contemporary art invoke a set of values, as I have suggested, they intend to denounce either the artists' action in making those works, the state's (or administration's) action in commissioning and exhibiting them, the critic's action in celebrating them, or the onlooker's action when visiting and admiring them.

If we want to explain rejection or, at the least, explicate the factors associated with reactions against contemporary art, we have to relate the values invoked (the general or public interest and universality, tradition and authenticity, work and morals) with the three dimensions of action: as objects, subjects and situations. To conclude this overview of the problem, let us consider how certain sociological traditions provide an understanding of explanatory factors. The objects of action involve, first, the products of artistic activity or art works. Although they are traditionally the concern of art history, they may also be analyzed by a sociology of art when it deals with the various ways in which contemporary art transgresses artistic expectations, such as the boundaries between art and non-art (Heinich 1990b; 1993). Second, inasmuch as publicly commissioned art objects involve arts policy that emanates from the state, acceptance may often best be understood through the approaches of political sociology. Third, various attitudes are involved of what Alan Bowness called the "four circles of recognition" (1989): other artists, critics and art dealers, collectors, and, finally, the public. They constitute the domains of history, aesthetics, economics of the arts, and the sociology of reception (Zolberg 1990).

However, if we were to confine ourselves to the art objects alone, the treatment inflicted on an art work by the public would engender the same kind of reactions from different subjects in differing situations. But, as shown above, this aestheticist interpretation, based on the characteristics of the object, is not sufficient to explain reactions to contemporary art. That is why we have to consider another relevant dimension of action, that is the subjects. In this case the subjects are opponents of contemporary art. To explain their reactions and the values they invoke when arguing against contemporary art, we need to take into account their habits and the nature and level of their art education, as suggested by Pierre Bourdieu's framework of analysis (1990). Along those lines, by employing survey data and statistical analysis, we could relate the social characteristics of persons who become involved in protests of this kind with their degree of involvement in the situation. We would deepen our understanding of people's involvement in collective protest as a form of political mobilization by adducing aspects of Alain Touraine's analysis (1973). We might consider the way individuals happen to enter a public debate or action by choosing to exercise voice, or withdraw from it instead, by choosing exit, according to Albert Hirschman's formulation (1970). Finally, we may focus on the degree of involvement or emotional embeddedness, as opposed to detachment from a particular situation, by applying Norbert Elias's figurational theory (1956).

Yet even when we add the dimension of the characteristics of the subjects involved, these diverse public reactions cannot be fully explained. Faced with the same art objects, members of the same social categories – with the same level of education and position in social space – would not necessarily react in the same way. People's capacity to accept or to reject an art object appears to be strongly associated with the third dimension of any action: that is, the situation. The situation refers to the historical and cultural context in which the controversy arises. It may also refer to a more specific and situated setting, such as face-to-face interactions in a particular place, at a particular moment. Thus, exhibiting art works in a public space tends to generate certain kinds of reactions because the works are seen by a broad, uninitiated public rather than the usual specialized public of art museums. Consequently, the discrepancy between what is expected and what is seen is much greater than usual, and increases the probability of misunderstanding and rejection. An important way of grasping these situations derives from Erving Goffman's conceptualization, especially his structuralist approach in *Frame Analysis* (1974). He provides a precise, powerful set of tools to encompass situations: "frame transformations," "keyings," "fabrications," and "misframings." They are directly relevant to many exhibitions of contemporary art, especially when they take place in public space.

Rejections of contemporary art cannot be explained solely by the nature of the situation: otherwise the same situations would generate similar reactions. We conclude that only a three-dimensional study that takes into consideration the works proposed by artists and the artistic world, the characteristics of the participants, and the nature of the situation allows a more complete understanding of the differences between the values on which accusations and justifications rely. In this essay, I have considered three main value domains in which claims for purity may invite negative reactions to contemporary art: sexual morals, public heritage or artistic authenticity. All elicit reactions from the lay public that try to keep *outside* the boundaries of artistic value what art specialists and art lovers have long ago included *inside*.

Notes

1 This essay is part of a forthcoming study of the rejections of contemporary art in France and in the United States. An earlier version was presented at the Ninth International Conference of Europeanists, Chicago, March 1994.

2 In 1994 the name of Christo's wife, Jeanne-Claude, was officially added to that of Christo on the works made since 1961 (personal communication from Jeanne-Claude).

Selected References

Boltanski, Luc and Thévenot, Laurent 1991, *De la justification – Les Economies de la grandeur*, Paris: Gallimard.
Bourdieu, Pierre 1990, *The Love of Art*, Stanford University Press [originally 1964].
1992, *Les règles de l'art: Genèse et structure du champ littéraire*, Paris: Le Seuil.
Bowness, Alan 1989, *The Conditions of Success: How the Modern Artist Rises to Fame*, London: Thames and Hudson.
Castelnuovo, Enrico and Ginsburg, Carlo 1979, "Centro e peripheria," *Storia dell'Arte Italiana*, vol.1, Turin: Einaudi, 285–352.
Douglas, Mary 1966, *Purity and Danger: An Analysis of Concepts of Pollution and Taboo*, London: Routledge and Kegan Paul.
Elias, Norbert 1956, "Problems of Involvement and Detachment," *British Journal of Sociology* ll: 226–52.
1993, *Engagement et distanciation: Contributions à la sociologie de la connaissance*, Paris: Fayard.
Goffman, Erving 1974, *Frame Analysis*, New York: Harper and Row.
Heinich, Nathalie 1988, "Errance, croyance et mécréance: le public du Pont-Neuf de Christo," *L'Ecrit-Voir* 11: 3–18.
1990a, "L'Art et la manière: Pour une cadre-analyse de l'expérience aesthétique," *Le Parler frais d'Erving Goffman*, Paris: Editions de Minuit, 110–20.
1990b, "Perception esthétique et catégorisation artistique: comment peut-on trouver ça beau?," *La mise en scène de l'art contemporain*, eds. André Ducret, Nathalie Heinich, and Daniel Vander Gucht, Brussels: Les Eperonniers, 30–50.
1991, "Pour introduire à la cadre-analyse," *Critique* No. 535: 936–53.
1992, "La partie de main-chaude de l'art contemporain," *Art et Contemporanéité*, ed. Jean-Olivier Majastre and Alain Pessin, Brussels: La Lettre Volée, 81–111.
1993, "Framing the Bullfight: Aesthetics versus Ethics," *The British Journal of Aesthetics* 33: 52–58.
Hirschman, Albert 1970, *Exit, Voice and Loyalty*, Harvard University Press.
Touraine, Alain 1973, *Production de la société,* Paris: Le Seuil.
Zolberg, Vera L. 1990, *Constructing a Sociology of the Arts*, New York: Cambridge University Press.

PART III

Living in the cracks

Art has served, and continues to serve, many purposes historically, and can, on occasion, have mixed or confused identities. Art is capable of existing between two (or more) worlds, or in an ambiguous state within an art world.

Social service art lives between two worlds, bearing an ambiguous identity. As a case study, Judy Levine describes the funding problems encountered in keeping alive a theatre group for prison inmates, "Theatre for the Forgotten." Art in the carceral network, where it attempts to normalize deviance and rehabilitate the inmates, is an outsider both to the arts and the social services. Levine traces the changing political scene, attitudes towards these confined populations, and changing funding sources for Theatre for the Forgotten from the Great Society programs of the 1960s to the present. In their quest for survival, hybrid outsiders, such as Theatre for the Forgotten must be tenacious, creative, and adaptive. Social service arts have lobbied over the years with some success to become an established and funded genre. Will this hybrid spawn a "new," accepted artistic genre? Asylum art, it will be recalled, transcended its status as "social service art" and became a recognized fine art form.

In Anglo-dominant Australia, where other ethnic groups were for decades unwelcome, Italian and other southern European immigrants gained support from a more friendly, post-War political regime. With the support of public monies, immigrants and their descendants established bilingual community theatres as a means of dealing with their minority positions. Community theatre allowed for the identification and exploration of common issues they experienced as outsiders. Maria Shevtsova describes three bilingual theatre groups, their programs and, on the basis of responses to a questionnaire survey, the impact of their productions on their intended audiences. She questions whether these interactive theatre experiences enhance cultural inclusion, and whether multicultural theatre will ever become part of the theatrical mainstream, rather than remain marginal to it.

Ana Mendieta was an artist whose works defied classification, linking a number of nooks and crannies within the art world. Irit Rogoff describes Mendieta's biography and work, exploring the several ways in which she was outside as well as inside the mainstream art world. Mendieta's "reterritorialization" was her conscious attempt to break the boundaries of what she perceived as a Eurocentric, urban, New York City-based, commodity-oriented artistic culture. Her work blended natural topographies, earthworks, the female body (her own), into an art meant to negate boundaries and to stress temporality and cultural displacement, as a means of opening up new artistic, political and personal possibilities.

8

Art as social service: Theatre for the Forgotten

Judy Levine

Introduction

Many arts organizations committed to providing "services for the unfortunate" were created as part of President Lyndon Johnson's "Great Society" program of the 1960s. But most of these organizations have since folded under the dual pressures of an expanding professional arts field in which the competition for funds increased dramatically, and an escalating nationwide economic downturn, which resulted in a decline in philanthropic dollars. "Theatre for the Forgotten," which is based in New York City and works in prisons, with juvenile offenders and with other of "society's outcasts," is one group that has persevered.

Arts for prison inmates – those considered so antisocial that they have been sequestered from everyday social intercourse – is, in a sense, the ultimate nonprofit activity. Arts groups that service those whom society incarcerates depend primarily on unearned income. Unlike most performance companies which derive all (if commercial enterprises) or some (if not for profit) of their earnings from ticket sales, arts for inmates is by its very nature a financial loser. And arts for inmates arouses conventional social negative attitudes toward "society's failures."

Rather than clearly an art enterprise, Theatre for the Forgotten sports a nonprofit mind-set of "benevolence for the needy" with a barely hidden social agenda. A duality of purpose – benevolence and art – makes for an ambiguity that threatens the definition of art as an end in itself. But this very ambiguity has become a tool to keep the troupe alive despite the precarious nature of its support.

As arts for inmates lost its appeal as a fashionable – or fundable – activity in the 1980s, and as government-induced austerity has come to be the norm in the 1990s, groups such as Theatre for the Forgotten have been obliged to seek diverse sources of support: local government, corporations, foundations. Requiring unending flexibility, Theatre for the Forgotten's organizers have engaged in a multiple presentation of self appropriate to available funding sources.

That Theatre for the Forgotten has been obliged to adjust its presented identity to match the priorities of potential funders may not in itself be surprising, since artists have historically depended upon the goodwill of their patrons. But in this case, marginality pervades every aspect of the group's work. As quintessential outsiders, these producers of art must muddy the categories that provide their fundamental legitimacy. The constraints and possibilities made available by the generosity of support structures, and the multiple self required by this dependency, have become the defining feature of Theatre for the Forgotten's work – and its mission.

The prison as a performance site

Theatre for the Forgotten was founded by Akila Couloumbis and Beverly Rich in 1967 in New York City. Having decided to form a theatre company, they came up with the idea of performing in prisons almost by chance.[1] Theatre for the Forgotten's first production (an evening of the one-act plays *Lou Gehrig Did Not Die of Cancer* by Jason Miller and *Hello Out There* by William Saroyan) was performed at the Riker's Island House of Detention, winning an enthusiastic response from both inmates and prison officials. A week later the group presented the same productions at the Women's House of Detention, with equal success. Their positive reception encouraged Rich and Couloumbis – and prison officials – to persist with Theatre for the Forgotten's activities, and to seek funding for additional programs. Couloumbis invited Vinette Carroll, of the newly formed (1967) Ghetto Arts Program set up by the New York State Council on the Arts, to see the production at the Women's House of Detention. Carroll was enthusiastic, but because of the Council's policy of not funding organizations without a track record, she was unable to help the group at that time. However, optimistic that funding would come in at some point, Couloumbis and Rich made plans for a new production.

The next play they selected, Robert Noah's *The Advocate*, was a dramatization of the Sacco-Vanzetti trial. Incorporating forty-five inmates into the cast as well as sixteen outside actors, the play was performed at Riker's Island in October 1967. *The Advocate* was the production that established Theatre for the Forgotten in the eyes of the outside world. Because its engagement of inmate actors was central to its purpose, Theatre for the Forgotten was unable to take *The Advocate* on tour. Instead, the company brought busloads of invited guests, including press and potential funders, to Riker's Island. Joan Davidson of the Kaplan Fund was part of this audience, and she awarded Theatre for the Forgotten its first grant, of $1,000, in early 1968.

Until then, Theatre for the Forgotten had operated entirely as a volunteer organization. Not only had the actors and director worked without pay, but Couloumbis and Rich "hustled everything we could think of." The Department of Corrections was extremely supportive of their activities, with Commissioner of Corrections George McGrath going so far as to suggest in 1968 that "the idea of instituting a full time dramatics section of our rehabilitation program is not far-fetched." The Department did not, however, offer the company financial support. Instead, the publicity from *The Advocate* allowed Rich and Couloumbis to begin cultivating a small base of individual contributors. And, in 1970, the New York State Council on the Arts awarded the group $5,000.

Rehearsals began for a second evening of one-act plays, which was taken to Riker's

Island, the Bronx House of Detention, and several other New York City prisons. In the light of its success in working directly with inmates during *The Advocate*, the group also started conducting acting workshops in prisons. For the next few years Theatre for the Forgotten developed a repertoire of presentations that utilized no more than three or four actors which toured prisons throughout New York State, New Jersey, Connecticut and Pennsylvania, as well as acting workshops and prison productions involving inmates. Acting as a vehicle for self-expression and personal development was in full vogue in the late 1960s and early 1970s, according to Helen Cash, Director of the Special Arts Services Division of the New York State Council on the Arts (a 1976 renaming of the Ghetto Arts Program); Theatre for the Forgotten's programs extended that philosophy to the prison population.

In 1972 Couloumbis designed a Work Release Program in which inmates were put into his custody on a daily basis to rehearse and perform with the group. The company's youth workshops also grew during the 1970s, and the group began a program which traveled to institutions such as Spofford Juvenile Detention Center, Baychester Diagnostic Center and other youth facilities. These workshops were funded by a combination of grants from the New York State Council on the Arts and the National Endowment for the Arts (NEA), contracts from New York City's Criminal Justice Coordinating Council and the New York City Youth Bureau, and private-sector funding from the Kaplan Fund, New York Foundation, Rockefeller Brothers Fund and other foundations, along with various small corporate contributions.

In 1978 Theatre for the Forgotten was awarded a Comprehensive Employment and Training Act (CETA) grant under a Title VI contract to hire fifty artists. As Beverly Rich explained,

> We did basically dance, music, and plays. We would perform those city-wide and to communities again who were in prisons, hospitals, senior centers. Group homes for kids, community centers – any place where theatre was not so available . . . We were very good at it because we knew the community so well.

The following year, Theatre for the Forgotten kept the CETA Title VI arts funding and also applied for a Title III CETA grant to train disadvantaged youths in employment skills such as building maintenance, office work, and financial systems such as entry-level bookkeeping.

The progression from the CETA arts program, which was closely related to the group's prison theatre activities, to an employment training program with only a slight arts component (twice-weekly workshops in communication skills utilizing theatrical training techniques and improvisation) was not difficult, according to Rich: "Being around government funding . . . when you hear that one thing's happening, you go 'OK, how are we going to be creative?' . . . [to] bring something new to a program like 'youth career job training.' One way to be creative is to use [the arts] within your work, because in order to get a job, you have to be able to communicate; to be able to communicate, you have to be able to move well and speak well and sell yourself." Nevertheless, the subtle realignment of the group's focus from theatre-as-art-activity to theatre-as-socialization-skills was to have profound effects on the company's future.

The decline in art funding – the rise in social support

After being supported throughout the 1970s under the Arts Exposure category of the NEA's Expansion Arts Program, which had provided funding to "community-based organizations that brought performances, exhibitions and festivals to people who were normally denied access to cultural events because of economic, geographic, or physical restraints" (Taylor and Barresi 1984: 212), in 1980 the Expansion Arts Program cut Theatre for the Forgotten's funding from $10,000 to zero. Couloumbis was told that the NEA no longer considered prison inmates to be "part of the community." According to A. B. Spellman, Program Director of the Expansion Arts Program, the shift that eliminated Theatre for the Forgotten's funding was part of an adjustment of the Expansion Arts Program into classifications based on artistic criteria instead of on community activities or social benefits. While Theatre for the Forgotten's constituency still fitted within the Expansion Arts Program mandate to assist arts organizations serving "culturally diverse, inner city, rural, or tribal communities" (National Endowment for the Arts 1989: 4), the Expansion Arts Program began evaluating applicant groups more on artistic content and less on social benefits.

A. B. Spellman noted (June 21) that while the Expansion Arts Program "did have a number of organizations prior to 1979, 1980, who did prison work, it was not in a particular category . . . often under arts exposure there would be prison programs." He explained the Program's 1980 shift:

> We eliminated categories based on activities like arts exposure, instruction and training, and organized the program according to discipline, largely to enhance competitive application review. [In order to] make sure that the [Expansion Arts] Program funded art, and that we could defend our grants in art terms, the language of the [new] guidelines described eligibility for instructional projects that were intended to develop pre-professional skills [for] people [who] were serious about pursuing careers in the form – as opposed to activity whose intent was to introduce people to the form, or to enhance community self-image, or to offer some creative work for kids.

Cast in terms of a guidelines modification, the Expansion Arts revision was actually a much subtler – yet broader – move for the Endowment. Turning from an emphasis on the audience to the professionalism of the performer, the Endowment moved into conformity with the "bottom-line" orientation of the Reagan years.

Because Theatre for the Forgotten's mission was to be "a comprehensive arts service program operating a variety of cultural workshops, performance and training programs in correctional facilities, community centers, senior citizen homes, and other related institutions" (Theatre for the Forgotten 1986) – rather than a program defined in artistic terms, as a theatre company – its mission lay outside the realm of the Expansion Arts Program. Its applications to the NEA Theatre Program in both 1982 and 1983 were rejected; after eight years of NEA funding (1972–1980), Theatre for the Forgotten received no further NEA support.

The Special Arts Services Division of the New York State Council on the Arts continued to fund Theatre for the Forgotten's prison tours at a level of $30,000 per year.

Covering three productions per year, this became the touring program's only funding. Support for the youth workshops slowly dribbled away during the 1980s, until only the New York City Youth Bureau remained as program sponsor. The workshops were run at such a low level, however, that Theatre for the Forgotten finally discontinued the program in 1989, hoping that the remaining penal institutions would hire its instructors, a strategy which has seemed to work.

At the same time that fundraising for prison arts activities was becoming more and more difficult to obtain,[2] the New York City Department of Employment picked up the funding for, and expanded, the CETA Title III Youth Employment Program, now called the Job Training Partnership Act (JTPA). Foundations also pulled back on their support for prison programs, and Theatre for the Forgotten discovered the seductive nature of government social service funding.

Beverly Rich now sees that period as one of confusion for the theatre. They discovered that: "There is a period of time that [foundations] fund you, and [then] they want you to seek other sources." The company got discouraged at the "limited sources for prison work, especially bringing plays to prison – and we were getting more governmental funding in other areas." With the aid of hindsight, she speculated that the rush to a "safe" governmental funding base might have ultimately set the theatre back.

Theatre for the Forgotten was running two CETA programs at the same time, a Youth Program and the Arts Program, in addition to attempting to maintain its prison activities. Beyond the practical aspect of not having enough time to fundraise, run full-time programs – especially governmental programs with their attendant red tape – and plan new activities, they realized that the drain of coping with the government programs caused the theatre to lose the enthusiasm it had earlier on: "We were stretched out trying to maintain the programs that employed a good number of people for whom we had some kind of a debt to maintain." Jerry Cofta, Associate Director of Theatre for the Forgotten, put it more succinctly on March 28: "It's the old story of the money is there, it sucks you down a particular path, and you become dependent."

In 1984 Theatre for the Forgotten began planning a completely new program, entitled Changing Scenes. This targeted juvenile offenders, a notoriously difficult penal population composed of youths who have committed serious crimes at the ages of fourteen or fifteen, or first degree murder at age thirteen, and who are processed through the criminal court system as if they were adults. Michael Greene, Juvenile Justice Administrator for the New York City Co-ordinator of Criminal Justice, worked closely with the group throughout the planning and implementation stages of the program. Greene explained (April 3, 1989):

> Somebody recommended Theatre for the Forgotten as running some of the best social service programs around, mainly for the Department of Employment, and that they had this technique of running theatre workshops as a counseling technique . . . [We] met and they said, "Look, you want to deal with tough kids, we've been to prisons, we have done theatre in prisons, we've been around for sixteen years and this is what we do . . ." And I said, "OK, I'll pick out this population of real tough kids – juvenile offenders. Deal with these kids once they are [on] probation or parole."

Greene added education, employment-readiness training and counseling components to the program. This cooperation of government social service agency and nonprofit organization in the process of program design is not uncommon. Often, as government agencies receive changed mandates (such as new target populations), they turn to non-profit organizations to help them fulfill their revised mission. By 1984, Theatre for the Forgotten was a known entity in the governmental social service arena. The innovative programming of Changing Scenes was a result of a confluence of funder, agency and population in need.

Changing Scenes was given substantial start-up funding from 1985 until 1988 by the New York City Criminal Justice Coordinator's Office, along with a smaller grant from the New York Community Trust. As Changing Scenes entered its fifth year in 1989, Theatre for the Forgotten was able to shift its funding to yearly contracts with the New York City Youth Bureau and Department of Employment, while obtaining several small private grants for the program. It ended the 1980s almost entirely a social service institution. Its increasing concentration on government-supported social service projects had the advantage of obtaining a stable source of income with a proliferating catchment area – the base to which the group's services can be applied. But it ended the decade with a narrower scope of resources and programming, bequeathing it a legacy of vulnerability.

By 1993, Akila Couloumbis estimated the portion of Theatre for the Forgotten's funding which was dedicated to arts activities at between 4 and 10 percent of the company's budget. The group's Changing Scenes program was still funded by the New York City Youth Bureau, and JTPA was still supported by the Department of Labor, but Theatre for the Forgotten's prison touring program had undergone a 70 percent drop in support from the New York State Council on the Arts. While Theatre for the Forgotten continued to bring theatrical productions to prisons, the company visited fewer sites each year. On the occasion of Theatre for the Forgotten's twenty-fifth anniversary in 1992, the company ran a small fundraising campaign, but there were no plans to continue the effort.

Art in the carceral net

Arts/social service practitioners tackle problems and populations that make society at large extremely uncomfortable. Struggling to survive, the arts/social service field has become a nexus of larger cultural concerns about inclusion, social obligation and the very nature of art.

The groups on which arts/social service groups focus are deemed marginal by the larger society: "the mentally, physically, sensorially disabled, or institutionalized [and] the isolated – socially, economically; the disadvantaged – socially, economically, culturally; those at risk, or threatened by economic and social circumstances; the unemployed; the elderly; the homeless; the homebound," as described by a 1983 conference on the healing role of the arts (Rockefeller Foundation Conference Report 1983: 8–9). Organizations providing arts services to the marginal have been affected by the same patterns as "pure arts" groups in the 1980s. Reduced governmental arts support in the

1980s made all arts organizations look elsewhere for primary funding. A difficult adjustment for any arts institution, this was especially painful for groups servicing populations unwilling and/or unable to support the arts on their own. During the late 1980s, as arts groups were obliged to rely increasingly on earned income (ticket charges, product sales and contracted services), those involved in art-for-art's-sake had trouble adapting. But socially oriented arts organizations had an even harder time, because they often served communities not only lacking discretionary income (prisoners), but also facing funding cuts for essential services such as counseling centers. While government funders and private foundations tried to mitigate the results of funding cuts on politically sensitive constituencies such as traditional minority communities, they gave arts for inmates a much chillier reception. As traditional funders withdrew, no new sources stepped in to fill the gap.

From his vantage point as Director of the National Endowment for the Arts Expansion Arts Program, A. B. Spellman has watched the arts/social service field evolve over the last three decades. He has seen a dialogue develop with funders in which community-oriented arts groups have been encouraged to focus on quality as opposed to service (June 21, 1989):

> The guerrilla theatres basically came indoors during the 1970s. They went back to proscenium, they got very much concerned with doing professional quality work. Nobody told them to do that, but I think that there [was] a subliminal pressure from funders to have that kind of orientation. It got to be apparent as people were competing for grants, and as the seventies' general social attitude became less committed to change, that organizations [which] were going to be rewarded by funders were going to be those who could produce the strongest work, and not necessarily those that could claim the greatest social good. "If we're a New York theatre company, we [have] to have reviews in the *Times*" pervaded the field. Whereas during the sixties and in the very early seventies, people didn't care a whole lot about that. But that was largely what you had to have to be able to get: foundation support, Arts Endowment support, New York State Council on the Arts support.

This change in values had a concrete effect on Theatre for the Forgotten when its NEA support was eradicated in 1980. But the progression toward professionalism and art for art's sake had far-reaching consequences for the field as a whole, as it struggled to redefine itself and survive through the politically conservative 1980s.

Foucault's notion of the "carceral network" is useful in understanding the link between services to such seemingly disparate populations as the institution-bound elderly, juvenile offenders, and children living in welfare hotels. In addition to the true penal institution, charitable societies, moral improvement associations and organizations handing out assistance utilize carceral methods, according to Foucault: "The carceral network links [the] multiple series of the punitive and the abnormal . . . The social enemy [is] transformed into a deviant, who [brings] with him the multiple danger of disorder, crime and madness." These carceral mechanisms "seem distinct enough – since they are intended to alleviate pain, to cure, to comfort – but all tend, like the prison, to exercise a power of normalization" (Foucault 1975: 293–308).

Promoting the arts as a normalization, or healing mechanism, however, implies illness as well as the implication that something can be cured. In many human service settings, this is often not the case. Sometimes, all that can be hoped for is "improvement" – the overcoming of psychological and emotional barriers within the individual and with others (The Rockefeller Foundation Conference Report 1983: 3–4). But if, as is often the case, rehabilitative improvement is all that the arts can promise – as opposed to a total regeneration of the deviant population – then in times of financial constraint, the arts will fall prey to a budgetary axe which considers not philosophy or social equity but the extent to which an individual can be normalized. And, indeed, when measured against a yardstick of such socialization barriers as poverty or homelessness, the arts are judged "soft" (as opposed to "hard" barriers such as drug addiction), and are considered a luxury of earlier, more liberal times.

In the 1980s a conservative law-and-order mentality denied the legitimacy of the provision of art to the homeless (the "cots and coffee" philosophy of homeless shelters) or of theatre activities for prisoners, preferring, instead, to build more prisons or advocate the death penalty. Helen Cash, Director of the Special Arts Services division of the New York State Council on the Arts, which has continued to fund groups concerned with the arts and social service, sensed that this work was "out of vogue – out of style. That humanistic attitude has dissipated to a great extent. There's so much tragedy going on, [that we're] not going to make life better for those accused of a crime" (interviewed on May 25, 1989). Michael Spencer, Executive Director of Hospital Audiences, Inc., an organization providing access to the arts for people in hospitals, prisons, or nursing homes, in drug treatment and prevention programs, and in other health and social service settings, believes "there is a widespread feeling in our society that people sent away to institutions either ought not to enjoy themselves or are incapable of enjoyment" (The Rockefeller Foundation Working Papers 1978: 3). At issue, according to Richard Mitchell of the New York State Department of Correctional Services, is "the manner in which society treats its failures" (Rockefeller Foundation Working Papers 1978: 41).

Social ambivalence about providing care for spoiled populations has extended to the support of the arts groups who work with them. In some cases, arts groups working with special populations are the only attention those populations receive. Spencer has found that to funders, to the institutions he works with, and to the public at large, "our funding is sort of peripheral to the focus" – on the punishment of deviance (June 6, 1989).

Groups servicing the carceral net have had to combat a dual resistance to their work: (i) a social reluctance to focus on those individuals with "spoiled identities";[3] and (ii) a feeling that the arts are a frill. Indeed, as Spencer has pointed out in speaking of Hospital Audiences' work with the homeless, "It's not popular and it's not socially acceptable – just as one doesn't entertain inmates and make things too cozy for them, in the public view one doesn't want to make shelters too cozy, because then people might stay."

Philanthropic priorities

Funding and acceptance of arts activities for social populations at risk or already within the carceral net were more available in earlier years, when many of these groups were formed. Spencer recalled when arts funders began to pull out of the field (June 6, 1989):

> [Starting around 1980] there weren't many sources to go to. It became unpopular to fund this kind of thing. There were some corporations that were reliable [in the arts], like Philip Morris, and Con Ed, [but] others have come and gone, or come in and stayed in for the blue chip area . . . The traditional big dollars tended to go to the more prestigious [arts organizations], and [those of] us on the front lines of humanity, or down in the trenches or sewers of humanity, are not really blue chips, except some elements of our work which appeal to "arts for the poor unfortunates," and then you may get corporate money that way.

While it is not surprising that corporations were some of the first funders to withdraw – what did they receive from funding society's marginalized? – foundations and government sources have also retreated from supporting arts/social service organizations.

Many groups which combined the arts with social service during the sixties and seventies have fallen by the wayside. Others have switched to concentrating on "pure arts" activities or to arts-in-education, a haven that was relatively benign. Those arts/social service groups that kept their dual focus have found themselves, according to Spencer, falling into "philanthropic cracks, especially between the health authorities and arts funding agencies in terms of qualifying or being eligible for funding" (Rockefeller Foundation Conference Report 1983: 14). Often, large established arts groups such as museums or symphony orchestras have been maintained on foundations' funding rosters, while groups combining arts activities with social services have been shifted into the same applicant pool as purely social service organizations. Richard Mittenthal, Vice-President for Programs of the New York Community Trust, explained his foundation's priorities (May 4, 1989):

> We have an arts program, the purpose of which is to encourage and nurture the growth of cultural institutions and individual artists in New York City . . . There are 150–200 off-Broadway theatres in New York City [that are] in business to put on art. Now there are also some theatres that are in business to employ ex-offenders or to employ handicapped people with putting on art as a secondary purpose . . . Those are not going to get much of a priority in our arts program. On the other hand, we have a program for handicapped children and one of the major purposes is mainstreaming. In that regard it is obviously an attractive idea to get people involved in the arts. We make a grant to the Queens Museum to bring blind kids out there and have them experience art. That receives a high priority in our blind program but would not receive a high priority in our arts program.

While Mittenthal is using social service funding as a source for arts support, the fit between program and support can be awkward, especially when measured against filling purely social service needs. Added to the dilemma for Mittenthal is New York Community Trust's continual prioritization of social services over arts services (May 4, 1989):

> Our Board deliberates every February about whether to spend [our unrestricted] money in education, drug abuse, AIDS, homelessness; nobody ever says let's make the arts a priority. There are homeless arts projects that make [the homeless] feel better about being homeless. It's nice if they feel better about being homeless, but they should feel better about not being homeless . . .

We don't have enough money for everything . . . [so] my preference as head of the grant program is to spend our homeless money figuring out ways to get the homeless not to be homeless.

New York Community Trust's impression that social service needs are more critical than arts needs is common – and may indeed be correct after a decade of restricted governmental spending on social programs. However, the "limited pot" thesis implies that if social needs are judged important, the arts – even those combining art and social purposes – will suffer.

Mittenthal's judgement is that while the arts are dropping generally in philanthropic priority, arts/social service programming is plummeting further still (May 4, 1989):

In private foundations and in corporations my sense is that money [has been] moved away from the arts to social purposes, but not to arts programs for social purposes, and in fact when foundations and corporations have reduced their arts budget because their money has gone to the homeless, their arts programs have then focused more on pure cultural institutions like the ballet and the symphony.

While pure social service programs receive preference over arts-oriented social services, pure arts institutions are accorded super-status over arts programs with social objectives.

The curse of the double agenda – arts and social service – has followed the arts/social service field as it matured. Not only have funders not issued guidelines oriented to this dual concentration, but as resources have become more limited, they have used restrictive functional categorizations to knock organizations out of competition. Often funder demands for clarity have functioned as cloaked requests for the traditional.

Arts/social service groups have found that using the correct language – social service jargon – is critical if they wish to be placed in an appropriate funding category. Far from a side issue, terminology signals professionalism, seriousness and a link to a body of practitioners assumed to have the proper solutions. Professionalism, for some arts funders, has become a code word, standing in for the requirement that grantees be arts-trained and interested solely in "pure art." Social service funders, on the other hand, tend to focus on a different set of professional qualifications. Artists working in this field often have a hard time overcoming suspicion based on their lack of formal credentials in social work. In addition, the benefits to be gained from an arts-oriented program can seem dubious when measured by the standard criteria of social work.

The arts are often perceived as a foreign object by those accustomed to operating solely within a social service universe. While the devaluation of art in the social service world, especially in the funding arena, is not universal, this view is so widespread that many arts/social service institutions have proposals and brochures that barely even mention the arts – the basis, supposedly, for their unique existence.

On the other hand, arts funders are upset that arts money, limited as it is, is being requested for what they see as social goals that ought to be funded through social service programs. Speaking in 1978, Joan Davidson, then Chairman of the New York State Council on the Arts, observed that an arts program involving murals on tenement walls "cover[s] up the fact that they don't have decent housing in the city," and concluded "the arts are important but they are not a substitute for housing" (The Rockefeller Foundation Working Papers 1978: 55).

Arts funders often feel helpless when confronted with huge social problems that social service funders aré accustomed to dealing with or have come to accept as normal. They react by retreating further into arts-directed priorities which do not include social service components. Moreover, while their hostility is muted, the arts community strongly resents the assumption that arts activities which serve social service functions are more valuable to society because of their dual mission. This assumption deprioritizes the making of art, and revokes the arts community's ability to establish its own priorities.

Art or social service

By channeling arts/social service groups into distinct funding categories, or requiring program descriptions in pure social service terminology, or résumés with extensive professional arts backgrounds or social work credentials, both the arts and social service communities are asking arts/social service groups to choose between the arts and social service. The demand for either/or categorization is almost ubiquitous. The conception of a program as only art or only social service, according to Bill Cleveland, an arts/social service practitioner working in the California penal system, poses the fundamental question: "Can [something] be art if it has a purposeful benefit above and beyond creation of a fine work?" (interview on June 26, 1989). An assumption about the proper role of art in society – that it should be admired, observed, separate – underlies the difficulty of the arts community in accepting the potential of art to fulfill extra-artistic social functions.

The 1980s shrinkage of arts resources has had the effect of narrowing the definition of what art is and what art is not. This restricted notion of pure art dovetailed with the prevailing conservative political ethos of the 1980s. Jim Mirrione, a playwright working in this field, has noticed that the idea of arts activities serving social purposes is disquieting to the art world (May 24, 1989). He interpreted this unease as "people's idea that art should stand on its own without any restraints, or should not come from a source that would imply dictation of a certain amount of values or service." While by the end of the 1980s the art world as a whole had become politicized as a reaction to the reigning political conservatism, art as social service had not taken on a similar cachet.

Helen Cash (Director of the Special Arts Services division of the New York State Council on the Arts) noted that "there seems to be a slight disparaging connotation to the term social service when you're talking about arts activity. Some people feel, if it's social service, it's not high [quality] . . . [It's] lesser quality because it doesn't result in anything tangible [a professional performance or art object]." What is at stake in the denigration of the arts/social service field is the notion that only pure art, the most valued art in the hierarchy of Western art, is really art.

The issue of "the arts [being] used in an instrumental fashion to assist in the achievement of other ends" (Arts, Education and Americans Panel 1977: 179) has been debated since the beginnings of public arts funding in the United States. While some functions have clearly been viewed as acceptable – statues glorifying Revolutionary War heroes, for example – other have been seen as suspect, often in direct relation to their subversive influence on the status quo. The multicultural and community arts sectors are two other cultural movements that have been subject to extensive attacks on their status as art.

The conflict between art-for-the-elite and art-for-the-culturally-deprived is part of a deepening twentieth-century struggle to redefine mainstream American culture. Across a wide spectrum of social arenas, a late twentieth-century campaign for inclusion has been waged by the traditionally excluded. The arts/social service field is one mechanism for waging that campaign within the arts community.

The notion that "access to artistic experience is a basic human right" (The Rockefeller Foundation Conference Report 1983: 5) is at the core of the arts/social service movement. While some groups in this field engage special populations in artistic activity, and others provide access to professional productions created originally for a mainstream stage, the entire field is concerned with "reaching out for the unreached audience," as Alvin Reiss, arts consultant and author, wrote at the heyday of this activity (Reiss 1972: 157). Late twentieth-century arts activities connected with social service goals extend a broader philosophy that connects the function of art to a service mission. This philosophy stretches from the public service mandate of government arts agencies, to the community service orientation of such public-sector projects as WPA and CETA, to the community arts movement's drive to localize art creation, distribution, evaluation, and support, and finally, in its most radical version, to the part of the arts/social service field in which the arts are simply utilized towards extra-artistic goals.

The impact on organizational identity

As early as 1978, C. Douglas Ades, Director of Urban Affairs at Chemical Bank, noticed a funding phenomenon that was resulting in "the tail" beginning to wag the dog in a funny kind of way. "[Groups] are coming up saying 'Okay, we'll call this program crime prevention because that's the way the money is coming down now'" (The Rockefeller Foundation Working Papers 1978: 60). Sally Charnow, former Co-Executive Director of Elders Share The Arts, discussed the schizophrenic nature of fundraising for the group as art/social work/psychiatry/participatory theatre and the problem of "going for bucks." She concluded, as do most arts/social service practitioners, that "if you don't go for bucks, you don't have a program – you can't survive."

But while adjusting program descriptions to a particular funder's interest is a time-honored fundraising technique, the issue is larger than "naming." As groups that started out with plentiful 1960s arts money became, of necessity, dependent on scarce 1980s social money, their agenda changed. As arts/social service practitioners matured as a field, the very nature of the programs shifted, and with it the perspective of the practitioners. Artists formerly concerned with aesthetic issues became preoccupied with social service criteria.

Given a range of government agencies with varying mandates, an arts/social service group in the 1970s could easily find a few programs which fitted its interests. Not any more. Even though the condensed size of the funding field has sometimes worked in favor of Theatre for the Forgotten, such as in 1984 when the group's reputation preceded it to the Office of the Co-ordinator of Criminal Justice and helped Theatre for the Forgotten initiate the Changing Scenes program, the reduction in the size of the funding community has led to the current situation of a buyer's market. Funders are calling the tune, by setting social priorities, issuing detailed RFPs (Requests For Proposals) which stipulate the exact nature and scope of the desired services, and evaluating vendors (non-profit organizations) on funder-relevant criteria.

Theatre for the Forgotten is a prime example of a group whose programming is determined by funder priorities. While it seemed to some that the group was simply identifying its program as "art that also does socialization training," an actual shift in the programming itself was inevitably occurring over time. But the far-flung nature of Theatre for the Forgotten's activities is not idiosyncratic. Many organizations in this area carry on a wide range of activities only marginally related to their main focus. Often, art/social service groups take on these additional activities at a funder's request. Theatre for the Forgotten, however, is strongly dependent on only one agency – the New York City Department of Employment, for the Job Training Partnership Act – and has found itself struggling to maintain its focus in the face of that program's demands. Couloumbis noted: "When most of your money comes from a singular agency, in order to insure that you have that funding, you give it the amount of time that's necessary, which then leaves you not as much as you'd like to have for other stuff."

While Theatre for the Forgotten has survived, its endurance is at the cost of obscuring a clear programmatic identity. A collection of individual interests, Theatre for the Forgotten's activities developed in response to specific historical eras (such as the programs originating under the CETA mandate) which have outlasted their initial impetus, and a general sense of "wanting to do good." Rather than programs following from mission, as in standard nonprofit procedure, Theatre for the Forgotten's mission has evolved to keep up with its programs – which arise, for the most part, in response to funding opportunities.

Strategies for survival

As arts/social service practitioners enter their third decade in the field, many are becoming increasingly savvy about "working the bureaucracy" to ensure their groups' survival. Perhaps because of the field's dual focus, arts/social service practitioners have an astute sense of how their groups can fit into guidelines and meet agency priorities that were not written with them in mind. And as arts/social service organizations outlast government bureaucrats, they are even gaining influence over how regulations are written.

In the analysis of Bill Cleveland, an arts/social service practitioner working in the California penal system, arts/social service advocates are taking a tip from the way arts-in-education proponents manipulate the general concern with improving the country's educational system into an emphasis on resources for arts-in-education. In the same way, says Cleveland, advocates for arts/social service programs are beginning to work with corporate, foundation, and government social service funders to create funding guidelines for arts/social service programming. According to Cleveland:

> [Arts/social service groups] are learning the bureaucracy, and seeing how the bureaucracy could serve them. Instead of seeing bureaucracy as an impediment, they're seeing bureaucracy as an absolute playground – they're seeing everything as an opportunity, rather than an obstacle. [What we're seeing now] is the insinuation of a foreign object in a bureaucracy – much to the chagrin of powers-that-be. (Cleveland, forthcoming)

As arts/social service veterans are gaining professional credentials, some are even crossing over into the funding field, and to the institutions contracting for services. A side benefit of the field's contraction has been that many ex-practitioners have entered the mainstream. Former CETA workers, in particular, are ensconced in government agencies around the country. Sympathetic to the field's point of view, they are often extremely helpful.

Theatre for the Forgotten's smooth transferral of Changing Scenes' funding base is one instance where the company used the bureaucracy to aid a transition. The company collaborated closely with Michael Greene, Juvenile Justice Administrator for the New York City Coordinator of Criminal Justice, on shifting Changing Scenes' funding from the initial start-up grant from his office, to the Department of Employment. Greene found out the division of the Department of Employment in which the program was likely to belong, used the power of his office to set up an initial meeting which he attended along with the group, and helped Theatre for the Forgotten lobby successfully when it seemed at the last moment that they might lose their hard-won funding.

Arts/social service groups are increasingly devoting their attention to understanding the nooks and crannies of government entitlement programs. Spencer has hired a lobbyist to represent Hospital Audiences, Inc. before the New York City Council and the New York State government; he reasons that since so much of the organization's support comes from government sources, he could either hire a publicist, or retain someone to protect the group's interests in the decision-making bodies most responsible for the climate in which the group operates.

Determining the future

While funder priorities have had a tremendous impact on the arts/social service field, arts/social service practitioners are also developing the capacity to determine the field's future. Charting a careful course through the diverse agendas of the various players, arts/social service organizations that outlasted the shake-outs of the 1980s have become adept at carving out their own unique service niches. Meanwhile, the funders who have remained committed to the field have also clarified their interests and become better attuned to the potential offered by the hybrid form. While still dictating in large measure the shape of the field, funders have grown more sensitive to the special possibilities – and restrictions – of artists committed to social service.

Continuing to embrace both artistic and social goals, Theatre for the Forgotten has stumbled through twenty-odd years of organizational life. Remarkably tenacious in its desire for the betterment of humanity even as the larger society has seemed to give up, Theatre for the Forgotten has obeyed the institutional imperative toward survival at all costs. While the constraints and possibilities made available by the generosity of support structures have helped to define Theatre for the Forgotten's work, the creativity of its practitioners will ensure its survival.

Notes

1 Akila Couloumbis, Co-Executive Director, Theatre for the Forgotten, in reminiscing about the group's happenstance beginnings: "I had no incredible desire to change the lives of the people inside the prisons. I didn't think it was my problem. I had never been arrested, I'd no reason to have any connection to prisons . . . I just looked at it to be something that would occupy a group of actors doing a play they wanted to do." Additional motivation, he confessed, was that "I was an actor and I wanted an audience" that outnumbered the people on stage. Unless otherwise noted, this and all subsequent quotations are from interviews conducted by the author during March to June 1989.

2 Couloumbis referred to the process as "beating a dead horse."

3 See Goffman 1963, for a discussion of the many forms of spoiled identity including linkages of more and less socially acceptable stigmas (divorce, a criminal past, or simply being elderly and hard of hearing).

References

Arts, Education and Americans Panel 1977, *Coming To Our Senses: The Significance of the Arts for American Education*, New York: McGraw Hill.

Cleveland, William forthcoming, *Art In Other Places: Artists Working In American Community and Social Institutions*. New York: Greenwood.

Foucault, Michel 1975, *Discipline and Punish: The Birthplace of the Prison*, New York: Vintage Books.

Goffman, Erving 1963, *Stigma: Notes on the Management of Spoiled Identity*, New York: Simon & Schuster.

McGrath, William 1968, "Forgotten Theatre Brings Down The Jailhouse," *New York Daily News*, April 13: 16.

National Endowment for the Arts 1989, "Application Guidelines for FY 90/91 Advancement," Washington, DC: National Endowment for the Arts.

Reiss, Alvin H. 1972, *Culture and Company*, New York: Twayne Publishers.

The Rockefeller Foundation Working Papers 1978, *The Healing Role of the Arts*, New York: The Rockefeller Foundation.

The Rockefeller Foundation Conference Report 1983, *The Healing Role of the Arts: A European Perspective*, New York: The Rockefeller Foundation.

Taylor, Fannie and Anthony L. Barresi 1984, *The Arts At A New Frontier – The National Endowment for the Arts*, New York and London: Plenum Press.

Theatre for the Forgotten, "Historical Papers," 1968–1989.

9

Multiculturalism in process: Italo-Australian bilingual theatre and its audiences

Maria Shevtsova

Contextualizing bilingual theatre – bringing outsiders in

Theatrical activities by immigrant communities in Australia must be understood in the context of the society within which they exist. Despite the construction of immigrant theatres, made by and for outsiders, the works produced under their aegis concern the whole of Australian society, not merely its ethnic enclaves. This study deals particularly with immigrants, especially from Italy, illuminating the role that they have played in the history of the country, and their response to theatrical art forms that have been created by and for them.

Specifically, theatrical productions were created for Italian-born immigrants (especially from the south of Italy), who arrived in Australia during the mass migration of the 1950s and 1960s. For economic, linguistic and related sociocultural reasons they did not attend mainstream or even "alternative" theatre. The questions asked by this study were: Can community theatre made by and for a specific minority change that group's status? Under what conditions does minority group theatre move from being the preserve of outsiders and begin to lead them into the aesthetic mainstream? Furthermore, beyond symbolic meanings, to what degree does ethnic theatre actually facilitate the sociopolitical inclusion of those whose presence and importance it acknowledges? When does multicultural theatre stop being a matter of outsideness and become included in the dominant culture, where difference becomes an accepted part of a heterogeneous society, and not inextricably intertwined with hierarchical rankings?

The focus of this study is Italo-Australian bilingual theatre, which uses Italian and English in the same production. This type of theatre is represented by the the Sydney-based Federazione italiana dei lavoratori emigrati et loro famiglie (Federation of Italian Migrant Workers and their Families – FILEF) Theatre Group/Gruppo teatrale FILEF (FTG), Adelaide's Doppio Teatro, and the Melbourne Workers Theatre. From a sociopolitical standpoint, these three performance groups have common objectives: they tackle material directly relevant to immigrant communities, which has been neglected by mainstream theatre. They show that the issues raised concern the whole of Australian society and are not restricted to ethnic ghettoes. They validate the history of immigrants – Italian immigrants in particular – by bringing to light the positive role they have played in the history of Australia. They make theatre accessible to the Italian-born, who have been marginalized. They reach the children of these immigrants, the second and third generation of Italo-Australians who, while being more or less assimilated in the dominant Anglo/Celtic culture, are losing or have lost touch with the language and culture of their origins. Finally, they help to revalorize a cultural legacy that has virtually been driven underground and derided by their adoptive country.

Although their goals are similar, the three groups do not have a uniform outlook and direction. All three are community theatre in the sense that the content and style of their performances are based on the experiences of their targeted audience. What this entails, particularly in the case of the Melbourne Workers Theatre and the FTG, is culling sociobiographical stories from individuals through conversations and interviews. Members of the production team, actors included, share the task of gathering the information required. Oral history is then transformed into productions that function like living documents. The essentially collaborative nature of these theatre workers further amplifies the sense of community for the immigrants.

The Melbourne Workers Theatre has been especially committed to exploring the untold life of factory workers. Both its preparatory methods and stage procedures accentuate class rather than ethnicity. The company conceives of a working-class history that is not contingent upon ethnic distinctions. Its approach may aptly be described as activist. Besides Italian and English, on occasion it also uses Greek and Macedonian or even Turkish, depending on the immigrant community targeted specifically by this or that production.

The degree to which particular languages are used and how they are mixed varies. Written accounts, including newspaper items, are also incorporated into the productions when appropriate. Workers' histories include those of Italians, Greeks, and Macedonians, and Australians of Irish/English/Scottish descent (henceforth referred to as Anglo/Celts), consistent with its aims of creating a working-class theatre that, in order to be characterized as such, includes the entirety of post-war immigrants to Australia from southern Europe.

Equally consistent with its goals is the company's choice of performance time and space – lunch hours in factory canteens, as well as on building construction sites. Performances, however, are not confined to the workplace. All sorts of other venues are used, from warehouses to bars, as well as reasonably established theatres.

The FTG does not have quite the same charge. Its activities are centered around an inner-city suburb which is the heart of Sydney's Italian community. Performances are held in a local school, making them easily accessible, not least to the pensioners of the neighborhood. Performers are recruited from anyone who is interested in joining, of whatever age or background. Those who are not fluent in Italian deliver lines in English. Unlike the Melbourne company, the FTG is vocationally uneven. It is composed of a few professional and semi-professional people who are outnumbered by amateurs. Although presentations are of a high standard, they lack the polish and finish expected from professional companies. This, together with the fact that their

Figure 24. Melbourne Workers Theatre production. *No Fear*, with Senol Mat as Shop Steward (1991). Photographer: Lis Stoney.

themes might be termed the "Italian experience" rather than the "Italian working-class experience", helps to explain why their productions are not as sharply focused as those of the Melbourne Workers Theatre.

While its productions accentuate differentiation by ethnicity, the FTG realizes that all Italians in Australia are not united by ethnic identity. Most Italians who settled in the neighborhoods across Sydney and other cities, and in rural areas during the fifties and sixties, supplied the country with the factory, rail, road, construction and farm labor it urgently demanded. Australia's agenda for economic growth was expressed clearly by her immigration policy at the time. Migration in the seventies and eighties, a trickle when compared with the previous decades, brought better-educated Italians who filled white-collar or professional positions. The Australian-born children of foreign-born parents who had emigrated out of economic necessity (though without instantly finding the riches promised them) are generally upwardly mobile. The socio-economic difference between generations is also a significant element for any discussion of the Italian community as such. The Group's stage work, while not impervious to these distinctions, is concerned above all with taking Italians and Italo-Australians as a composite whole and promoting the cultural visibility denied them for so long.

Figure 25. Melbourne Workers Theatre Production, *The Ballad of Lois Ryan*, with Kate Gillick as Lois and Laura Lattuada as Georgina (1988). Photographer: Sylvia Tur.

Doppio Teatro, by contrast, is a fully professional company. It is community-based and oriented insofar as it relies on Italian neighborhoods, associations (which generally group people from a specific region in Italy) and clubs for its inspiration and audiences. At the same time, it does not turn down invitations from other prestigious organizations, such as the Adelaide Festival or other institutions that belong to the world of "official culture." Indeed, Doppio's appearance at venues usually attracting well-heeled or practiced theatrical spectators of whatever ethnic group draws members of the Italian community who would probably not otherwise have gone there. It extends audiences for both the ethnic community and mainstream theatres, and merges the boundaries between them, a measure of Doppio's public importance and success.

Doppio does not focus on the working-class component of the Italian and Italo-Australian community. Its primary concern is with recovering the cultural heritage attenuated, fragmented and dissipated by immigration. Not surprisingly, then, it concentrates on the problems of cultural identity: the imprint of peasant origins on the values, attitudes and behavior of southern Italians who, along with skilled industrial workers from Italy, emigrated soon after the Second World War; the binding strength of shared traditions, notably of rural traditions, and their dislocation in an alien society; the cultural stasis brought about by living according to memory; the difficulties of integration, where pressures to conform collide with incomprehension, resistance or rejection on both sides; Anglo/Celts urging adaptation while denying the channels for it and Italians fearing to let go of their "identity," in that it assisted their survival.

Doppio productions powerfully dramatize the confrontation between past and present. Similarly, they show the gap between generations, where the children of dispossessed parents struggle to affirm their social, cultural and psychological independence from them. The productions are elliptical and poetic in their style of presentation. Legends, tales, songs, masks and other aspects of southern Italian popular culture take pride of place, endorsing the validity of the old culture on its own terms and as part of the artistic heritage of Australia. As such, Doppio succeeds in having social impact since it challenges negative conceptions about southern Italians among Anglo/Celts.

As the foregoing remarks indicate, the theatre practices of these three groups are a form of social intervention with and for disadvantaged minorities. By being on the *offensive*,they challenge prevailing ideas as to how community theatre should service an amorphous social category, which is presumed to understand and speak English fluently. *Bilingual* (indeed, bicultural) theatre, in other words, not only insists upon the existence of ethnic diversity in Australian society, but also pushes ethnic cultures out of the debilitating confines of what might be termed "pasta-pizza folklore." By this I mean a risk-free, unproblematic consumer culture whose pleasures completely mask the pains of its producers.

Bilingual theatre groups did not begin to appear until the early 1980s, whereas monolingual, English-only community theatre had flourished a decade earlier. While explaining this time-lag is beyond the scope of this study, several points may nevertheless be sketched. The first had to do with the election in 1972 of the Labor government of Gough Whitlam, the second with the establishment in 1974 by Whitlam of the Arts Council (now known as the Australia Council), whose mission was to finance, encourage and legitimate the development of the arts, and the third with the notions of multiculturalism addressed by Whitlam and his cabinet.

The multicultural focus involved reassessing Britain's pervasive domination – political, socioeconomic, linguistic and cultural – over her former colony. Thus it entailed reckoning with the genocide of Aborigines on the one hand, and the denigration, by contempt and neglect, of non-Anglo/Celtic immigrants on the other. Paradoxically, by taking a more global view of Australian society, multiculturalism homed in on its heterogeneity and ethnic differences. Instead of being tantamount to a primordial sin, they began to be understood as a source of national wealth. The delay in the emergence of bilingual community theatre is linked with both the timidity of non-Anglo/Celtic groups in exercising the empowerment opened up officially to them (timidity being an outcome of scapegoating and exclusion), and with the hesitations of the population at large in accepting realities that it had been living with daily but which government decree was now making unavoidable.

Plays, audiences, and politics: the spectators' reactions

The core of this essay is based on an audience questionnaire study conducted by me in the course of FTG presentations. I attempted to assess audience reactions to specific productions, and identity the audience composition. The audiences studied attended *L'Albero delle rose*/*The Tree of Roses* in 1987, and *Storie in cantiere*/*Stories in Construction* in 1988. Two years earlier the FTG had mounted an anti-war play entitled *Lasciateci in pace*/*Leave us in Peace*, and its first production was *Nuovo paese*/*New Country* in 1984.

New Country was a landmark in the twin histories of multiculturalism and bilingual theatre. An ambitious work, it involved about a hundred performers, counting among them grandparents, parents and schoolchildren living in an inner-city suburb which is the hub of the Italian community in Sydney. It began in a park, took to the streets, as occurs with Italian festivals, religious and secular, and finally filled the local school which was jam-packed with the spectators who had accompanied it (thus being actors in the performance) or had simply waited for its arrival. As its title suggests, the production was a theatrical account of Italian migration to Australia. Its journey to the school played out stories about the sea voyage. The entry to the school symbolized the port of entry into the new country. Scenes inside the building were devoted to tales of settlement.

Drawing on a variety of Italian popular traditions, *New Country* was a great success by virtue of its apparent spontaneity, street-theatre dynamic, novelty, and most importantly because it announced a theatre commensurate with the goals of multiculturalism. A minority culture seemed at last to be included in the national culture. Its movement from the ghetto-ized periphery to an operative social network announced a considerable structural change. Multiculturalism, in other words, signified a reordering of institutions, perceptions and values as well as prospects for the future.

The Tree of Roses picked up some of the themes of *New Country*, depicting them through the lives of three generations of women. Its narrative starts in Italy in the 1920s, goes through the rise of fascism, resistance to fascism, the Second World War and the postwar period of reconstruction and emigration, and ends at the date of the production. It also looks at the daughters of the seventies propounding feminism to their mothers. A collage full of flashbacks of the past converging with scenes from the present, it revolves around protagonists whose names are a compound of Rosa (Rosalia, Rosalba, etc.). Besides generating humor, the play on names shows that each woman is one facet of a collective story. More humor comes from the male and female comperes of the show who comment on scenes or prepare the audience for the special point of scenes to follow. Neapolitan songs, dances, shadow-plays, circus acts, puppet shows and skits in the style of commedia dell'arte break up the dialogue. The performers' mimicry and physicality help non-Italian speakers understand the action, as do summaries in English of the main ideas debated by the characters. The shift from one language to the other not only shows generational differences between grandmothers, mothers and daughters, but also points out to spectators that, if they have to make an effort to understand a foreign tongue, as did Italian immigrants, they are nevertheless not being excluded.

Stories in Construction relies on similar montage and performance techniques. The initial idea for the production came from an accident on a city construction site where one worker died and several were injured as a result of inadequate safety precautions; the employers were held to be at fault. The play takes up the theme of the accident but changes its location to a building complex being completed for the 1988 bicentennial celebrations. This complex was a showcase for the then Labor Government of New South Wales which trumpeted loudly and with much pomp the "celebration of a nation," that is, the 200 years since Australia had been colonized as a penal settlement by the British Crown.

The hoopla over Australia's bicentenary allowed the production to comment satirically on how non-Anglo/Celtic groups, and Aborigines in particular, were being cheated by the bicentenary celebration since they had not enjoyed the equal rights that make disparate groups one nation. The labor-ethnic issues involved with the construction accident merge, then, with issues of racism and the genocide of Aboriginal peoples, especially as this was assumed to be continuing, given the disproportionate number of deaths of Aborigines held in police custody. The number, the nature and the unclear circumstances of these deaths had been controversial issues throughout the bicentennial year. *Stories* thus attempted to broaden current discussions on multiculturalism by placing at their center the problematical, historically loaded and explosive issue of the Aboriginal peoples, the most excluded of all outcast groups in Australia.

The questionnaire

The questionnaire I constructed consisted of forty-two questions in Italian as well as English. It was distributed before performances began and collected when they had ended. Some were returned by mail. Questions covered eight areas:

(1) the social composition of the audience (ethnic group, gender, age, level of formal education, occupation);
(2) spectators' contact with Italy (frequency of travel to Italy and date of last journey, reading Italian newspapers);
(3) their awareness of and contact with Italo-Australian sources of information (knowledge of FILEF activities, reading newspapers in Italian published in Australia);
(4) their "cultural" level (number of plays, films, concerts, and operas attended annually, number of books read annually in English and Italian. This does not include other cultural events such as festivals, fairs, national and regional celebrations);
(5) the cross-section of theatres attended (last production viewed and where);
(6) spectators' interaction with and assessment of *Tree* and *Stories*;
(7) what spectators considered to be suitable material for future FTG productions;
(8) whether the FTG was performing to its own, perhaps restricted, audience or whether it had succeeded in broadening its audience base, as intended.

My survey embodied a host of concerns. What did spectators value in FTG productions? Did bilingual community theatre provide access to theatre for any particular ethnic group? What other purposes did it serve and for whom (edification, entertainment, platform for social debate, impact on perception of another culture)? Did it fulfill needs not catered for by other types of theatre? Did it create new needs? How did "minority" theatre stand in relation to "majority" theatre? What role did it play in the lived reality of multiculturalism as well as in the formation of multicultural policies?

Publics and their cultural experience

The sample involved 315 respondents, not all of them replying to all 42 questions. Of this total, 39 percent were Italian and Italo-Australian, 43 percent were Anglo/Celts, and 18 percent belonged to the "other ethnic" category. Asked how often they attended the theatre each year, of the 289 respondents to this particular question, a surprisingly large number turned out to be relatively active theatre goers: 118 attend 1 to 3 times a year, 108 of them 4 to 10 times, 21 went 11 to 20 times, and 14 over 20 times. What should be highlighted, given the FTG's commitment to intervention and cultural democracy, are the lowest and medium rates of attendance. Twenty-eight respondents stated that they never went to the theatre: *Tree* or *Stories* was the very first production they had seen in their life. All the Italians in this group, except for one, were from the working class. Thirteen other respondents, mostly Italian and Italo-Australian, stated that *Tree* or *Stories* was the first production they had seen in Australia. Combining these two groups showed that they made up 13 percent of the total of 315. These novices were being serviced in the strongest sense of the word by the FTG. They also represented an untapped resource for creating audiences. The 118 who said they went to the theatre infrequently (one to three times a year) represented 37 percent of the total. Italians, Italo-Australians and "other ethnic" were the most represented at this rate, while Anglo/Celts went to the theatre more often than the rest. At medium attendance rates (4 to 10 times), 63 percent were Anglo/Celts, 10 percent Italians, 13 percent Italo-Australians, and 14 percent "other ethnic." If the figures are taken as a micro-image of Sydney's theatre-going public at the time, the conclusion is that Italians and Italo-Australians were a small part of this public.

Combining the spectators who did not go to the theatre at all with those who went infrequently (1 to 3 times a year) showed that they made up 50 percent of the total. The figure is likely to be higher in real terms for Australian society as a whole – a major justification for the existence of community theatre as such.

It is interesting that while cinema is viewed as a mass medium accessible to everyone, the attendance rate of Italians was concentrated at zero. Even Italo-Australians appeared for the most part to be going only 4 to 10 times annually, whereas Anglo/Celts attended more than twenty times, as did "other ethnics." A number of respondents stated they watched films on television, perhaps explaining why they did not go to the cinema often. By contrast, avid filmgoers stressed their interest by adding that they also watched films on television.

The response for attendance at concerts tended to follow the pattern of theatregoing. Thus the heaviest concentration was in the category of 1 to 3 times annually. Only 5 percent of all respondents went to concerts more than 20 times a year, whereas 31 percent of all respondents go to the cinema over twenty times a year. Consistently, 41 percent of respondents rarely attended the theatre and concerts or did not go at all, while the figure was only 19 percent for films. Anglo/Celts went to the theatre, the cinema and concerts more frequently than others. The sample indicates, then, that Anglo/Celts benefited most from institutionalized cultural events.

Even in the case of opera Anglo/Celts came out first. Opera attendance by Italians fell into the medium category, as did their attendance at other arts. Overall, opera is the least attended of all the arts surveyed: 63 percent of all respondents never went to the opera.

It is worth noting the socioeconomic status of Italian and Italian-Australian opera-goers in the sample. Those who attended 1 to 3 times a year were mainly blue-collar workers, tradespeople, salespeople and secretaries, and pensioners. Opera, whose origins lie in popular culture, could still be said to reach the Italian popular classes. However, Italians and Italo-Australians who went more than 3 times a year were more likely to be professional people. Anglo/Celts and the category of "other ethnic" groups who went to the opera were invariably professionals and paraprofessionals, which suggests that for these ethnic groups opera was a "high" art enclave. Many watched opera on television or listened to it on the radio at home.

Spectator likes and dislikes: the FTG productions

Starting with *Tree*, 104 respondents explained what they liked. The most striking feature was their receptivity to what might be described as the production's reality principle, stressing the "real life" of the stories and their "truthfulness". Most of the spectators who noted the production's verisimilitude were Italians and Italo-Australians.

Italians identified strongly with what they saw to be an accurate picture of their own experience, *realtà* ("real life") or *vissuto* ("truthfulness") recurring frequently in their response and often being the sole word used in their positive reaction. When Anglo/Celts said the play was "true to life", they were possibly referring to their knowledge of the problems faced by Italians in Australia. Some Anglo/Celts noted the "women's issues," "problems common to all women, irrespective of nationality," "women's liberation," "feminism," or the "feminist perspective" of the production. No Italian or respondent of any other ethnic origin generalized in this way.

The tendency to identify personally with the material was also the case among Italo-Australians, who often said they could "relate" to it "from their own background and family."

Only two respondents, both of whom were Anglo/Celtic and university-educated, spoke about the production's historical dimension, one explaining it gave "insight into early Italy," the other noting it presented a "non-Anglo side of history." Few mentioned cultural differences. One praised those aspects of the production dealing with "cultural traditions, difficulties in transplantation of culture to Australia and extra difficulties of being ethnic in Australia." Yet even where direct reference to history and culture was lacking, there were implicit references to them, notably by Anglo/Celts who stated that the production was "informative" or "educational." One said that *Tree* was her "introduction to multicultural theatre." Another explained that it "lets non-Italians understand problems associated with not understanding a language."

Regarding the production's bilingual presentation 6 percent of respondents commented favorably. By contrast, when respondents stated what they did not like, 12 percent of Anglo/Celts cited the "language barrier." Some said they "couldn't understand all the Italian jokes" or "felt left out" or "frustrated."

Respondents were usually more vocal about content than staging. When talking about staging they referred to the music and songs or to the "energy," "vitality," "pace," and "action" of the whole. Many Anglo/Celts made such general remarks as "well-staged," "well-shaped," and "well-acted." An Anglo/Celtic male arts administrator described it as a "strong ensemble piece." Few Italians made any comment at all regarding staging, and details were noted only by those with higher education, all professionals.

Negative reactions (apart from the complaints of "not enough English") came from respondents who found the characters "confusing," mainly because the women's names were all variations on Rosa. Some criticized the "absence of men," and a few thought the feminist "philosophy" a "bit dépassé," veering towards caricature. An Anglo/Celtic female objected to its critical view of "housewives" on the grounds that such criticism was "demeaning of human potential." Four percent thought the production was "too didactic," an opinion expressed at some length by an arts administrator: "it tended to be overcome by didactic qualities and ceased to engage the sensuous emotional qualities which persuade an audience more subtly of the arguments." An Italo-Israeli felt the whole production was based on the naturalistic assumption that "things are as they are" and cannot be changed. This idea was echoed by two Anglo/Celts, who disliked how the ending affirmed the values of marriage and the family.

Very few Italians made critical observations and even then they were slight. One felt the costumes did not adequately show the differences in age between the women. Another detected some racism in the production, presumably against Anglo/Celts.

A total of 133 respondents answered qualitative questions concerning *Stories in Construction*. On the whole, respondents made very general statements which suggested they had caught the gist of the production in terms of its substance, tone, mood and perspective. For example, some spoke of its "relevance." Others said it was "topical" or "modern." Some saw it as "political," remarks ranging from "politically sound" (in one case "ideologically sound") to a "politicized script. What a relief!" Those who referred to its topicality and politics were Anglo/Celts in professional occupations, with the exception of a sales assistant who was also more explicit ("left wing; the workers got together; militant").

Surprisingly few commented on the family scenes or scenes focusing on the younger generation. Compared with *Tree,* very few saw the production from an educational point of view. One Anglo/Celtic university student said she "learned a lot." Another, a university-educated unemployed woman, said she liked the production very much because "it provided information about issues that usually do not concern me and which I know little about."

Approximately the same number as for *Tree* referred to the bilingual presentation, and in much the same terms. Two respondents are worth quoting in full. An Italo-Australian explained: "I liked the bilingual speech because what I missed in Italian I caught up with in English." Secondly, an Anglo-Australian female doctor stated: "The combination of both languages means you can follow most of the story without necessarily being able to speak good Italian. Also gives me a chance to practice and improve my Italian." The doctor's second remark confirms my impression that non-Italians welcomed the opportunity to hear Italian as well as try out their Italian by writing on the questionnaire in Italian. Pleasure in expressing themselves in Italian, or simply in testing it, was particularly noticeable on the part of individuals from the "other ethnics" as well. Anglo/Celts writing in Italian were generally fluent in the language.

Fifty percent fewer than those responding on *Tree* commented unfavorably about the bilingualism, again for similar reasons. An Anglo/Celtic male accountant made this astute observation: "I don't speak Italian so some sketches were lost to me, but this I realize is my problem, as the purpose of the group indicates."

Of the several respondents who alluded to the "great stories," all were Anglo/Celts. One thought the script was "too heavy-handed, too preachy," adding that several actors did not know their lines or moves. Otherwise, when Anglo/Celts referred to the acting, they either used the adjectives "good" or "talented" or, more frequently, talked about the "vitality," "energy" and "liveliness" of the performance as a whole. Italians, once again, were conspicuously absent in comments on performance aspects, though some noted the production was "lively" or "spontaneous."

Italians and Italo-Australians were much more forthcoming about the enthusiasm of the performers or, in the words of one Italian teacher, the feeling of solidarity they conveyed. Respondents across the board appreciated the music and songs, often adding superlatives. Given the importance of dance, notably in a disco sequence and the tarantella closing the performance, surprisingly few chose to comment upon it.

Among those who liked the performance, more indicated a mixed response than for *Tree*. Respondents gave a developed critique of the production in subsequent answers. The few who did not like the work were usually brief, as was the case of an Aboriginal film-maker who said the production was "noisy, predictable, a bit amateuristic."

Comments were varied. Among those who offered a critical evaluation several cited the "unclear delivery of lines" and the "hurried and shouted expression." Some claimed they were not able to hear the dialogue of the scenes played outside the auditorium, adding they did not think these scenes were necessary. Thirty-three percent of respondents gave some thought to the script's substance and structure. The most common observations were that the script was "a bit diffuse," "weak," "slack," or "messy." One Anglo/Celtic woman explained: "There were too many issues presented on a plate not tied together convincingly: feminism, racism, class issues, etc., etc." A few found it difficult to "grasp the meaning of each scenario" and found the building site scenes "a bit repetitive." Several Anglo/Celts thought the script was "dogmatic," "a bit heavy-handed at times with some of the issues," or objected to what they believed were overworked stereotypes. Respondents from the "other ethnic" group were particularly vocal on these points. For example, one stated firmly that she did not like the clichés: "The dialogue amongst the workers around the scaffolding was banal. The workers were stereotyped and it was hard to understand what they were trying to say as a group of workers." Others felt the story was too unilateral: "The ideas are too one-sided; both points of view are not presented in the workers versus bosses struggle."

The observations of Italians and Italo-Australians, especially the former, were particularly striking because they were usually reticent about offering a critical opinion. For example, an Italian thought "some things were over-stated" while another commented that "some things were not right," that the Group should not be "too against Australians" because Australia had provided a reasonable standard of living for Italians. Other Italians who had emigrated in the mid-1970s echoed those sentiments: "I felt that the people [on stage] were totally against Australians."

What distinguishes the assessments of *Stories* from those made of *Tree* is its reflective character. Respondents were far more prepared to offer their opinions. Those who stated unequivocally that they liked *Stories* were more willing than in the case of *Tree* to jot down what they believed was not successful in the production. They were also remarkably persistent in formulating their thoughts, most of them elaborating upon them in the space left for the follow-up questions asking them what they would change in the production and why. *Tree*, by comparison, yielded a series of unfilled spaces, suggesting that respondents were happy with the production as it stood. Some stated firmly that they would change "nothing."

It should be clear, even from this brief summary, that the spectators were engaged with the productions, relating them, in one way or another, to their life in society. What also emerges is that Italo-Australian theatre serves a community purpose, a service to many ethnic groups and not only to the group assumed or perceived to be its "special" audience.

This raises the question as to whether community theatre made by and for a specific minority changes its status because of its interactive power. When does the theatre of a minority group cease to be on the "outside"? Does interactive theatre enhance cultural inclusion? Does it facilitate, in actual (rather than symbolic) terms the sociopolitical inclusion of an "outsider" group? When does multicultural theatre stop being considered theatre for "others" and become accepted in the theatrical mainstream without being considered hierarchically inferior to it?

The data raise another important issue. From the point of view of an inclusionary governmental cultural policy there is the greatest need for intervention, mobilization and renewal among the disadvantaged and disenfranchized who are concentrated in the lower classes – the working class or the modern under-class. Arguably, community-multicultural theatre fulfills its vocation properly when its audience encompasses those who suffer any degree of exclusion because of ethnic and/or class factors and when it brings them in as protagonists equal to others on the stage of society.

Respondents have made it clear that they see ethnicity not solely in terms of identity (let alone of an essentialist concept of identity), but as a springboard for personal and collective empowerment. Theatre coming out of the same source is, consequently, viewed by them as an ally, a partner that can indicate where and how they might look in order to make their own way.

This perception, which emerges from spectators' commentary on FTG productions, also coincides with the goals and intentions of the Melbourne Workers Theatre and Doppio Teatro, irrespective of the shift in emphasis between the two groups. As was noted earlier, the Melbourne Workers Theatre is unashamedly militant, while Doppio

Teatro's poetic theatricality operates on a more subliminal, more elusive level. The Melbourne Workers Theatre prefers to stay on the margins of the establishment and its culture without, however, foregoing its right to engage with, and intervene in, the latter's affairs. Doppio Teatro, by participating in such artistically serious, up-market, and internationally prestigious institutions as the Adelaide Festival, walks with official culture, but does not comply with its social selectivity, especially where audiences are concerned: Italians, Italo-Australians and spectators from various other immigrant groups rub shoulders here with their more affluent and more powerful neighbors. Nevertheless, like the FTG, Melbourne Workers Theatre and Doppio Teatro set something of an example for ethnic theatre in Australia, in general. Most of all, they show that multicultural theatre need not always be on the outside looking in, but can definitely be on the inside looking out.

Acknowledgement

Acknowledgement for its assistance is due to the Australian Research Council (ARC) Small Grants Scheme.

10

In the empire of the object: the geographies of Ana Mendieta

Irit Rogoff

The empire of art

"Mysterious Death in the Art World" screamed the headline of a recent book review (Eaton, 1990). The book itself is circulating under a similarly sensational title: *Naked by the Window – The Fatal Marriage of Carl Andre and Ana Mendieta* (Katz 1990). A multiplicity of articles have, over the past several years, attempted to deal with the unclear circumstances of Ana Mendieta's death in 1985 (Endell 1985). It would seem that both her life and her death have somehow been contained within a very particular geographical location, that of the art world. While the art world cannot claim for itself a fixed and concrete location, a mapped terrain with distinct boundaries, it is nevertheless a world unto itself, with a distinct cultural and linguistic tradition and a vehement sense of territoriality.

In spatializing the cultural narrative that has emerged around the work, life and death of Ana Mendieta, I am claiming that these have been constructed out of a set of territorial imperatives which continue to privilege a Eurocentric, urban and commodity-oriented artistic culture whose center is professed to be the New York art world. Mendieta herself, Cuban, female, a conceptual artist working in geographically peripheral areas, not only rejected such centrist organizing principles but sought to replace them with alternative geographies, which brought together natural topographies with the landscape of a female body imposed, inserted and cast upon them. The folkloric location of her work and her life by the press has served to characterize it in a particular way, one reserved for the defiant outsider.

By invoking the concept of "geography," of what Edward Soja terms "the politicized spatiality of social life" (Soja 1989: 2), I am attempting to reframe, or relocate it within a cultural sphere which is concentric and multicultural rather than centrist and hierarchical. This discussion is related to my larger project, entitled "Terra Infirma – Geographies and Identities" which is a semiotic attempt to deconstruct the assumed relations between geographies and identities within the post-colonial world. Instead of geography I would like to posit a set of linked categories formulated through the discourses of race, gender and site (which is critical and contingent as opposed to the fixed and naturalized concept of geography). It is only by attempting to undo such specific locations that we can begin the process of critically interrogating the terms which attribute value and prominence to cultural products.

Any critical examination of the relationship between geographical materialities and the representations of coherent identities reveals that, contrary to expectations, these neither complement nor construct one another in a direct or causal manner. The mere appearance of flags or of other recognized national entities within identifiable boundary lines, of landscapes which invoke the attributes of national, regional or continental characteristics, or the representation of specific linguistic practices, do not necessarily signify a set of shared homogeneous values operating from within one shared collective identity. While critical discourses have dealt with such inconsistencies at great length, the world of visual representations has continued to mask the possibilities for difference which exist within the locus of geographical signification.

Contrary to readings which conflate geographies and identities and link both to a historical determination of the homogeneous, collective and shared nature of cultural enterprise, the following discussion posits the strategic function of cultural displacement and dislocation and the ways in which these are pictorially constructed and signified.

Focusing on the work of Ana Mendieta, I attempt to look at issues of both iconography and of the situating of the art object in relation to the art world, each with their critical view of the positivistic logic of the sign, of temporality as opposed to concrete objecthood and of the extreme art world preoccupations with establishing a "center," as the main platform on which pictorial cultural coherence has been founded.

Furthermore, I argue that the disruption of such traditions, through geographical and cultural exile and dislocation, opens up possibilities for the incorporation of alternative and plural perspectival vantage points and pictorial references which forge new cultural conjunctions. They are constructed out of difference and disjuncture rather than similarity and continuity. Within the realm of visual representation the issue of materiality, of alternative modes of visually codifying specific, located and named entities, is central. Above all else the issue to which these visual discourses of place and identity point is that of positionality – the newly arrived at, oblique and circuitous ways in which the self is positioned in relation to the great traditions, be these of epistemic structures, the signification of specific location and its national/cultural identification, or gendered narratives and histories.

It is precisely because this effort cannot be contained within conventional systems of sign interpretation that it opens up possibilities of the representation of displaced identities. If the representations of geographies in Mendieta's reconstruction of acculturated earth plots do not work toward the signification of traditionally identified affiliations and locations, perhaps their resistance works towards a revised understanding of identity. The fact that these can be further differentiated by gender-related issues and practices opens up possibilities for visual discourses of gender and culture which work across one another.

Traditionally, coherent cultural identity has been seen as transcending such aspects of difference as gender or language while anchored in a shared participation in an overall historical narrative. Introducing these as further degrees of inherent difference with clear cultural manifestations may help to redefine positionality away from the traditional concept of rootedness within one specific and coherent given culture. How to make the invisible fragmentation of the subject which works against traditions of cultural coherency visible is the question being asked by many contemporary artists, and how to do so within the inherited language of signification and therefore disrupt its supposedly simple legibility is equally the subject of much of contemporary critical discussion.

A death in art – retold

Early in the morning of September 8, 1985, the well-known minimalist sculptor Carl Andre was charged with murdering his Cuban-born wife Ana Mendieta by flinging her out of the window of their 34th floor Greenwich Village apartment. Art world luminaries of the male sex gathered around Andre in support. The $250,000 bail demanded by the New York District Attorney for the charge of second degree murder was posted by a who's who list of the great names of the art world of the sixties and early seventies. Andre was after all what artspeak terms "museum class," a founding father of Minimalism, his massive installations of bricks and copper tiles bought for hundreds of thousands of dollars by the great modern art collections of the world. Mendieta on the other hand was an inhabitant of the feminist subculture of the art world, an exhibitor in publicly funded arts projects of short duration and a contributor to such journals as *Heresies*, definitely not "museum class."[1]

The tragedy served as the focus of one of the quintessential art world circuses, the stuff from which myths of the excesses of bohemian life are made. Here were two prodigious drunks, she "boisterous and euphoric," he "sullen and taciturn," both of firm though wildly divergent leftist politics, notorious for their constant fights and reconciliations. "A Death in Art," screamed the cover of *New York Magazine* (December 16, 1985). "Did Carl Andre, the renowned minimalist sculptor, hurl his wife, a fellow artist, to her death?" He has a name and a stylistic affiliation, she is anonymous and affiliationless. The article continues, "The case is causing a deep rift among artists. There was one light moment at Puffy's, the artists bar at Harrison and Hudson streets [this information is essential to ground the action in New York, center of the art world, and to provide practical information for *New York Magazine*'s readers, who will all undoubtedly rush out there immediately] when a beer pitcher labelled Carl André Defense Fund appeared on the bar and someone contributed a brick." But for the most part, feelings were running high: "I think there's a division between Carl, who is a white and super-successful artist and Ana who was a rising but not too successful female Hispanic," says one woman in the art world. "I think it's coming down to a class struggle; the memorial service was like two hundred of the disposessed of the art world. The only two prominent people I recognized there were Claes Oldenburg and Leon Golub." The art establishment, this woman claims, is coming down on Andre's side: "There's a whispering campaign . . . here's this loony Cuban and what can you expect." The possibilities for suicide are also discounted by all of the articles which appeared immediately after the death: the consensus was that she was "too ambitious, too pushy" to do herself in.

After two trials Andre was acquitted in December 1986 of all charges pertaining to the death of Mendieta. This horror and the sensationalizing trivialization – racist, sexist, snide and mercenary – which I have tried to document here, do serve one purpose and that is to help problematize the issue of situating that is central to the fascinating record of work Mendieta left behind her.

The geographies of Ana Mendieta

I have been carrying on a dialogue [she wrote in a letter to a woman friend] between the landscape and the female body (based on my own silhouette). I believe this has been a direct result of my having been torn from my homeland (Cuba) during my adolescence . . . I am overwhelmed by the feeling of having been cast from the womb (nature). My art is the way I re-establish the bonds that tie me to the universe.[2]

In another letter written in the early 1980s Ana Mendieta tells of an "African custom which I think . . . is analogous of my work . . . The men from the Kimberly go outside their village to seek their brides. When a man brings his new wife home, the woman brings with her a sack of earth from her homeland and every night she eats a little bit of that earth. The earth will help her make the transition between her homeland and her new home" (Barreras del Rio 1987: 28–41). Mendieta and her own sack of earth had gone through a process of "deterritorialization." Caren Kaplan describes this as "A term for the displacement of identities, persons and meanings that is endemic to the postmodern world system" (Kaplan 1985: 187). The idea is founded on Deleuze and Guattari's use of the term "deterritorialization," to locate the moment of alienation and exile in language and literature (1986). This is the thread that will guide my analysis, below. Now, however, without wanting to privilege biography as an analytical tool in any way, I put forth a few biographical facts that seem significant.

Mendieta grew up in middle class comfort in the Havana of the late forties and fifties; her father was a highly politicized lawyer; a great-uncle had been president of Cuba; a great-grandfather, Carlos de Rioja, was a general in the 1895 war of independence. In 1958, when Fulgencio Batista was still in power, Ignacio Mendieta, Ana's father, was working secretly against the government. The revolution came but things did not go well for Ignacio Mendieta. Though pro-Castro he was anti-Communist, a devout Roman Catholic who considered the Communists anti-God. He refused to become a member of the Party and quickly fell out of favor and out of work. With money increasingly tight and suspicion becoming a way of life, the Mendietas sent their two daughters to the United States for what they thought would be a short sojourn. Armed with a letter giving power of attorney to the Catholic authorities, and a vision of America founded on Troy Donahue and Sandra Dee, the Mendieta sisters found themselves first in a camp in Miami and then an institution in Dubuque, Iowa. This was in essence a reform school, whose inmates were orphans and socially disfunctional children subjected to brutal beatings and other horrors. Over the next eight years a series of foster homes were to follow, until her mother and brother finally joined them, while her father remained in prison in Cuba. Ana later said that by the time she was seven-

Figure 26. Photograph of Ana Mendieta by Nereyda Garcia Ferraz. Source: "Ana Mendieta: A Retrospective," the New Museum of Contemporary Art, New York (1987).

teen she knew she had two choices, either to be a criminal or to be an artist, the only two sources of power available to her (Barreras del Rio 1987: 33).

Violence remains central to her early work, body art in which she encased her form in mud or blood or grass or flowers. After the occurrence of a rape at the University of Iowa, Mendieta did a violent rape series. In one she lay nude in the woods, her backside bloodied.

In another, for which she invited the members of the workshop to come over to her apartment, she was tied to the table nude from the waist down and there was blood all

Figure 27. Ana Mendieta, *Untitled* (earth body work with tree and mud, Old Man's Creek, Iowa City, Iowa) 1977. Collection of Ignatio C. Mendieta. Source: "Ana Mendieta: A Retrospective," The New Museum of Contemporary Art (1987).

Figure 28. Ana Mendieta, *Untitled* (earth body work, Old Man's Creek, Iowa City, Iowa) 1977. Estate of Ana Mendieta.

over the floor and the door. Both trauma and dislocation were converging on the geography of her own body.

Karen Caplan (1985: 189) suggests that deterritorialization describes the effects of a radical distanciation between signifier and signified in which meanings and utterances become estranged. Such a process of defamiliarization enables the imagination, even as it produces alienation, in Deleuze and Guattari's words, "to express another potential community, to force the means for another consciousness and another sensibility" (1986: 17; cited in Kaplan: 188).

Mendieta's actual displacements were numerous and repeated: from Cuba and her family at the age of thirteen she moved to the United States, then to studies at Iowa university, to life in New York City's SoHo, to work in Mexico and Cuba and finally to work in a studio in Rome as the recipient of the prestigious Prix de Rome. The geographic migrations were accompanied by a series of artistic moves, from a minimal mode to an increasingly conceptual art involving actions, objects and documentation. The changes taking place within her artistic practice were thrown into sharp relief by Mendieta's increasing awareness and incorporation of the emergent discourses of cultural criticism involving gender, race and the cultural signification of certain sign systems, into her overall understanding of her art.

There is little nostalgia or illusion about the regaining of previous cultural coherencies in any aspect of her work. As an adult she actually returned frequently to Cuba on working visits. She had prepared works in the Cuban section of Miami where she made a figure-like form out of the hair of Cuban exiles in Miami collected from local hairdressing salons. This figure she attached to a local tree much used in ceremonial rituals by the immigrant population of the city. Every aspect of this complex project is inscribed with an understanding of loss, transition and emergent immigrant realities that build on but do not emulate or continue the original practices. Within this artistic project in Miami we can observe no nostalgic hankering after some semblance of either the "real" or "original" culture, but rather a recognition of its supposedly secondary level of existence as a displaced immigrant community, and as a potent cultural reality. Of her actual return to Cuba as an adult Mendieta wrote "I was afraid before I went there because I've been living with this obsessive thing in my mind – what if I found out it has nothing to do with me?" Between these lines we can read the presence of conflicting cultural traditions and of the artist's own location of herself within entirely opposite and conflicting political and ideological systems of state communism and capitalist democracy.

Interludes in Mexico and Rome thus assume a form of cultural mediation, Mexico being a host to many exiled Latin Americans who found that they could relocate their own preoccupations within a Spanish culture which has sustained itself continuously and has an acute and fully articulated awareness of its own heritage. Rome on the other hand is the source of the other culture which made up Ana Mendieta's world of reference, the Western tradition founded in classical antiquity and Roman civic practice. All of these journeys speak not only of disruption and cultural fragmentation, but also of the collecting of tools, images and references which would help the work transcend the boundaries the artist wished to dissolve. These include narrow definitions of the type of work which qualifies for the category of "art," the sites and locations which are considered credible for its display as art objects and, above all, the conventional linear histories into which this artistic practice could be slotted.

Mendieta's process of deterritorialization had been effected through a framework of feminism, Third-World cultural politics and first-world avant-garde art practices of the late 1970s and 1980s. The relationship of these elements to the great traditions and to her own work had gone through a series of sharp dislocations which were brought to an abrupt halt with her violent death at thirty-six. The scope of the project she had begun was enormous and can be seen as only partially completed. Transience and discontinuity are inscribed in every aspect of this project and its untimely ending does not in any way diminish or qualify its significance. Both her premature death and her declared state of exile can, in hindsight, work in a derogatory way to sentimentalize readings of her work rather than move towards a recognition of the critiques of concepts of time and space as traditional cultural values, which she was working to deconstruct.

Outsider works and becoming minor

Mendieta's work of the last decade of her life had been closely bound to the earth. Often she traced the silhouette of her body on earth, sand, tree trunks and fields in the environs of Iowa City where she had pursued her studies and in the Oaxaca region of

Figure 29. Ana Mendieta, *Untitled* (gunpowder and silver, at Old Man's Creek, Iowa City, Iowa) 1977. Collection of Ignatio C. Mendieta.

Mexico and the hills of Jaruco near the city of Havana, Cuba. The works themselves use a rich variety of materials including gunpowder, fire, wood, paint mixed with blood, cloth, metal foils and many others.

Some of these have been eased into place with a great delicacy that works to echo the existing lines of rock or earth formations, while others have been etched through blasting with gunpowder or set up by fire with the intention of imposing their form on the landscape through extreme contrast. Free-standing silhouettes raised high onto the skyline and set alight like the military banners of ancient armies on the march, served to illuminate and transform the horizon for a series of eerie moments and then collapse into small piles of ashes and charred fragments.

The transient status of the works, sites abandoned either to destruction or to change, according to climatic and other conditions, echoes other states of transience all linked to an earth which defines everything but cannot be adhered to in any way. They function like a contemporary production of site-specific archaeology which proceeds to play havoc with conventional notions of cultural time, of past and present and yet, in defying cultural time as a progressive sequence, they do not attempt to impose some other non-specific notion of timelessness.

The project which Mendieta embarked on might best be described through a concept parallel to Deleuze and Guattari's "deterritorialisation" – that of "reterritorialisation" (Deleuze and Guattari 1986: 17). As Caren Kaplan understands this conception, its value "lies in the paradoxical movement between 'minor and major' – a refusal to admit

Figure 30. Ana Mendieta, *Anima* (fireworks silhouette series, earth body work and performance, Oaxaca, Mexico) 1976. Collection of Raquel Ol Mendieta.

either position as final or static. The issue is positionality. In modern autobiographical discourses for example, the self that is constructed is often untenable or, at the very least, in tension with competing issues . . . Much of contemporary feminist theory proposes a strategy of reading and an analysis of positionality similar to Deleuze and Guattari's conception of 'becoming minor.' In working with issues of race, class and sexualities, as well as gender, feminist discourses have come to stress difference and oscillation of margin and centre in the construction of personal and political identities" (Kaplan 1985: 188).

Mendieta's process of reterritorialization is the construction of a collective history based on gender as well as on race and on alternative cultural specificity. The artistic materials and tools that she employs in this project are: matter versus contour as the essence of a personalized geography and place, or "site" (i.e. determined by choice rather than fate) as opposed to location. In these she is working against the grain of the dominant artistic traditions in her total negation of all forms of boundaries.

Her works are made predominantly out of doors and remain there, thus (their photographic representations excepted) rejecting the social boundaries within which works of art are produced and displayed: studios, galleries, museums. This was in clear defiance of the art world's obsessive concern with "the center" out of which small colonial offshoots could be tolerated but no more. In the immortal words of Joe Helman, an art dealer, "If your work is traded in Prague, Bogotá, Madrid, Paris and LA but not New York – you're a provincial artist. But if you're traded in New York and anywhere

Figure 31. Ana Mendieta, *Untitled* (earth body work with cloth, Oaxaca, Mexico) 1977. Collection of Raquel Mendieta Harrington.

else, you're international" (Woodward 1989: 33). Thus the issues of cultural centrality and marginality take on a new twist with this emphasis on the siting of the work as an index of its value.

Mendieta, who was culturally displaced between her Latin heritage and her American education and who increasingly attempted to employ models of analysis gleaned from Third-World feminism in her own Western artistic practice, also displaced herself in relation to the art world by making ephemeral objects which were exhibited in distant and little known rural spots. Generically too these works defy definition and containment within a given style or mode, since they differ from both earth works and from pure body art by combining the two and by playing on the tension between a performance art and a continuous slow deterioration of the pieces in nature. The works themselves too are without boundaries within their sites since there is no exact place in which they either begin or end, thus they cannot be framed or bound within conventional artistic or geographical territorialities. Their extreme materiality, sensuous, brutal, culturally and physically suggestive, plays the role of foregrounding quality, texture and substance as opposed to definition.

Lest all of this sound like an attempt at an archetypal "feminine" artistic practice, I hasten to say that Mendieta's work cannot be summed up as a representation of the dreaded biologically essentialist "feminine." This is due primarily to her unceasing preoccupation with and ability to find and visually articulate different balances between

Figure 32. Ana Mendieta, *Guanabancex* (rupestrian sculptures) 1981. Estate of Ana Mendieta.

universality and specificity. She carved, sculpted, dug, blasted, fired and painted figures inspired by the mythological metaphors of the Great Mothers, Gaea, Hades, Mother Earth, and so on, in and on her many sites. But their universality is purely a function of their reception by western European traditions. For Mendieta, a rigorous student of the religions and rituals of Spanish and Latin American cultures, predominantly the Santeria in Cuba in the Middle Ages, these have a concrete historical specificity (Barreras del Rio 1987: 28).

Such cultural and historical concreteness is in turn echoed in the ways that her work repeatedly negotiates sets of images and sets of materials with different sites. Her own vigilant insistence on concretizing the experience and its representation points to the fact that our responses to specificity require that it be within an acculturated hand's reach, a historical tradition in which we ourselves are positioned, a museum or an accessible or recognizable location. The fact that these works take place in little known hills and river banks in Mexico or Cuba does not make their location any less specific.

Nor does their historical moment take the form of a nostalgic hankering for the primeval, the ahistorical and the timeless. The predominance of female figures in the iconography is not an attempt to repopulate the world with a universal female form on which every mythical narrative and allegory can be hung, but rather to give concrete visual forms to lost narratives by "siting" them.

This supposedly lost, timeless quality has been projected on them by a Western historical narrative that constructs and determines place, that designates time, and excludes other narratives that cannot be located parallel to itself. I find Mendieta's restless travels, her constant search for sites, her insistence on named geographical locations for her work, to be the most telling part of her historical reterritorialization. Her very playfulness with regard to the transposition of culture in time and place leads to a new understanding of the strategic sense of knowledge and its deployment. Her invocation of myths, religions, symbols and materials seems to me, for all their transience and ephemerality, to stress the strategic and geographical as opposed to the temporal dimensions of human historical narratives. Geographies and their signification thus emerge not as the sites of secure and coherent identities but rather as disruptive interventions in the historical narratives of culture.

Mendieta's process of reterritorialization, of constructing what Edward Said characterizes as the general European effort to seek new worlds to rule (1978), takes the form of making a collective gendered history. Rooted in a particular Latin America tradition, and then consciously displaced again and again, this history is attractive precisely because it points to future possibilities rather than to closure. In "becoming minor," exploring the revolutionary potential of that recognition of difference and of negation of boundaries, Ana Mendieta simultaneously confers a rich potential reworking of the condition of exile and of artistic innovation.

Notes

1 The series of quotations from art world luminaries and hangers-on, gossips and socialites is taken from Endell (1985).
2 Ana Mendieta, unpublished statement quoted in Perreault (1987: 10).

References

Barreras del Rio, Petra 1987, "Ana Mendieta: A Historical Overview," *Ana Mendieta: A Retrospective*, New York: The New Museum of Contemporary Art, 28–51.

Deleuze, Gilles and Guattari, Felix 1986, *Kafka: Towards a Minor Literature* (translated by Dana Polan), University of Minnesota Press.

Eaton, Kathryn 1990, "Mysterious Death in the Art World," *San Francisco Chronicle* February 16: 16.

Endell, Kay 1985, "A Death in Art," *New York Magazine* December: 38–46.

Kaplan, Caren 1985, "Deterritorialization: A Rewriting of Home and Exile in Western Feminist Discourse," *Cultural Critique* 2: 187–98.

Katz, Robert 1990, *Naked by the Window: The Fatal Marriage of Carl Andre and Ana Mendieta*, Atlantic Monthly Press, 1990.

Perreault, John 1987, "Earth and Fire: Mendieta's Body of Work," *Ana Mendieta: a Retrospective*, New York: The New Museum of Contemporary Art, 10–23.

Said, Edward 1978, *Orientalism* , New York: Pantheon.

Soja, Edward 1989, *Postmodern Geographies: The Reassertion of Space in Critical Social Theory,* London: Verso, 1989.

Woodward, Richard 1989, "For Art, Coastal Convergences," *New York Times* (July 16): 33.

PART IV

Genre switching

Artistic change is unceasing, but patterns and rates of change vary from one era and art form to the next, and from one place to another. Art in its many forms may change slowly and subtly, or with an enormous, almost revolutionary sweep. Thus, innovation was barely perceptible in Egyptian art over three millennia, whereas modern European history is replete with examples of artists and art traditions that have experienced quantum shifts both in standing and meaning. For instance, many French academic painters, whose works formerly graced the corridors of important buildings and mansions, came to be relegated to museum basements, their works considered historically interesting but aesthetically unimportant. Photography, with its mixed origins in technology and its early commercial and documentary uses, over the last half-century has gained entry to the domain of high art. Tableware, including flatware and dishes, the furnishings of artisans and design schools, have found their way into elite households, and thence into craft and art museums. Frequently, new forms of highly valued art arose from the meanest origins.

Leila Sussman takes us into the physical education programs of the elite women's colleges in the late nineteenth and early twentieth centuries, as the nursery of modern dance. A cultural preoccupation with health and exercise led to the incorporation of gymnastic exercises and dance classes in certain of these colleges. They provided fertile soil for the development of theatrical modern dance led by innovative women choreographers such as Martha Graham. Sussman traces the turbulent introduction of early modern dance to the public, its assorted ad hoc venues, the formation of companies, their search for funding sources, and its initial public reception. She notes that preservation of its repertoire is insurance for survival, yet most of the repertoire remains unrecorded. This is curious, given the unprecedented success of modern dance in this era.

The tango was a mandance, born in the bordellos of Argentina of the demographic imbalance between the sexes as a result of rapid immigration. Desire and social caste were encoded into body language, music and song. Juan Corradi traces the evolution of the tango as an aesthetic form, its overseas journey to post-First World War Paris, and the personages who transformed and promoted this Latin dance via Paris to international prominence. Corradi's essay posits an affinity betweeen the tango and various of its social circumstances, which through conscious social manipulations resulted in the emergence of a dance form of elegance and high repute.

11

Colleges and companies: early modern dance in the United States

Leila Sussmann

Introduction

Modern dance in the United States was a cultural movement led by women who were artistic innovators. Their goals were aesthetic, not feminist, but they pursued their choreographic careers with striking persistence, even though the composing, if not the performance of dances, was usually reserved for men. Through their determination to create a new kind of theatrical dance, and their collective genius, they succeeded in creating an art.

Retrospectively it is clear that early modern dance actually was deeply involved in feminism.[1] The dancers were almost exclusively women, their dances were in part about themselves; and their innovative way of moving presented a new image of woman. Their art was also associated with the campaign for women's higher education. Dance compositions by the first generation of moderns might never have found a sustained following had their work not been taken up and disseminated through the women's colleges. How the colleges and the new dance converged to forge a self-renewing audience for modern dance is the main topic of this essay.

Secondly, the essay analyzes the organizational characteristics of the early modern dance companies, and demonstrates how the companies' structure, born of poverty, had advantages for an avant-garde art form. Beginning with the context of the late nineteenth century it takes its subject up to the 1960s, tracing how modern dance came to be produced by a particular set of institutions and how these institutions, in turn, were critical in shaping modern dance.

Considering that they started with insignificant resources, the success of the proponents of modern dance is remarkable. At their beginnings they had few followers, no subsidies and no knowledgeable critics to interpret their way of dancing. They created their art in unmapped territory. Performance venues ranged over concert stages, musical revues, union halls, college gymnasiums. All these factors lent ambiguity to their project: were they making popular or high culture, art for art's sake, or art as a tool of politics?

Women's colleges and women's health: from exercise to modern dance

From the middle to the end of the nineteenth century, the period when women's colleges were founded, Americans were preoccupied with health and exercise. Exercise, in particular, was a cure prescribed for "neurasthenia." The term neurasthenia, introduced into medicine in the late 1860s, applied to symptoms such as asthma, chronic fatigue, weakness and fainting spells. Medical writers attributed the spread of neurasthenia to the strain of industrialization and of urbanization. It was said to be distinctively an American "nervousness" (Beard 1869: 217).

While neurasthenia was defined as a general medical problem, it is clear in hindsight that its causes were conceived differently for men and women. Its symptoms constituted behavior that deviated from accepted gender roles. For men the cause was "too much passivity," indicating a weakness stemming from over-refinement. Neurasthenic women, on the other hand, were suffering from "too much activity," squandering their limited energy on inappropriate mental and physical tasks. "Excessively passive" men and "excessively active" women were behaving too much like the opposite sex.

The treatments for this gendered disease were also gender-related. For men the cure was Theodore Roosevelt's "strenuous life" – large doses of physical activity along with a passionate devotion to work. Roosevelt overcame a childhood plagued by asthma, insomnia and gastrointestinal trouble to command during the Spanish-American War the Rough Riders brigade of cavalry, whose feats, notably the charge up San Juan Hill in Cuba, were legendary. For neurasthenic women, on the contrary, the cure was prolonged bed rest and deprivation of visitors, reading, movement – any form of mental or physical stimulation. Women needed to recoup energy for procreation and mothering (Lutz 1991: 21,32). In 1873 the prominent Boston physician Dr. Edward Clarke wrote a treatise, *Sex in Education*, in which he told of a Vassar student who fell gravely ill from "excessive study" while experiencing menstrual irregularity. He deplored the "propensity" of college women to remain single, claiming that the consequence of these tendencies would be "race suicide" (Clarke, 1873, quoted in Gay 1984: 214).

In spite of the success of Clarke's book, which went through seventeen printings, the project of providing high quality higher education for women was coming to fruition. Vassar College had been in existence for just eight years when his book was published; Wellesley College was founded in 1874, one year after its publication; and Radcliffe College was founded in 1879. The early women's colleges could not ignore the body of opinion that Clarke represented; it was a threat to their dream of excellent higher education for women. They rejected the idea that study was harmful to women's health, but at the same time they took unprecedented steps to guard the good health of their students. Their concern was built into campus architecture in the form of ample gymnasiums (Helen Horowitz 1985: 169), and it was built into the curriculum in the requirement that all students take courses in hygiene and physical education. There was no parallel requirement in men's Ivy League colleges:

> The field of study in which the women's colleges clearly pioneered was health. Courses in hygiene and physiology were standard offerings in nearly every woman's college from the beginning . . . Such courses were reinforced by required physical education. (Newcomer 1959: 10)

These requirements implied acceptance of a need to protect studious women from neurasthenia, but the acceptance had its irony. While appropriating the male prerogative of higher education, the women's colleges also appropriated the male, not the female, cure for neurasthenia: plenty of work and plenty of exercise. The element of defensiveness in their stance appears clearly in statements carried by the early catalogs of some leading women's colleges. Smith College's Official Circular of 1877 said:

No student has thus far received the slightest apparent physical injury from her college work. The majority have decidedly improved in health since entering college.

The Wellesley College catalog of 1878 was more militant:

For many years the charge has been made, in public and in private, that the health of girls is destroyed by hard study in schools and colleges. It is the favorite argument of those who oppose the higher education of women. We will not submit in silence to this odious injustice. Hard study, properly directed and regulated, promotes physical health.

Given this background, it is no surprise that dance entered the college curriculum as a kind of exercise intended to promote health. Only after it had gained admission into the curriculum did it gradually evolve as a form of self-expression with aesthetic dimensions. Furthermore, dancing was thought to be a risqué activity, one which the American Puritan heritage condemned as "immoral." When, around 1853, the president of Mount Holyoke, Mary Lyon, published a book of exercises to promote not just health but "grace of motion and good carriage," she warned teachers that when done to music, her exercises should not be performed in a dancelike fashion or they would arouse opposition (Kraus and Chapman 1981: 112–113). Her goal was the same as that of eighteenth-century dancing masters who had taught graceful deportment to the upper classes, but she dared not call it "dancing."

Later in the century two physical culture movements, gymnastics and Delsartian exercise, included dancing as an aspect of their programs. Dr. Dudley Sargent introduced something he variously called "gymnastic dancing," "aesthetic calisthenics," and "classic dancing," into his normal school for physical education and into the Harvard Summer School of Physical Education. His follower, Emil Rath, wrote a book on women's physical education in which he not only advocated dancing to increase circulation and metabolism but struck a new note, saying:

Dancing is rapidly becoming a universal and popular form of expression. . . . This new spirit seems destined to burst the prosaic bonds of our present day materialism by giving the inner life of the people a medium for artistic expression based upon . . . all-permeating rhythm–dancing in its various forms. (quoted in Ruyter 1979: 89–92)

The expressive dance to which Rath referred grew out of Delsartian exercise as adapted to the United States. The Frenchman, François Delsarte, developed exercises to train singers and actors. A sort of expressionist who studied human movement, gesture and facial expression, he sought to codify the overt signs of inner states. Three precursors of modern dance, Isadora Duncan, Ted Shawn and Ruth St. Denis paid tribute to his work.[2]

An American interpreter of Delsarte, Genevieve Stebbins, popularized his system of exercise among middle-class American women concerned about their health. Stebbins's version formed a bridge between routines designed to relieve "nervous tension" and aesthetic routines of pantomime with rhythmic steps and statue poses. Used for entertainment in elegant salons, the aesthetic exercises had a large following in the 1880s and 1890s. Ruth St. Denis's mother, who was a physician interested in women's health, took her daughter to hear a Stebbins lecture; it left a lasting impression on the young girl. When Ted Shawn and Ruth St. Denis founded their California school of dance, Denishawn, they hired a teacher of Delsartian exercise (Kendall 1979: 12–27).

At Denishawn, upper- and upper-middle-class girls with strictly amateur intentions studied dance, along with professional hopefuls such as Martha Graham, Doris Humphrey and Charles Weidman. Thus both the founders of modern concert dance and their early devotees shared the experience of study at Denishawn. We shall see that a shared introductory training in their college dance classes also linked together the audiences and artists of modern dance in later years. Their colleges' insistence on a liberal arts education gave them a common cultural background as well. Those who were to become the core of their audiences and the artists underwent the same schooling.

Denishawn was attended mainly by students interested in practicing dance as amateurs and by professional dancers, while from the 1890s women physical educators were attracted to Sargent's Harvard summer school. The Perry-Mansfield Dance Camp which opened in Colorado in 1914, a contemporary of Denishawn, attracted a mixture of girls from the elite women's colleges and women physical education teachers. It taught acting, dance and horseback riding. Over the years of its existence, nearly all the leading modern dancers taught there (Bogue 1984: 11–34). The Harvard summer school, the Perry-Mansfield Dance Camp and other summer dance schools were precedents for the Bennington College summer dance festivals of 1935–1941, which became a landmark in the history of modern dance. They brought together four of the leading first generation choreographers – Martha Graham, Doris Humphrey, Charles Weidman and Hanya Holm – to compose, perform and teach. Not only dancers, but physical education instructors from colleges all over the country made up half the student body. They played a key role in disseminating modern dance to the colleges.

In the meanwhile, the word "dancing" appeared more and more frequently in prestigious college catalogs. The Smith College catalog first used the word in a course description of 1891, and the Barnard catalog in 1909. In 1913 Barnard offered a course in "interpretative dancing."

Despite this growing incidence of "dancing" in the curriculum, the art of dance lacked a prestigious intellectual rationale until John Dewey's educational philosophy provided one. Emphasizing active experience by the pupil as the basis for learning, Dewey underlined the need for control to be internalized as self-control (Dewey 1916). Dewey himself did not write about physical education, but a Deweyan, Thomas Wood, published an essay on health and education which favored team athletics and dance, as opposed to gymnastics. Gymnastics was too authoritarian; it imposed control from the

Figure 33. A Pageant (June 1925), Oberlin College Archives, Oberlin, Ohio.

outside; it did not give the opportunities for self-expression provided by sports and dancing (Newcomer 1959: 192).

Dewey also wanted schools to foster children's creativity. In dance curricula, that idea translated into a concern with having the students compose dances rather than cultivate a polished performance technique. Accordingly, during the 1920s the colleges developed a "natural dance" which used movements like walking, running, skipping and leaping. Teachers' College, Columbia, Oberlin College, and others taught natural dance in the 1920s. Its advantage was that it enabled young women to compose and perform without years of technical training (Ruyter 1979: 112).

The idea that creative composition was important, and virtuoso technique much less so ruled college dance programs until the 1960s. During the 1980s Bennington College maintained the stress on creativity and minimized the importance of performing technique. Its 1985–86 catalog stated that "The college stresses modern dance with an emphasis on choreography. . . . No particular level of [performing] proficiency is required for graduation."

As dance historian Nancy Ruyter was the first to make clear, the colleges evolved their own collegiate modern dance to meet the needs of their students even before the generation of Martha Graham came to dominate theatrical modern dance (*ibid.*: 117–124).

Figure 34. Margaret Palmer, Class of 1930, *c.*1926–30. Oberlin College Archives, Oberlin, Ohio.

Figure 35. Natural dancing, 1920s, probably first published 1928. Oberlin College Archives, Oberlin, Ohio.

Graham, over a long career, developed a technique systematic and comprehensive enough to be used by other choreographers. It appeared to a connoisseur of dance like Lincoln Kirstein to owe nothing to any dance tradition. George Balanchine called it a "classical technique," by which he meant that it provided a framework for composing dances. Doris Humphrey, too, developed a technique of great scope, but different from Graham's. The explorations of dance movement by these pioneers provided a substantial foundation on which talented successors could build. They demonstrated that dance had endless new possibilities for those willing to throw tradition overboard and to try to reinvent it.[3]

The alliance between the colleges and modern concert dance

Once modern dance had made its debut on the New York legitimate stage in the late 1920s and early 1930s, it came to have a symbiotic relationship with nearby women's colleges. They hired modern dancers as instructors, invited companies to perform on campus, encouraged formation of modern dance clubs and staged student recitals. In the year that Martha Graham and her company made their first appearance at the Guild Theatre, in 1929, Barnard College hired a Graham student as dance instructor.

The case of Randolph-Macon Woman's College in Virginia provides a graphic instance of the interconnections of the emergent art form and the colleges. In 1928, Randolph-Macon Woman's College hired Eleanor Struppa, a 1920 graduate, to be Professor of Physical Education and Dance. Struppa had received an MA at Teachers' College, Columbia, under Gertrude Colby, an originator of natural dance. Struppa had continued her dance studies later with Wigman and Kreutzberg in Germany and with Martha Graham. Soon after taking on her duties, Struppa founded a student dance group at Randolph-Macon (Randolph-Macon Archives). She choreographed the Greek choruses which the students danced in Randolph-Macon's annual Greek play, itself given in Greek. In addition, they gave recitals of Struppa's original dances.

The famous Graham dancer, Helen McGehee, began her career in the group, inspired by the leading dance companies Struppa invited to perform on campus. As Helen McGehee told me in interview in 1993, in those days, the best-known companies were affordable even by a small college.[4]

Radcliffe College introduced its first course for credit in modern dance in 1931 (Radcliffe Course Catalogue,1931). By 1932, the field had become so active that Barnard held a symposium on teaching methods for choreographers and teachers of modern dance in eastern women's colleges (Barnard College archives). During 1935, Doris Humphrey's company made a one-week tour of Virginia colleges which included Randolph-Macon, Mary Baldwin, Sweetbriar and Lynchburg (King 1978: 211). That year the company also appeared at the New School for Social Research and Columbia University in New York City, Southern Methodist University, the University of Michigan and Pennsylvania State College, in addition to many non-college dates. Humphrey biographer Marcia Siegel claims that Humphrey was the first major choreographer to tour the colleges, her success being due to her invention of the "lecture-demonstration" followed by a performance (Siegel 1987: 166–184).

Figure 36. Chorus of Thebans from *The Antigone* of Sophocles, presented by the Greek Department of Randolph-Macon Woman's College, 1931. Courtesy of Lipscomb Library, Randolph-Macon Woman's College.

There are no reliable figures on the growth of modern dance in American colleges and universities during the Bennington Festival years, ". . . but three surveys conducted between 1937 and 1941 show fifty to seventy-five colleges offering modern dance, most under the aegis of the physical education department . . . Modern dance was by far the most prevalent of all dance forms offered" (Kriegsman 1981: 34–35, 39–125).

The Bennington choreographers fiercely maintained their individual distinctiveness, with intense pressure on company members to be loyal. One did not lightly leave Graham to join Humphrey or vice versa. College teachers, however, were under the constraint of having to offer, and defend to their colleagues, a new field of study called "modern dance." To get it through their Curriculum Committees and win approval by voting Faculty members, dance had to have at least as much discipline as other fields in the curriculum. Whether or not they intended to, the college instructors striving for coherence melded individual styles into a generic modern dance.

The development of a generic modern dance was useful as well outside the campus. Young people who came to New York City on their own to study were obliged to throw in their lot with one or another choreographer, or try by themselves to integrate what they learned at each studio. New choreographers undoubtedly discovered themselves through that effort, but for most it was a daunting project. If college teachers had tried

Figure 37. *The Suppliants* of Aeschylus, presented by the Greek Department of Randolph-Macon Woman's College, 1936. Courtesy of Lipscomb Library, Randolph-Macon Woman's College.

to transmit the separate Graham and Humphrey techniques to their beginners, "collegiate modern" would probably have dissolved. Instead, the development of a generic modern dance smoothed its incorporation into the curriculum.

Equally important for the colleges was the fact that the leading practitioners of modern dance belonged to "the company of educated women" (Solomon 1985). Lectures to students by Martha Graham and Doris Humphrey were accepted by the faculty as being intellectually appropriate for institutions of higher education. That Graham and Humphrey were well read is shown by the intellectual emphasis they placed at the center of their working methods. They often assigned texts of readings to their companies to be studied in connection with dances they were rehearsing. They expected – indeed required – the dancers to understand the cultural content of the dance; it was necessary to good performance.[5]

The performance imperative

For modern dance companies, performing before a public is necessary. "We're performers. We don't perform in closets," says Judith Jamison, Artistic Director of the Alvin

Figure 38. *Cathedral*, from the Dance Recital by the Artist Students of Eleanor Struppa presented by the Physical Education Department of Randolph-Macon Woman's College, 1933. Courtesy of Lipscomb Library, Randolph-Macon Woman's College.

Ailey company (Program of the Public Theatre 1995). Dancers claim they outdo themselves before an audience (Sussmann 1985a). Without the electricity of at least occasional public appearances, no matter how small the audience, rehearsal seems purposeless; morale droops.

Besides colleges, other performance venues included auditoriums and gymnasiums in different institutions as well. In fact, New York City's immense cultural resources allowed the companies to appear in legitimate theatres, as well as in community centers such as the well-known "92nd Street Y" (YMHA), the Neighborhood Playhouse Theatre, the Henry Street Settlement and the St. Bartholomew Community House. A seemingly unlikely venue was the Bedford Hills Montefiore Sanitorium; hospitals, orphanages and other institutions for long-and short-term "shut-ins" engaged them as entertainment for their clients, especially during holidays. From private parties on large estates, where the audience numbered a few dozen, to outdoor concerts along with symphony orchestras, where the audience numbered in the thousands, all engagements were gratefully considered. Not least of the sponsors of modern dance were the private schools, schools of the arts and public high schools of New York City as well as the nearby colleges and universities. Washington Irving High School and the High School of Needle Trades presented modern dance regularly.

Sites such as these, however, did not provide much income. More earnings came from teaching at the choreographers' studios where classes were given for professionals and amateurs. Again, only New York City could furnish sufficient dance aficionadas to fill studio classes. Yet sometimes even that culturally rich city failed to live up to its promise.

Under the auspices of the Federal Theatre Project (FTP) of the New Deal, a short-lived dance project emerged in New York City during the 1930s. Dissension within the Works Progress Administration (WPA) arts programs arose as to whether their goal was providing relief for artists or providing a subsidy for the arts. Eventually, these subsidies were discontinued by Congress, partly because some of its members suspected the FTP of leftist tendencies. A leftist dance movement, in fact, existed in New York:

> By the late 1920s, a radical arts movement had spread to dance, as groups were formed with the political aim of raising class consciousness through dance. Inspired in part by versions of Marxism which called for art to be a tool of agitation and propaganda, early dances focused on the oppression of workers throughout the world . . . Groups such as the Red Dancers, the Rebel Dancers, the Theatre Union Dance Group, and the early version of the New Dance Group performed at union meetings, in May Day parades and political rallies sponsored by the Communist Party and other organizations. (Prickett 1994)

In contrast to leftists, the Bennington choreographers took the position that art and politics were separate; their revolution was aesthetic. Their "art for art's sake" ideology aroused leftist scorn (Prickett 1994). Only a few choreographers, notably Anna Sokolow and Sophie Maslow, bridged the two camps, combining their leftist sympathies with Graham technique.

Also, the line between commerce and fine art was equally imprecise. A number of groups sought their sustenance in commercial theatre. They were following the example of the impresario, Sol Hurok, who had presented Isadora Duncan on national tours in 1920 and 1922, both times with financial success. The venturesome Hurok, who had successfully presented the ballerina, Anna Pavlova, also brought Mary Wigman to the United States on tour in 1931–32 and 1932–33 (Robinson 1994: 86–93,148–153). He promoted Martha Graham on a national tour in 1946, but sold a large number of tickets only in New York City (Prickett 1994: 296–297).

Wigman's success in this country in the thirties was a source of tension for United States modern dancers. They wanted their work to be different from her German Expressionist dance (*Ausdruckstanz*). Doris Humphrey wrote:

> We must remember that German dancing is not for us. We must not copy in this country if we are to develop. Imitation is at once our greatest talent and our greatest vice. (Manning 1993: 261).[6]

Above all else, Hurok's role was as an impresario. His willingness to present Wigman and Graham on continental tours means that he thought they might be successful with large popular audiences, as Pavlova and Duncan had been under his management. Hurok's aspiration suggests that the final definition of modern dance as either popular or high art was still hanging in the balance. His entrepreneurialism was matched on the artistic side by innovative dancers, such as Helen Tamiris, Humphrey, Weidman and Holm, all of whom choreographed for musical comedy. Indeed, Graham, Humphrey and Weidman had earlier toured in vaudeville with Denishawn. Whereas the national vaudeville stage began to wither with the advent of movies, the Broadway musical comedy remained viable. Indeed, for a time, Humphrey hoped that musical comedy would provide her with a living. In the end, however, she gave it up because she did not want to subordinate her choreography to the constraints of collaboration (Siegel 1987: 127–128). Holm, on the other hand, enjoyed collaboration and had a very successful career in musical comedy, as did Tamiris. If more modern dancers had gone into the musical theatre, the "new dance"[7] might have become an ornament of musical comedy rather than an autonomous concert art. Regardless of its trajectory through the institutions associated with high culture, in the work of Holm, Tamiris and others, modern dance also left its mark on American musical comedy dance.

In the end, however, its association with elite women's colleges was what determined the social status of modern dance in the realm of high culture. Not only did the colleges provide venues and income, but they generated modern dance audiences with a cultured liberal arts education. Cohort after cohort of graduating students had seen performances on their campuses, taken classes and, possibly, both composed and performed modern dance themselves. Many continued after college as empathetic spectators.[8]

However, from an institutional standpoint, the colleges' contributions to the life of modern dance were not wholly positive. The fact is that physical education had low status on an academic campus, especially in women's colleges in which football was not an attraction. Keeping it for a long while in Physical Education departments actually tended to marginalize it. Doris Humphrey deplored the situation:

> She allowed herself to complain about the lack of interest that Physical Education sponsors showed in the dancers. In Greeley, she had to teach at one end of a huge gym with acrobats working out at the other end. She knew there were interesting people on campus there but felt isolated as a guest of the "despised" Physical Education Department. (Siegel 1987: 159)

More generally, dance has long been marginalized in Western culture as, on the one hand, a "woman's thing" and, on the other, a thing of the body rather than the mind. Even when embedded among courses in dance history, dance ethnology and dance aesthetics, dance offered by the Physical Education department lacked the academic prestige of "fine art," "serious" music, and literature. Clearly, if its standing was to be elevated, its practitioners would have to cut it out of that foundation.

One of the earliest dance departments to be made independent of Physical Education was established at Randolph-Macon Woman's College in Virginia. The student modern dance company had been a jewel in Randolph-Macon's crown for thirty years, yet granting dance the academic standing of a serious art met with faculty resistance. Finally, when in 1962 the faculty voted that it be severed from Physical Education, they carried the measure by a majority of only one (Randolph-Macon archives, Minutes of Faculty Meeting, December 10, 1962).

The choreographer's company

Despite the ties that linked them, neither the masterpieces of modern dance nor the great stylistic experiments were created in the colleges. Rather it was the one to two dozen small companies in New York City which produced the great early works. The structure of these companies developed mainly as an adaptation to poverty: they had no outside funding. Yet these organizational characteristics were well suited to an avant-garde art.

First, each company was built around the work of a single choreographer. In the beginning, there were no works to be performed. Artists had willy-nilly to compose their own material, and dancers who could not create had to depend on those who could. Consequently, the choreographer was the heart of the company. She founded it to perform her works, and she was its star performer. She gathered dancers around herself, taught them her movements, made dances for the company and arranged engagements to present them. Since she had no material rewards to distribute, other than the possibility of performing, the choreographer had to keep talented dancers in her orbit by sheer personal magnetism.

As a jack-of-all-trades, the choreographer made the artistic decisions and handled the business of the group. Equally important, she was the socio-emotional leader of the company. Her leadership had a determining effect on its cohesion. Early modern dance illustrates well Max Weber's theory that charismatic leaders enable a break with tradition. Powerful personalities who inspire devotion can bestow legitimacy on ideas that are radically new. Ernestine Stodelle's account of Martha Graham's career leaves no doubt as to Graham's charisma:

> In a simple straightforward way they (the company) worshipped her. They never questioned her judgment. They believed every word she said, considering it to be the truth – Martha's truth . . . She was dominated by a vision of the highest order. It was an honor to be dominated by her.
> (Stodelle 1984: 68)

To invent an art using movement not explored in the dance of the past was *the* task of the avant-garde. They were dedicated to the modernist imperatives, "Make it new!" . . . "Astonish me!" Audiences attended their concerts to see the choreographer's latest work, rather than to witness the interpretation of a familiar work by a new performer. The choreography was the thing.

That the first-generation dance groups were the choreographer's companies is in contrast to what happened later. An egalitarian ethos among young people in the sixties invaded dance companies, leading to more participation by the dancers in composing the dance (Sussmann 1985b). Gradually, this development reached a point in some places where, as is now more frequently the case, members of the company compose parts of the dance and the choreographer then puts the parts together. The choreographer still leaves her mark on the dance. Nonetheless, this a very different mode of composition from one which depends on an individual artist; it had significant consequences for the structure of a dance work.[9]

Second, the modern dance companies were small. The prominent companies of the thirties and forties had only twelve to fifteen members (Horosko 1991: 167–171). They were primary groups, based on close, personal relationships. The atmosphere of such a company is conveyed in the following quote from an interview in 1984 with a New York City choreographer. Asked how she felt when a dancer left the company, she said:

It's a huge event in my life and a difficult one . . . I get tremendously attached to them . . . I'm a person with strong feelings and strong attachments. I have strong effects on the dancers . . . It's not a cool relationship. It's not just a job . . . I think it's a very hot relationship.

(Sussmann 1985a: 55)

The antithesis of a primary group in sociological theory is the large secondary group, where relationships are impersonal, people play delimited roles, the group is purposefully organized to achieve specified goals, and members participate mainly for material and prestige rewards and only partly for the intrinsic rewards of the work and the friendships. The School of the American Ballet, as Joan Brady describes it, is a clear example of a secondary group:

We knew hardly anything about each other's lives because (Balanchine) was interested in us as dancers, not as people, and where his interest left off, ours in each other did too.

(Brady 1982: 117, 179)

Third, the community of modern dance companies was tiny. In the thirties their studios were concentrated close together in Manhattan. They shared the same dance roots. Graham and Humphrey came out of Denishawn. Cunningham and Taylor both danced with Graham before founding their own companies. Twyla Tharp danced with Taylor before founding her company and the Judson dancers were rooted in Cunningham. As late as 1958 the *Dance Magazine Annual* listed just 28 modern dance companies (Sussmann 1984: 25). A very small circle of talents, aware of each other's on-going work, created modern dance. In effect, it is almost always a small circle which constructs a new artistic style. Individual genius alone is rarely adequate to that task; it requires closely related work by a group[10] (Mannheim 1940: 84–85). Social support is emotionally necessary too. The indifference of the Establishment is bearable where there is approval by an intimate circle.

Fourth, the earliest companies were subsidized by the unpaid labor of their members. The dancers earned a living through waitressing, teaching, or any job which left them time for a schedule of class and rehearsal. Still more important, since they were young women of the upper middle class, many were supported by indulgent families who thought it was "all right" for a girl to dance in the years between school and marriage. Even if their families did not give them an allowance, they provided the young dancers with a safety net. The dancers' college education, too, provided them with occupational alternatives in case their dance careers should prove disappointing. With these resources, they could afford to spend a few years living in the subculture of "artists' poverty." That subculture persists. The *Poor Dancer's Almanac* is a contemporary guide to survival for dancers without money in New York City (Dance Theatre Workshop Publications 1983).

It is not that the early moderns cherished poverty. On the contrary, they sought funds wherever they might find them, including popular entertainment. They hoped a large, popular audience would come to appreciate their art, but that hope has not been fulfilled. Even supported by government and foundation funding, modern dance attracts an elite audience with college and post-college degrees. In Boston it is substantially better educated than the ballet audience, which itself is in the majority college educated

(Sussmann 1990b). Though governmental and foundation funding have expanded the public for live dance performance to cities in every region of the country, the audience remains predominantly a college-educated group (John Robinson 1993).

While it made existence difficult, poverty gave the first generation, avant-garde, modern dance companies freedom from the constraints of external demands. Whether it comes from public or private sources, support in the form of grants and funds requires its recipients to devote themselves to bureaucratic procedures that take them outside their creative projects. One such constraint is imposed by the requirement of "rational" financial management. Thus if choreographers had their way, they would insist upon countless hours of rehearsal. But few successful choreographers today are able to pay for as much rehearsal time as they feel they and their companies need in order to compose a dance. In contrast, the first-generation choreographers, like the nineteenth-century genius starving in his garret, spent time freely:

> When the rehearsal started, Martha [Graham] . . . faced the open center of the rectangular room...Along the margins of that space, the girls would be stretching quietly on the floor, or staring patiently out the window. Once in a while, Martha would speak. One of the girls would be called into the "sacred" center. Instructions would be given . . . the girl would strike a pattern in the waiting space. A despondent shake of the head . . . would stop her in her tracks . . . And silence would fall again . . . How did it feel to be called to rehearsal and then used so little? This was hard, no doubt, and a far cry from the fast action rehearsal of today when minutes count.
> (Stodelle 1984: 67)

Since they supported themselves, however much they might have preferred otherwise, the first-generation companies were beholden to no outsiders. No grant proposal guidelines bound them. They were not encouraged into "multi-arts collaborations" this year and "service to minority communities" next year by grant allocations contingent on adopting these goals. They were autonomous, the condition essential to an avant-garde.

Conclusion

Early American modern dance was feminist in the sense that it was related to the campaign for women's higher education. Its principal founders, teachers, students and performers were women. While the scenarios the companies danced varied, their way of moving portrayed strong women; they sent a powerful message about the New Woman. Strangely, this message of the movement style was not explicitly discussed at the time, perhaps because there was little in the way of politically organized feminism. The disquiet that early modern dance aroused was due, I believe, to the female assertiveness coded in its style. It is hard today to view a dance like Graham's *Chronicle* (1936) performed by twelve women, without thinking that, while the dance was made as an antiwar protest, it is also about women in revolt.

Modern dance became located in the domain of high culture through its association with privilege. The first women's colleges, which helped to invent and disseminate it, were elite institutions transmitting high culture to young women of high social status.

In the beginning modern dance was structured like most avant-garde arts. The tiny community of small companies was self-supporting, mutually involved, striving to be wholly original while building on each others' discoveries. Their collective work achieved a radical disjuncture with dance tradition, as they intended. Funding in the 1960s by public and private agencies produced an explosion of dance performance in the seventies and early eighties (Sussmann 1984: 23–28; Heilbrun and Gray 1993: 25–26, Table 2.2). But the institutional structure of modern dance has become considerably more complex. Since the late 1980s, as funding has contracted and the community of dance companies has shrunk, modern dance has evolved into a "postmodern" dance with an uncertain future.

The important question about this outsider art, as well as for any fleeting created form, concerns the durability of its situation in the realm of high art. For modern dance, as with dance in general, the problem is whether its masterpieces will be thoughtfully revived, recorded and preserved, both in archives and in performance. Whereas ballets have been preserved through an oral tradition of teaching and demonstrating roles by older to younger dancers, this kind of transmission rests on the relative continuity of ballet companies and, especially, their repertoires. The case of modern dance is different. Its orientation to the new has gone along with the short life of most companies, their discontinuity and a lack of concern for preservation. Only a few modern dances have been transplanted from one company to enough companies, and have been learned by enough dancers, to make their long-term survival a possibility. The idea that "dance is ephemeral" leads to neglect of past accomplishment. Joined to the avant-garde concern exclusively with the future, this may contribute to a self-fulfilling prophecy in which modern dance could vanish as the autonomous high art form it has with such difficulty become.

Notes

I dedicate this essay to the memory of Cynthia Novack, gifted composer, performer, teacher and anthropologist of dance. I thank the National Endowment for the Humanities for the grant that supported this research.

1 In the Postlude to his book, *Wagner Nights*, Joseph Horowitz says, "Wagnerism's residual reach into the early twentieth century was subtle and complex. One area that deserves study is its relationship to modern dance." Horowitz describes Ruth St. Denis and Isadora Duncan as the successors to the proto-feminist Wagner fans of the Gilded Age: "Brunnhilde and Isolde, Lili Lehmann and Lilian Nordica were influences en route to liberation. After 1900, Ruth St. Denis and Isadora Duncan . . . self-expressive, self-created solo dancers were individualists no corps de ballet could have satisfied. In effect, they capitalized on the New Woman's agenda . . ." (Horowitz 1994: 336).

2 The line, "Every little movement has a meaning all its own," memorializes this expressionism. It derives from the title of Ted Shawn's book, *Every Little Movement* (Shawn 1954).

3 For a codification of Humphrey's technique see Stodelle 1990; for Graham's see Horosko 1991.

4 The reader may want to compare the "natural dance" of the 1920s as practiced on the Oberlin campus (see Figures 33, 34 and 35) with the modern dance of the 1930s and 1940s on the

Randolph-Macon campus (see Figures 36, 37 and 38). "Natural dance" is plainly influenced by the many photographic images of Isadora Duncan that circulated in the 20s, while the modern dance of Eleanor Struppa's students looks Grahamesque. Working to look and move like Isadora and then like Graham must have had an effect on these college women's self-conceptions, especially their non-verbal self-images. Movement patterns are an important dimension of self-presentation. Movement can create a psychological state, as well as "express" one. A new way of moving in dance can flow over into daily life, becoming a force for social change and not merely a "reflection" of it.

5 The opposite attitude in the ballet world was one reason for the alienation of the colleges and modern dancers from ballet. Lincoln Kirstein, himself a leading intellectual in the arts world and mentor of George Balanchine, said it succinctly in an interview: "It is the temperament of dancers that they don't require a lot of intellectual stimulation" (Russell 1982: 57). Such an attitude toward the women college graduates in modern dance companies would have been untenable (Sussmann 1990: 21).

6 Susan Manning has called the Benningtonians "humanists" as compared to the "leftist" dance groups (Manning 1993: 265). She finds both feminism and "nationalism" in the humanists' dance as she does in Wigman's. Manning believes a revisionist history of American modern dance is needed to unveil the "nationalism" behind the "art for art's sake" ideology of the Benningtonians and the "constructed" nature of the claim that modern dance is essentially an art created on America.

7 "New Dance" is the title of a composition made by Doris Humphrey in 1935 that for many years served as a synonym for "modern dance."

8 A telling difference between the amateurs of ballet and modern dance lies in the fact that while the audience for ballet is larger (Sussmann 1990b), many more adult students and non-professional performers apparently "do" modern (Robinson 1993, Appendix C: 36–40). A Boston study of the modern and ballet audiences in that city showed the modern dance audience to be much smaller.

9 The contemporary Boston group, the Back Porch Dance Company, works in this way It is also a feminist and inter-generational company. As so often happens, its ideology is implicit both in the group's own organizational structure and in its dances.

10 Because she is very much more famous than other early choreographers it sometimes seems today that modern dance was the sole creation of Martha Graham. However, a number of her contemporaries, especially Doris Humphrey, were very important. Humphrey's movement style includes much that Graham's lacks and vice versa. People attracted to the one are often much less attracted to the other. Together, they make a stronger statement about modern dance's possibilities than does either alone.

References

Beard, George 1869,"Neurasthenia and Nervous Exhaustion," *Boston Medical and Surgical Journal* 3: 217.

Bogue, Lucille 1984, *Dancers on Horseback*, San Francisco: Strawberry Hill Press.

Brady, Joan 1982, *The Unmaking of a Dancer*, New York: Harper and Row.

Dance Theatre Workshop 1983, *Poor Dancer's Almanac*, New York: DTW Publications.

Dewey, John 1916, *Democracy in Education*, New York: Macmillan and Company.

Gay, Peter 1984, *The Education of the Senses*, New York: W.W. Norton.

Heilbrun, James, and Gray, Charles M. 1993, *The Economics of Art and Culture*, New York: Cambridge University Press.

Horosko, Marian 1991, *Martha Graham: The Evolution of Her Dance Theory and Training 1926–1991*, Chicago: A Cappella Books.
Horowitz, Helen Lefkowitz 1985, *Alma Mater*, New York: Alfred Knopf.
Horowitz, Joseph 1994, *Wagner Nights: An American History*, University of California Press.
Kendall, Elizabeth 1979, *Where She Danced*, New York: Alfred Knopf.
King, Eleanor 1978, *Transformations: the Humphrey-Weidman Years*, New York: Dance Horizons.
Kraus, Richard and Chapman, Sarah 1969, *History of the Dance in Art and Education*, Englewood Cliffs, New Jersey: Prentice-Hall.
Kriegsman, Sali Ann 1981, *Modern Dance in America: The Bennington Years*, Boston: G. K. Hall.
Lutz, Tom 1991, *American Nervousness, 1903*, Ithaca and London: Cornell University Press.
Mannheim, Karl 1940, *Man and Society in an Age of Reconstruction*, New York: Harcourt Brace.
Manning, Susan A. 1993, *Ecstasy and the Demon: Feminism and Nationalism in the Dances of Mary Wigman*, Berkeley and London: University of California Press.
Newcomer, Mabel 1959, *A Century of Higher Education for Women*, New York: Harper.
Prickett, Stacey 1994, "Structuring a Dance Realism: Form versus Content in the American Revolutionary Dance," paper for meetings of the American Studies Association.
Program of the Public Theatre 1995, vol. 2, issue 1, December, advertisement.
Randolph-Macon Woman's College 1916–1929, Lipscomb Library, alumnae and staff papers.
Robinson, Harlow 1994, *The Last Impresario: The Life, Times and Legacy of Sol Hurok*, New York: Viking.
Robinson, John P. 1993, *Arts Participation in America: 1982–1992*, National Endowment for the Arts.
Russell, John 1982, "Lincoln Kirstein: A Life in Art," *New York Times Magazine*, June 24: 57.
Ruyter, Nancy 1979, *Reformers and Visionaries: The Americanization of the Art of Dance*, New York: Dance Horizons.
Siegel, Marcia B. 1987, *Days on Earth: The Dance of Doris Humphrey*, New Haven and London: Yale University Press.
Shawn, Ted 1954, *Every Little Movement*, Lee, MA: Shawn.
Solomon, Barbara M. 1985, *In the Company of Educated Women*, New Haven: Yale University Press.
Stodelle, Ernestine 1984, *Deep Song: The Dance Story of Martha Graham*, New York: Macmillan.
1990, *The Technique of Doris Humphrey and its Creative Potential*, Princeton, N.J.: Dance Horizons.
Sussmann, Leila A. 1984, "Anatomy of the Dance Company Boom,1958–1980," *Dance Research Journal* 16/2: 23–28.
1985a,"Social Settings of Modern Dance," unpublished manuscript.
1985b, "The Work of Making Dances," *Sociologie de l'Art*, ed. Raymonde Moulin, Paris, La Documentation Française, 203–12.
1990a, "Recruitment Patterns: Their Impact on Ballet and Modern Dance," *Dance Research Journal* 22/1: 21–28.
1990b, "The Boston Audience for Dance," unpublished manuscript.

12

How many did it take to tango? Voyages of urban culture in the early 1900s

Juan E. Corradi

Choreography and demography

How many did it take to tango?[1] If we glean an answer from the scraps of evidence at our disposal, it would seem that at the beginning (but nobody knows where and when exactly it began [Zlotchew 1989: 273]), it was not two, but one: a lonely man, trying a few complicated steps, as if he were using his feet to write invisible graffitti on the floor. That lonely man only imagined his partner. The tango was, at its inception, a man-dance. And it mattered little that, at a somewhat later point, or simultaneously, a man chose another man to dance with. His male companion was the double of his solitary self, making the absent partner – the woman – all the more vivid in the imagination of each. Those two were not a couple; they were accomplices in a ritual in which the female half of the couple was the virtual *tertius gaudens*, always elsewhere. The two men would concentrate on their steps, on the recognizable patterns of the rite. The feet, the hips, the thighs, and the arched backs performed the rite. Their eyes were averted from each other. The gaze was fixed, intense and, at the same time, empty of desire. A furtive glance, the mere hint of pleasure, any move that could bring the two males close to what Aeschylus, in a less fastidious age, called "the sacred communion of thighs," provoked a duel, sometimes to the death. Far from enacting, or even mocking, any sort of copulation, the tango was an act of elaborate avoidance: it was dancing around something inaccessible.

How many did it take to tango? For men to dance, separately or together, around an absent woman was to choreograph the demography of immigration. Immigration shows an excess of males. This was the case in the United States during the decades of mass immigration, and it was true of Argentina during the same period, when the tango was born. By contrast, western European countries had fewer males than females in their population: In about 1910 there were 94 males to 100 females in England, 97 in France, Germany, and Switzerland, and 98 in Belgium and the Netherlands (Institut International de Statistique 1916: 40–43). The United States had 106 males to every 100 females in 1910, and Argentina 116 in 1914, no doubt because of the impact of immigration (Institut 1919: 40–41). The reason was simple: besides families of immigrants containing the average proportion of the sexes that prevailed in their home country, there came a good many unattached males, both on a seasonal and on a permanent basis. Data gathered on the sex of Italian immigrants to Argentina from 1876 to 1900 show an average preponderance of males by two to one; by 1900 the proportion was three to one (Malaspina 1902).

The imbalance between the sexes fostered an active market in native prostitution. Until approximately 1900 prostitution was a domestic enterprise, a supplement of income purveyed by women to the male "heads" of single or multiple households. Such husbands/pimps exploited, besides their wives, a few other, generally younger, "pupils" whom they had managed to ensnare. To yield an income, the quasi-domestic craft depended on a mixture of personalized coercion and seduction: the women seduced their clients, and the pimp seduced the women to work for him. If and when the women left him to work for someone else, he tended to mourn them (Danero 1971, Tallón 1964). The exploitation of sex was a cottage industry – somewhere between a feudal and a capitalist arrangement. Both the pimp and his "pupils," the boss and the workers, depended on their bodily skills and the management of gender-coded charms. The stereotype of the tango macho owes much to those arrangements: sex, good looks, brute force but also a winning smile, parasitism and sloth, and a tendency towards master/slave relationships which put the possessor of such attributes on the edge of role reversals. In due course, and in a different demographic context – hence, a different market – the macho too could be rented by a rich woman, for a good tip. In the 1920s, the *malevo* ("tough guy") of Buenos Aires became the taxi-boy of Paris (Taxil, no date).

So much changed in just two decades. After 1900, prostitution blossomed into a multinational enterprise, a network of organized crime that started in the *stettls* of Eastern Europe and ended in the brothels of Buenos Aires and the Argentine provinces. Women from Russia, Poland, Turkey, France, and Spain were cheated, trapped, auctioned, and forced to work for large-scale organizations like the infamous Zwi Migdal (Jozami 1930; Londres 1928; Korn 1989: 75–143). The tango became a regular feature in the many brothels of Buenos Aires and its suburbs, where it was danced in the patios of the houses of ill-repute by men alone or with the women who worked inside (Batiz 1908; Montero 1904, Starkenburg n.d.). The bordellos were outlawed in 1919, and this affected the practice and the sites of prostitution. Some brothels continued to function as clandestine establishments. At the same time, many prostitutes found their clients on the streets of the city, or in the palm-lined avenues of Palermo Park (Buenos Aires' replica of the Bois de Boulogne). The cabaret became the center for much of the activity related to the high end of the trade. The tango moved from the outlawed brothels into new urban spaces of entertainment: the Frenchified cabaret and the popular vaudeville theatre. These entertainment centers had a male dominated atmosphere. "Decent women" stayed at home after dark, while "other women" provided entertainment for upwardly mobile middle-class males (Castro 1986: 148). As part of these larger trends in the environment, the early emphasis on dance was replaced by a new emphasis on lyrics, on tango as song, written for a literate audience of a more cosmopolitan city, and reproduced as sheet music to be performed in the cabarets, the popular theatre and on the radio. A cohort of new tango poets emerged. "The false gaiety of the 1920s and the themes related to prostitution and to the cabaret were the primary topics for the tango poets of this era" (Castro 1989: 237).

How many did it take to tango? About the same time, the tango became the rave of cabarets in Paris and other European capitals. There, the demography of the sexes was exactly the reverse. The Great War deprived many women of their husbands, who were fighting at the front. Many women turned to the men who were not yet mobilized. These youths formed, in the words of Armand Lanoux, "le troupeau des gigolos, des hommes-objets" ("the herd of kept men, of men-objects") (Lanoux 1975). After the Armistice in 1918, nearly 20 percent of French soldiers did not come back. Those who returned were damaged, tired, angry men longing for quiet domesticity – a wish that did not exactly fit the habits of independence, self-assurance, and unabashed sexual initiative that women had acquired. The demographic imbalance and the mismatch of desires fostered the proliferation of new places and new practices: the renovated *thés-dansants*, the late dinners at the cabarets, and orgies as well, where a new class of worldly male dancers, with dark eyes and slick hair, were ready to embrace those *femmes desoeuvrées* and lead them on the floor, through stylized tango steps (Marguerite 1922). In an important way, demography had set the stage for Gardel and Valentino.

Representations of mobility

As a cultural manifestation, the tango combines and intertwines in a complex manner several dimensions. It is a piece of music; it can be danced, and it is a song, with a rich repertoire of lyrics. The relationship of the public to the tango is not merely that of a listening – and therefore passive – audience. To dance the tango is to participate in its production. The lyrics of the tango are parables of city life. The tango blurs the distinction between performer and spectator, between musician and listener. This blurring is further enhanced by the self-referential properties of the tango: the lyrics, and the dance, are also about the tango. And, as the saying goes, "everyone's life is a tango." In short the tango is, if I am allowed the use of semiotic jargon, *une structure en abîme*.

The tango often sings its own conditions of production, and the city looms large as the very site, the primal context of those conditions. A perusal of the tango lyrics in currency during the decade of the twenties (when the music of Buenos Aires, as well as the city itself, became sedimented into a more or less complete corpus) reveals a recurrent structure of space and time, a set of constitutive forms of intuition. In terms of time, there is a "before" and an "after." In terms of space, and supporting the division of time, there is "above," and "below," a "center" and a "periphery." These are all firm points of reference – the poles of a narrative that encompasses also intermediate zones, in both space and time: places where the extremes meet, zones of encounter and exchange, moments of transition. Since time flows only between fixed points, it is, in the end, patterned after space, and the entire structure displays the atemporal quality of myth – the myth of an ideal city.

Stylized Buenos Aires, the city of the tango, has several margins – suburbs, *barrios*, *arrabales* – and a center. The margins have both physical and moral characteristics.

They are open spaces – areas of urban defeasance, where the city blends with the countryside, a bit like the River Plate getting mixed with the waters of the sea. Because there is more space between the houses, and the buildings are low, the sky is very present during the day, dominated at night by the moon. Street lighting is weak and does not compete with the older, overwhelmingly rural, sense of the hours and the seasons. In this liminal ecology, the house is the primal structure, the space where the family meets to fulfill its institutional destiny, to enforce love among those whom coupling and the accident of birth have thrown together. Outside the home, there are the street corner and the other homes, that together form the *barrio*; also the mud, the weeds, the stars, the moonlight. These places are strongly cemented together into a sense of community. The *barrio* is the site of the first encounters outside the family, different from the home but also marked by "genuine" affect: first loves, friendships, fights to assert one's honor. Not all the spaces outside the home are in the open. There are enclosed spaces as well, where the rituals of friendship, extramarital love, and catharsis (the avowal of sorrow) are performed. They are: *el cafetín*, or *café de barrio,* places for men alone, where they sit and wait, where they take time to reflect upon existence, and linger over a cup of black, usually bitter, filtered coffee; the *cantina*, more Italian in origin and comportment, where men drink, standing, at the counter, talk, and also purchase goods that could be classified as groceries and hardware; finally, *el cotorro*, a room that is rented and reserved for amorous encounters between men and women, to make love and talk, without hope of forming a family but without the anonymity and barrenness of a cash nexus, for their relationship is not one of prostitution (Juan 1988; Congreso 1917). All those suburban spaces are suffused with sentimentality, but they are also sites of pain, which intrudes into the idealized community.

The deep injuries of class – poverty, exclusion, and abuse, are hard to heal. They push some – especially the young and the handsome of both sexes – to leave. If a woman:

> Se te embronca desde lejos,
> pelandruna abacanada,
> que has nacido en la miseria
> de un convento de arrabal,
> porque hay algo que te vende,
> yo no sé si es la mirada
> la manera de sentarte, de
> mirar, de estar parada,
> o ese cuerpo acostumbrado
> a las pilchas de percal. (Margot)
>
> One can spot you from a distance
> – upstart riff-raff –
> born in the squalor
> of a slum outside town.
> For something gives you away:
> perhaps it is your gaze,
> or the way you sit,

the way you stare, or stand up,
or perhaps it is your body,
so used to wearing percale rags.

If a man:

Sos el mismo que allá por mi barrio
el botón dos por tres encaró
porque había dicho el comisario
que piantaras de aquella sección.
Sos el mismo del negro pañuelo,
sos el mismo del saco cortón,
el del lustre aceitoso del pelo,
prepotente, haragán y matón. (Malevito)

You are the same guy who in my old neighborhood
the cop picked up two or three times,
because the sheriff had told you
to scram from the district.
You are that guy with the black kerchief,
the short jacket,
the slick oily hair
– bossy, a bully, and a sloth.

Mobility is both the promise of a better life and a betrayal of those who stay behind. In this respect, the tango is the ballad of street-corner society: it sings one's second thoughts about making it. It asks time and again: Is it really success? The tango bemoans, or denounces, mobility as fraudulent because it sings only movements of a special kind – the movements of the body as a site of pleasure: dressing, parading, dancing, drinking, doing drugs, and making love. If a woman:

Ese cuerpo que hoy se marca
los compases tentadores
del canyengue de algún tango
en los brazos de algún gil
mientras triunfa tu silueta
y tu traje de colores
entre el humo de los puros
y el champán de Armenonvil. (Margot)

Your body – today – follows
the daring steps
of a tango beat,
held in the arms of some sucker,
while your figure is victorious
and with your colorful dress you bask
in the smoke of good cigars
and Armenonvil's champagne.

If a man:

> Hoy parás en el Domínguez,
> te vestís a la alta escuela,
> jugás fuerte a la quiniela
> y hasta San Carlos te vás.
> Si caés a una carpeta
> hacés temblar al banquero.
> ¡Parecés el Trust Joyero
> por las joyas que cargás! (Malevito)
>
> Today, you hang out at Domínguez's;
> you dress in high style,
> gamble hard at the numbers,
> and you even frequent San Carlos.
> When you hit the casino,
> the house trembles at your sight.
> You look like a jewelry shop,
> with all the gems that you carry.

The tango never addresses conventional mobility, of the inter-generational kind, based on either educational and occupational advance. It addresses only a special sacrificial short-cut: the venue of a more or less disguised prostitution. The saga of the anti-hero then begins. A teenage girl from the *barrio*, already somehow predisposed to "take off," is picked up by an upper-class playboy, is seduced, and starts a new moral career as a kept woman in *el centro*. Her days are spent in the flat that has been rented for her, the *garçonnière*, and her nights are spent at the cabaret. The *centro* – the *garçonnière* – and the cabaret are intermediate zones, places where the high and the low meet, where spurious mobility takes place, and where the decadence of the characters begins. In these spaces the woman displays an adorned body. She is dressed and bejewelled:

> Justo a los catorce abriles
> te entregastes a la farra,
> las delicias del gotán.
> Te gustaban las alhajas,
> los vestidos a la moda
> y las farras del champán. (Flor de Fango)
>
> Just when you turned fourteen,
> you abandoned yourself to the fun,
> to the delights of tango-dance.
> You liked wearing jewels,
> dressing up,
> and partying with champagne.
>
> Empilchada,
> la boca pintada,
> cepillo de dientes,
> las uñas lustradas.
> Hoy vive en Corrientes,

muy bien instalada,
con baño caliente,
como una cocot. (Cocot de Lujo)

Decked out,
with lipstick on,
with toothbrush,
polished nails,
she now lives on Corrientes street,
in a good pad,
with a hot bath,
like a French call-girl.

Her easy smile, aided by champagne, if not cocaine, betrays a secret hurt:

Enviciada,
tomando pavadas
porque es deprimente
no andar endrogada
como anda la gente
que es bien educada. (Cocot de Lujo)

She is full of vices,
she takes silly stuff,
she reckons it's bad
not to do drugs
like all the fancy folk.

Her happiness is as shallow as it is short. She slides down into a hell of degradation, first as cheap cocotte, and finally as a bitter and wasted hag:

Después fuiste la amiguita
de un viejo boticario,
y el hijo de un comisario
todo el vento te sacó . . .
Y empezó tu decadencia,
las alhajas amuraste
y una pieza alquilaste
en una casa e'pensión.
Te hiciste tonadillera,
pasaste ratos extraños
y a fuerza de desengaños
quedaste sin corazón. (Flor de Fango)

Then – you became the girlfriend
of an old pharmacist,
and then, the police chief's son
took all of your dough;
you started going downhill;
you walled up your jewels,
and took a room

in a boarding house.
You walked the streets,
had some rough times,
and so many disappointments
finally broke your heart.

If she is a he, the saga is not so different. He starts as a young and tough *malevo* who pleases women but holds them at arm's length:

Era un malevo buen mozo
de melena recortada;
las minas le cortejaban
pero él las trataba mal.
Era altivo y le llamaban
el Taita del Arrabal. (El Taita del Arrabal)

He was a good-looking tough guy
with a well-trimmed mane;
the chicks came up to him,
but he treated them bad.
He was haughty, and so they called him
the Boss of the Slum.

At some point he too becomes seduced by the world of the cabaret, of easy money, in return for sexual favors as gigolo. His clothes are finer, but also more effete. He does not dance the tango as he used to in the brothels, with *corte*, but in a softer, easy way: "the French way." Which means that, for a sort of metatango that many of these tangos construct, the tango that moved to Paris followed a similar path of moral decay:

Pero un día la milonga
lo arrastró para perderlo:
usó corbatita y cuello,
se emborrachó con Pernod,
y hasta el tango arrabalero
a la francesa bailó. (El Taita del Arrabal)

But one day by dint of dancing
he was lost.
He wore a tie and a collar;
he got drunk on Pernod,
and he even did the tango
the French way.

For a while the *malevo*, now just a *malevito*, "looks like" the rich playboys who feign to be his pals, but he too ends without love, without money, and without friends:

Cuando empiece a nevarte en el mate
y la línea entrés a perder,
si no has hecho como la hormiguita.
¡Malevito! ahí te quiero ver,
sin amor, sin afecto, sin nada

que en el mundo te haga de puntal.
Malevito tal vez sea ésa
la venganza del triste arrabal.(Malevito)

When your hair turns snow white,
and a paunch spoils your shape,
if you did not save enough like the little ant,
then I'll see you, tough boy,
without love, without affection, with nothing
to prop you up in this world.
Maybe that is, tough boy,
the revenge of the sad slum.

La linda vida antigua
por otra abandonó
y cuando acordarse quiso
perdido se encontró.
Pobre Taita, muchas noches,
bien dopado de morfina,
atorraba en una esquina
campaniao por un botón.
Y el que antes daba envidia
ahora daba compasión. (El Taita del Arrabal)

He left the old ways
for a different life,
and before he knew it
he was lost.
Poor Boss, many a night.
high on morphine,
he hung out in the corner,
tailed by a cop.
He who once was the envy of many
inspired pity at the end.

Tango lyrics tell the story of spurious mobility that takes the characters from the painful but authentic world of the *barrio* or the *arrabal* to the dangerous and mundane space of the *centro* where the familiar signifiers are lost, and new, free-floating, signifiers take their place. Worldliness is a mirage where the men and women of the *arrabal* get lost. There is an erotic exchange with figures of the upper class, who also act *extra muros*. But the tango does not represent the structured, "normal" habitat of the upper class. The tango was danced, quite early, and of course clandestinely, in the very rooms of the sumptuous homes, but, unlike the modest rooms and patios of the *conventillos* (tenements), the abodes of the rich are not described or evoked by tango lyrics. The record of the early incursions of the tango in those mansions are found not in songs but in the memoirs and recollections of the upper class.

Who narrates these stories with such sorry endings? It is the voice of someone – generally a man – who has stayed behind, rooted in the *barrio*, but with a panoramic and disabused perspective on the illusions and dangers of mobility – a mix between

Tiresias and Cassandra. The narrator's pose is a moral suit that anyone can wear. It makes one feel, if not happy, at least reassured in the affirmation of traditional values. The tale of (apparent) social success and elevation is balanced by the counterweight of moral degradation. The end in loneliness or death restores the broken social equilibrium, and avenges the betrayed suburb. Most tangos put together form a polyphonic odyssey, in which the *barrio* is the poor man's Ithaca. Always pessimistic and often also cynical, tango lyrics project, in their individual parts and as a whole, a deeply conservative world view (Castro 1986: 147).

By dint of repetition, the basic elements of tango lyrics become tedious. The morphology of the tango tale is simple: low/high, periphery/center, spurious success/failure. The tale is wrapped in an aura of resignation. Is there a way, within the very terms of the tale, to escape the gloomy fate, to make the formula work, not as a bitter revenge of the *arrabal* upon the hero who has transgressed, but as a (vicarious) collective revenge of the *arrabal* upon the *centro*, and hence, indirectly, upon the upper classes? There is indeed a way, but it depends on a further escalation of the strategy of representation. The sung becomes the singer. The successful tango star controls the cabaret, instead of being its victim. He will seduce the upper class, instead of being seduced by it. As singer and performer he will represent the world of the arrabal in a complex, almost political way. Instead of betraying his origins, he will redeem them. His millions, his car, his champagne, his entire life will be admired, and endorsed by those "left behind" in a physical not moral way. He will become "our man" up there. This happened with Gardel. *El morocho del abasto* ("the dark kid from the Central Market") became "our *Gardelito*."

The tango's cosmopolitan round trips

Buenos Aires es una gran ciudad. Yo siempre añoro tanto esas calles, los amigos . . . pero, en verdad, cuando me encuentro en ella me dan deseo de volverme, de irme lejos . . .

No te vayas, quédate aquí y volvé a Buenos Aires de cuando en cuando, como hago yo, como quien va a visitar los restos de una novia querida, que se lleva en el corazón y a quien no se puede olvidar.

Buenos Aires is a great city. I always miss those streets, my friends . . . but, to tell you the truth, when I am there I want to take off again, go far away . . . Don't go back; stay here and visit Buenos Aires from time to time, like I do, like someone who goes to visit the grave of a dear sweetheart whom he cannot forget. (Carlos Gardel to Julio de Caro, in Paris, 1929)

The great success of the tango in Paris, whence it spread through the rest of Europe, is one of the most colorful patches in the crazy quilt of the 1920s, when it truly came into its own as valid and universally known music. It was only matched, and preceded, by the success of jazz. But whereas jazz had, as a logistical backdrop, the support of the many Americans who had arrived in France as fighting troops, and who had decided to stay after the Armistice, the music of Buenos Aires counted only on the tenacity of a few musicians who had crossed the ocean, plus the nostalgic fidelity of diplomats (from Argentina, Peru, Uruguay) and a substantial community of free-spending expatriates (some 5,000 in those days) who liked to patronize the cabarets of Pigalle (Kaspi and Mares 1989: 14). These *argentins de Paris* – somewhat profligate and rather well connected – gave the tango the needed boost, as a ready-made audience.

In the twenties the tango acquired a wider, more diverse audience. The music started to attract fans from all walks of life. It evoked toughness, exoticism, and sex. The themes were: nostalgia, solitude, lost love, erotic resentment, the passing of time (*le temps perdu*). The Parisian cabarets produced a new myth for Buenos Aires, a bizarre but effective bricolage of rhythms, lyrics, and costumes borrowed a bit from everywhere (Leenhardt and Kalfon 1992: 44), and embodied in the figure of a slick and irresistible Latin *gigolo de luxe* – even though some of the quintessential Argentine machos were born in Naples or Toulouse.

The music was strong. It could be listened to (though the lyrics, in Paris, were seldom understood) but also danced. Part of its secret, like jazz, is that it demands to be felt. Enrique Santos Discepolo, a celebrated composer, described the tango as "a sad thought that one can dance." It was ideal material for cabarets. These centers of night life became the cornerstone of a system that extended far beyond it, through the new techniques of reproduction of sound and image: the gramophone record and the cinema.

In Paris, the tango assumed a new folkloric persona, fabricated with elements that had little to do with the original article. Because of regulations designed to protect French performers from foreign competitors in situ, the latter were required to present themselves on stage dressed in their "national costumes," not as regular musicians but as *artistes de variétés*. They were thus legally forced to stereotype themselves. The French state had in fact sanctioned a social pressure that every expatriate has experienced in his or her host country: to become the expected caricature of him or herself. Argentine tango players appeared dressed as gauchos – which was tantamount to having jazz players wear cowboy chaps. In exchange for this travesty, Paris gave the tango something more precious: it gave the tango world renown, it made it chic, fashionable, legitimate. Success in Paris meant that all barriers to its acceptance back home, in Buenos Aires, would be dropped. The tango of Buenos Aires became truly Argentine only after it became the rave in Europe: first in Paris, then Barcelona, Rome, Athens, Moscow, and Berlin.

The transvaluation of the tango, the process of its simultaneous distortion and legitimation in Europe, had begun more timidly in Paris a good decade before the "crazy years" – in the fullness of a gentler belle époque. Nobody knows exactly how and when the music was introduced in France. At best, there are a few hunches and anecdotal hints, mostly the recollections and musings of musicians like Francisco Canaro, whose memoirs venture two or three versions of the first voyage of the tango from Buenos Aires to Paris (Canaro 1957). The first, and more attractive, version, has the tango titled *La Morocha* (composed by Enrique Saborido) transported and distributed by the officers of the Argentine tall ship, the frigate *Sarmiento*, in one of her early circumnavigations at the turn of the century. The second version is a variant of the first: the tango in question was not *La Morocha* but *El Choclo* (authored by Angel Villoldo), and it was distributed clandestinely by the crew, and not the officers, of the ship. The third version is more banal. A French businessman visited, on a trip to Buenos Aires, a tango parlor of dubious repute, where he heard *El Choclo*. In a fit of enthusiasm, he acquired several copies of the sheet music and took them to France.

These stories put the arrival of the tango in Paris sometime during the first decade of the century. Other conjectures by tango historian Horacio Salas suggest that the tango arrived neatly with the century. In 1900, the Uruguayan singer and composer Gobbi was left stranded in Paris, when the theatre company for which he worked dissolved. Forced to earn his keep through odd jobs, it is quite likely that he played tangos in the cabaret circuit – mixed, no doubt with other more conventional music pieces. But if this part of Gobbi's life is shrouded in the mysteries of his mediocrity, some later episodes can be ascertained with more precision. Gobbi went back to South America. In 1905 he married the Chilean singer Flora Rodríguez. In 1907 the great Buenos Aires department store Gath and Chaves, sent the couple to Paris with the mission of recording their voices on gramophone discs. They travelled in the company of the composer Villoldo, and stayed seven years, during which they composed tangos, taught people how to dance them, and worked for the music firm of Pathé (Salas 1986: 112–113), recording comic dialogues and Argentine country music, plus some tangos.

As a last shred of information about the arrival of the tango in Paris, we can report that Ms. Georgette Leroy, the widow of tango pianist Alberto López Buchardo, told a newspaperman from *La Prensa* in 1953 that, fifty years before, in 1903, her husband and the writer Ricardo Güiraldes had danced the tango, as a demonstration, in Paris. Yet, given the advanced age of the lady, and other statements by her in the same interview, she could have meant 1913 instead of 1903. Be that as it may, and considering the upper class extraction of both Messrs. López Buchardo and Güiraldes, it could well have been they who appear demonstrating the tango in an elegant Parisian salon, circa 1905, in a silent short film which is kept in the Paris Cinémathèque. If that is so, then one of the two gentlemen was in drag. Yet other details of the film suggest otherwise, namely that this "first" tango was danced by a real couple, except that they were both cross-dressed, as if to stress the perverse aura of the novelty that surrounded the music. In any event, the figures in the background who watch, with an air both refined and blasé, the strange convolutions of the transvestite couple on the dance floor, could well have been Anna de Noailles, Marcel Proust, and Robert de Montesquiou.

Whatever mysteries surround the arrival of the tango in Paris, one thing is certain: whereas in Buenos Aires its origins were in the modest brothels of the suburbs, in Paris, the début took place primarily in aristocratic circles (Bioy 1963: 181) before it reached the circuit of cabarets (Leenhardt and Kalfon 1992: 42). At the beginning, "proper" Argentines, and diplomats in particular, were shocked at the ready acceptance of the tango among the beau monde. Europeans, for their part, did not understand what the fuss was all about. In a letter to Victoria Ocampo, written at the beginning of 1914, Count Pier Desiderio Pasolini, an elderly Italian senator, had this to say:

> . . . And the tango? There is much talk about it, did you know? The Argentine Ambassador in Paris has declared that it is a completely special dance, limited to plebeians, to the lowest and most corrupt classes of Buenos Aires, who exist, of course, in that city as in all large capital cities, but Argentina cannot admit that the tango be considered the national dance of the Argentine people.

The Church authorities, the bishops, have forbidden it in France, and henceforth it is also banned in all of Italy as something immoral and dangerous for good morals. It is possible, however, that so many protests and prohibitions have actually helped advertise the tango, because it is danced everywhere.

One night, after dinner, I was at the Excelsior Hotel in Rome, watching other people dance. What they danced did not seem to me different from any other dance. It is true that I have never danced, not even when I was young, and I am not a good judge in the matter. I thought that what I was observing was just another dance, when someone warned me that it was a tango. I was not particularly impressed, and could not understand what the fuss was all about.

(Ocampo 1965)

Despite the vast distance that separated those two worlds – European aristocracy and Argentine low life – they had something in common: they had little to do with ordinary men and women, they were ex-centric to the worlds of the family and regular jobs (Salas 1986: 120–121). It was only in the late twenties that the tango was received, and finally accepted, by the working and the middle classes as "their" music. This "popular" music form came in fact, from the sides to the middle, from the extremes to the center. And in such displacements and metamorphoses, the comings and goings, the return journey Buenos Aires–Paris–Buenos Aires, played a crucial role. But the generalized triumph of the tango, beyond the fancy milieux, was a bit more hazardous.

At the beginning of the fateful year of 1914, as war approached, four young Argentines – three musicians and one dancer – decided to build upon, and expand, the previous attempts, in 1912, by another dancer and composer – Enrique Saborido – to introduce and teach the tango to the Parisian public. The newcomers were Celestino Ferrer, Eduardo Monelos, Vicente Loduca, and Casimiro Ain. The first three formed a tango trio, while Ain demonstrated the dance steps. They started a show on the first floor of 6 bis, rue Fontaine, at a cabaret, then called "Princesse." Years later, it was given the Argentine slang name of "El Garrón" ("The Pimp," according to Andrade and San Martin 1967: 39). At the same address, at street level, functioned the theatre "Deux Masques," which later on would also become a tango cabaret, with the name "Palermo." After the Great War, these cabarets, and a few others, would form a well known network of tango places in Montmartre (Cadícamo 1975: 19–20). But 1914 was a bad time for the musicians, and their luck soon ran out. One of them left for Brazil, where he found a job as a juggler. Another fell gravely ill, returned to Buenos Aires, and died soon thereafter, of tuberculosis. A new *bandoneonista*, called Filipotto, replaced the sick man. But the war made their situation precarious, if not outright dangerous, and did not augur well for business at the "Princesse."

The pioneers finally left for New York, prompted by a Mr. Ryan, an American who owned horses which he raced at Longchamps, Auteuil, and Chantilly, and who promised to help them in Manhattan. New York would prove, alas, even more indifferent than Paris (Malnig 1992: 47). They were only offered odd jobs that had nothing to do with music. In this indifference they shared a room in a tenement on Tenth Avenue, with a fifteen-year-old Italian immigrant, very handsome, Rodolfo Guglielmo d'Antonguolla. This young bricklayer would make, seven years later, a name for himself in the movies (Malnig 1992: 27–28). The high hopes for the tango that began in Montmartre thus ended, rather shabbily, in Hell's Kitchen. Only with the end of the war would Paris become ready to listen again, and to applaud. A few years after the Armistice, the same Antonguolla would "fake," with exquisite grace, a few tango steps, with Jean Acker, in the same old cabaret of Montmartre, the "Princesse" – now "El Garrón," and to great success. The young man's name was now Rodolfo Valentino. *Le tango argentin* for the general public was then born.

The "roaring twenties" were the golden age of ocean liners, and Bordeaux and Marseille were the two principal ports that connected France to Buenos Aires. In 1920, the *Garonne* discharged in the port of Marseille two Argentine musicians holding a contract to work at a local cabaret, called "Tabarin." Their names were Genaro Exposito and Manuel Pizarro, and they played for a French orchestra directed by a M. Lombard. They received the meager sum of 50 francs per day. Pizarro would not last long: after a short time, he was released from the contract after having reimbursed M. Lombard the 500 pesos (well over 1,500 francs) the latter had invested in Pizarro's round-trip ticket. At the Gare Saint Charles, Pizarro boarded a train for Paris, where he would soon become the Diaghilev of *le tango argentin*.

The culture of the twenties cannot be understood, in Europe, except in terms of the shock and horror that preceded it. The Great War seemed even more repulsive when seen in retrospect. It had definitively shattered the facile illusions of progress in which Europeans had basked at the turn of the century. Those illusions ended in a sudden, senseless carnage of vast proportions. They lay buried in the trenches and mass graves. After the War, the spirit that presided over the work of reconstruction was the passion to forget. When prosperity arrived again, it prompted, among the rich, a propensity to spend that went far beyond the conspicuous consumption of the 1890s. The twenties would engage, instead, in frenetic, anxious spending, as interpreted by Georges Bataille and the Surrealists. It was the era of the metropolis. Three cities marked it, as the favored sites of cultural experimentation and social change: Berlin, Paris, and New York. New York was the new Babel, and Berlin Babylon. They were characterized, essentially, as *villes-chantiers* (cities under construction) – the very embodiment of speed, boldness, efficiency, utopia. Paris, however, had not physically changed. The war had not ravaged it: neither Big Bertha nor the Zeppelins produced much rubble, or too many dead. Plans for radical reform were shelved. The city remained her Haussmannian self. Le Corbusier's radical proposal to build 18 towers in the middle of the city did not prosper: it won him the reputation of murderer of the past. Parisians preferred to redefine the urban space rather than rebuild it. They embraced novelty in something other than plaster and stone: primarily in the arts, fashions, and mores.

Buenos Aires too progressed, but culturally lagged behind. Argentina had been spared the War. As in all the major conflicts of the century, the country remained neutral – a position that suited not only the Argentines but the European belligerents as well. Buenos Aires consolidated its European look, but tended to wallow in the complacency of her mimicked *juste milieu* (mediocrity). It became a spectator-city of the periphery – in strict geopolitical terms, a rich European suburb, complacent, as if assenting to Borges's opinion (Borges 1972):

Figure 39. "Photograph of Argentine tango (dance)." Buenos Aires, *c.* 1920–21. Call # MGZEA #1. The Dance Collection, the New York Public Library for the Performing Arts. Astor, Lenox and Tilden Foundations

Ahí está Buenos Aires. El tiempo que a los hombres
Trae el amor o el oro, a mí apenas me deja
Esta rosa apagada, esta vana madeja
De calles que repiten los pretéritos nombres.

There is Buenos Aires. Time, which brings to men
love or gold, merely left for me
this faded rose, this futile skein
of streets which repeat the bygone names.

As for novelty, Buenos Aires exported it in the form of a cultural commodity. The tango was her unwitting gift to Europe and the world. When Pizarro arrived in Paris from Marseille, he went straight to the foothills of Montmartre, where he took a room in the modest Hôtel Pigalle (55, rue Montmartre). Henceforth, that address became the hub of tango musicians from the River Plate. Ferrer, Filipotto, Ain and Chutto were already there, back from not making it in New York. They used the little hotel to deepen their friendship, to exchange experiences and information, and to build a network of contacts that could turn into contracts. The first contacts made by the aspiring musicians were with young members of the community of affluent Argentines, especially those who made the rounds of the nightclubs as part of their lives of leisure and adventure in a city that offered all sorts of pleasures for foreigners at prices that seemed low and which the favorable exchange rate made even more attractive (*Le Figaro* 1920). These high living Argentines were avid consumers of champagne: not just the simple Pommery, but also the famed 1914 vintage of Veuve Cliquot *rouge*. The fact was not lost on Monsieur Elio Volterra, owner of the "Princesse," when he met Pizarro at the behest of Vicente Madero, the wealthy scion of an elite family of Buenos Aires, known by all the waiters for his spectacular tips, and enthusiasm for the tango (Ocampo 1965: 15). It occurred to M. Volterra that giving the musicians a chance to play the tango, unpaid and on probation, in his establishment, could please the *porteño* (denizens of Buenos Aires) clientele that arrived around midnight.

For the cabarets of those days led a double life. Before midnight, their clientele was humdrum: salesmen from the *grands magasins* in search of adventure, call-girls and gigolos. After midnight, the big spenders arrived, and the expensive bubbly flowed. The decor changed. The atmosphere turned elegant, worldly, even ceremonious. Many diplomats attended. To please the Argentines, the supper that was served after the show included dishes from back home: steak, the pot-au-feu called *puchero,* with corn on the cob and bone marrow. The men wore dinner suits, the women of the elite wore dresses by Christian Dior and jewels by Lacloche. As Argentine males caught the fancy of the French demi-mondaines, scenes of jealousy by the offended wives were not infrequent.

The promise of a trial show at the "Princesse" energized Pizarro, who summoned his friend Volterra from Marseille. Within a week Pizarro had formed a tango orchestra, with an Argentine core composed of himself at the piano, a violinist, and three accordeon players. The rest were French musicians. He also suggested that, at least for the occasion, the cabaret's name be changed to "El Garrón." The request was honored, the orchestra started its rehearsals, and the requisite gaucho garments were commissioned, in order to satisfy the requirements of the union of French musicians (part of the French Veteran's Union) that foreign players be dressed in "national costume." The tango would be presented to the public as a folkloric attraction. The owner of the cabaret made sure that his select Argentine clientele was invited and spared no effort to provide an appropriate *mise en scène*: red velvet, special blue lighting, spots on the musicians and their instruments, a carefully staged assortment of tables, placed according to the rank of the guests. Past midnight, they arrived: the members of the resident elite of Argentines, playboys, de luxe tourists, sympathisers, and the Argentine Ambassador himself: Marcelo T. de Alvear, accompanied by his wife Regina Paccini. The opening tango was *El Entrerriano*. Its last chords were swamped by applause. Many others followed, until the early hours of the morning. Pizarro had prepared a repertoire that included the latest pieces from Buenos Aires, many of which made reference to France: *El Marne*, *Sans Souci*, *La Cumparsita*, *La Tablada*, *El Cencerro*, *Agua Bendita*, and *Chique*. Most of the audience stayed till the very end. The show ended with a real ovation. The doors of Montmartre were now wide open for the tango.

The first tango show was, nevertheless, a bit contrived. It was a ceremony of recognition and validation, an exercise in nostalgia – real, perhaps, for the Argentines, and vicarious for the French. But nobody had *danced*. Like every good host, Pizarro knew that clients and guests have to be prompted with finesse to take to the dance floor, in particular to the sounds of a very exotic melody. The genius of an impresario consists, besides charm, of an uncanny alertness to opportunity. And opportunity came on the night of the second show. Rodolfo Valentino and Jean Acker were sitting at one of the tables. Very few people in Paris then knew the novice actor from Hollywood (he had just finished acting in "Out of Luck" and "Passion's Playground"). Valentino was better known in the night clubs of Los Angeles, as dancer of *sui generis* tangos. He too liked to dress in gaucho garb for those displays. Argentina/gaucho/tango formed one set in the image repertoire of the showbiz of the twenties. Pizarro, with a good intuition of suspense, asked for a pause, told the audience who was among them, then turned the spot-light on Valentino, and asked the "rising star" to demonstrate the tango. Valentino, for whom this was an opportunity too, led Jean Acker to the dance floor and started moving to the compass of *El Choclo*. His steps would not have passed muster in any of the dance academies of Buenos Aires, let alone satisfy the standards of the famous El Mocho, but they were perfect for Paris, for they were easy to imitate. Others soon joined them on the dance floor, and soon many Parisians would feel experts in the art of performing a parody of the dance. The tango became the occasion in which Paris mimicked Buenos Aires. Henceforth, at "El Garrón" the tango was the main attraction every night, only followed by jazz.

Pizarro's great accomplishment was not just the correct steering of the tango through to success, but, and more important, the assembly of a complex organization to consolidate and expand that succcess. He called on his four brothers, also players of tango, and two other musicians, from Buenos Aires. They formed the solid core of the cabaret's *orquesta típica* (standard tango band). Stung by "El Garrón's" tango hit, other cabarets followed suit, and started playing tangos as part of their shows. Pizarro soon placed his brothers at the head of new "satellite" tango orchestras in some of these night clubs. Pizarro's success in the cabaret circuit allowed him to try something more ambitious, namely the presentation of the music of Buenos Aires on a national, republican stage. Every year the Paris Opera organized a music show for the benefit of the Patronat de l'Enfance. It was called *le bal des petits lits blancs* (ball of the little white beds). Many French stars performed, and the highest authorities attended. In 1920, Pizarro managed to be asked to open the show, with *La Cumparsita*. From that moment on, the tango bore the highest official seal of approval, and *La Cumparsita* became, to this very day, its flagship. The public roared and asked for more. The Spanish star Antonia Mercé, already well-known in Paris, danced both *El Choclo* and a very different "tango": a classical Spanish piece by Isaac Albéniz.

For the tango to have traveled the distance, within a period of six or seven months, from Buenos Aires to Paris, and within Paris, from Pigalle to the Opera House, was no mean feat. Pizarro deserved most of the credit: he combined with supreme confidence the art of the stage with the management of the backstage. He secured music of good quality while he ceaselessly built a support network for it. He was a headhunter and an impresario. In short, Pizarro intuitively understood that popular art was a form of collective action, an iceberg-like structure of which actual performance was the small visible (and audible) part. Pizarro published the tangos he composed with Garzon, a publisher in the rue de l'Echiquier, and recorded many others for the gramophone, with Pathé. He joined SACEM, the copyright association, so as to secure royalties, which in

Figure 40. "The Valentinos, in an Original Dance, 'The Russian Tango': Rudolph Valentino and His Wife, Natacha Rambova Hudnut, in Their Exotic New Dance," *Vanity Fair*, February 1923 issue, photograph by Abbe. Courtesy *Vanity Fair*, copyright © 1923 (renewed 1951) Condé Nast Publications Inc.

a few years would become quite significant. He even devised an ingenious stratagem to promote tangos: he rented a truck for his orchestra and played at a number of street corners one 14th of July. Parisians learned to dance the tango on the streets, on the boulevards, and on the public squares. Pizarro also colonized other cabarets and nightclubs by having each one of his four brothers head an orchestra at such places as the "Hermitage" in Champs Elysées, the "Hermitage" at Longchamps (near the race track), the "Washington Palace" in the rue de Magellan, not far from the Etoile, and at the Claridge Hotel in the 8th arrondissement. His friend Casimiro Aín trained a woman from Marseille to be his partner in dance, and together they set up a tango school, and also gave private lessons in their homes to people of means. Last, but not least, Pizarro taught two Spanish singers and a Peruvian – Gracia del Río, Eva del Erso, and Alina – to be tango vocalists in his orchestra. In short, Pizarro "touched all the bases" to secure the promotion of the tango and its reproduction as a musical form.

In 1922, Marcelo T. de Alvear, the Ambassador of Argentina in Paris who graced "El Garrón," was elected President of his country. The President-elect, who was described by critics as "he who goes to all the parties," sent his secretary to invite Pizarro, with his full orchestra, to join him on board the liner *Massilia*, for his triumphal homecoming (Korn 1989: 19–20). Pizarro hesitated, for fear of putting his hard-won achievements in Paris at risk. But he had done sufficient groundwork to allow himself a grand interruption. He accepted the invitation, and joined the presidential party in the port of Bordeaux on August 19, 1922. With Alvear, Pizarro, and the tango, Parisian Buenos Aires returned to Argentina. The voyage was pleasant, with good seas. The ship was new, and quite luxurious (*La Razón* 1922). There were parties, conversations, entertainments, plus grand receptions awaiting Alvear and his entourage in Rio de Janeiro and Montevideo. The tango was played and danced during the passage. The *Massilia* finally docked in Buenos Aires on September 4. Waiting at the pier stood the outgoing president and radical caudillo Hipólito Yrigoyen and a large crowd. The sound of many sirens, the honking of car horns, and the flight of a thousand pigeons greeted the passengers. Alvear went home, not far from the port, near Plaza San Martin – the same Parisian *barrio norte* (the elegant Northern section of Buenos Aires) that saw him grow up as a child and that would see him decline in old age. Pizarro had farther west to go, to his *barrio* of the Abasto (the Central Market of Buenos Aires) – the haunts of family and friends, of Calabrian taverns and tango players, among them Gardel. Both men, the president and the impresario, were at the peak of their success. They would see each other again, during Alvear's inauguration on October 12. Alvear had a country to run. He would return to Paris six years later, after his term of office. In the meantime, his beloved *manoir du Coeur Volant* would wait, basking in the foliage and the light of Marly-le-Roi. Pizarro had a business to run, in Paris. After two months in Buenos Aires, he went back. Now a man of means, he rented a spacious apartment at a prestigious address: 93, Boulevard Haussmann, next door to the Argentine consulate, close to the Chapelle expiatoire (the memorial chapel for Louis XVI) and not far from the building across the street, where Marcel Proust had lived until 1919.

Thanks to Pizarro's efforts, the popularity of the tango spread far and wide between

1922 and 1925. More Argentine musicians arrived from Buenos Aires – among them one of the most admired composers, Arolas. Other names were: Schumaker, Bianco, Cosenza, Bachicha, Pettorossi, Contursi. The tango conquered more nightclubs. Their names: Capitol (rue Notre Dame de Lorette), Le Perroquet (rue de Clichy), Le Narguilé (rue Frochot), Palermo, and many others. By 1925 the tango was more than music, it was a style, a fad, a signature: one could read, in advertisements "couleur tango," "thé-tango," "Champagne-tango," "Whisky-tango," and similar silly terms. Everything associated with the dance – the melancholy looks, the slicked-down hair style pasted *a la gomina* (pomade), of idealized macho stars – was suddenly chic. In 1925, an elegant cad from Buenos Aires, aged 25, who did the round of cabarets, introduced that hair-fixer for men. He was Carlitos Arce. When properly applied, the perfumed glue left the hair smooth, stretched, and shiny. The hair was combed backward, and it was parted on one side with razor-like precision. For a man who chose the style, the Ebony effect contrasted with the pale face and white teeth, but matched the solemn black of the tuxedo, and of the patent-leather shoes. If the man was young, even middle-aged, and had good looks, he became an explosive *beguin*, a dangerous sex object. Like Josephine Baker's spit curl – a question mark hanging upside down on her forehead – Arce's hairdo was imitated by the French. Unlike Josephine's, Carlito's name was lost, but the look remained, made even more striking by Paul Colin's posters plastered on every kiosk in Paris. (A more venal Argentine, named Gonzalez Roura, manufactured the concoction, and started a profitable line of men's cosmetics in Paris.)

The tango finally became an international sedimented cultural form: recognizable through an elaborate sign system. The tango was announced in all the kiosks, represented in poster images, and played in public spaces. It rang in the ears of many passers-by on the pavements of Paris and Buenos Aires, as if accompanying their steps in the broken rhythm of metropolitan bustle.

Note

1 This manner of interrogating the tango was suggested to me by the text of Pedro Cuperman in his collaborative work with Nancy Graves (Cuperman and Graves 1991).

References

Andrade, Juan Carlos and San Martin, Horacio 1967, *Del debute chamuyar canero*, Buenos Aires: A. Peña Lillo.

Batiz, A. 1908, *Buenos Aires, la ribera y los prostíbulos en 1880*, Buenos Aires: Lito.

Bioy, Adolfo 1963, *Años de mocedad*, Buenos Aires: Librería y Editorial Nuevo Cabildo.

Borges, Jorge Luis 1972, *Obras Completas*, Buenos Aires: Emecé.

Cadícamo, Enrique 1975, *La historia del tango en Paris*, Buenos Aires: Corregidor.

Canaro, Francisco 1957, *Mis bodas de oro con el tango, 1906–1956*, Buenos Aires.

Castro, Donald S. 1986, "Popular Culture as a Source for the Historian: Why Carlos Gardel?" *Studies in Latin American Popular Culture* 5.

1989, "The Soul of the People: The Tango Poets of the 1920s and the 1930s and their Use of Popular Language," *Studies in Latin American Popular Culture* 8.

Congreso de la Nación, República Argentina, Dirección de Información Parlamentaria 1917, *Prostitución y represión de la trata de blancas*, June 20.
Cuperman, Pedro and Graves, Nancy 1991, *Tango*. New York: Iris Editions.
Danero, E. M. S. 1971, *El cafishio*, Buenos Aires: Fontefrida.
Jozami, N. J. 1930, *¡Vendida! Memorias íntimas de Cosia Zeilon: la Zwi Migdal vista por dentro*, Buenos Aires: Tor.
Juan, María Victoria 1988, "La prostitución en Buenos Aires a través de las obras literarias 1890–1930," *Jornadas de historia de la Ciudad de Buenos Aires*, Municipalidad de Buenos Aires: Instituto Histórico de la Ciudad de Buenos Aires IV: 207–33.
Institut International de Statistique 1916, Etat de la Population (Europe). *Annuaire International de Statistique* I, The Hague.
1919, Etat de la Population (Amérique). *Annuaire International de Statistique* III, The Hague.
Kaspi, A. and Mares, A. 1989, *Le Paris des étrangers*, Paris: Imprimerie Nationale.
Korn, Francis 1989, *Buenos Aires: los huéspedes del 20*, Buenos Aires: Grupo Editor Latinoamericano.
Lanoux, Armand 1975, *Paris 1925*, Paris: Grasset.
La Razón 1922, *Anuario*, Buenos Aires.
Le Figaro 1920, Financial Section, Paris.
Leenhardt, Jacques and Kalfon, Pierre 1992, *Les Amériques latines en France*, Paris: Gallimard.
Londres, A. 1928, *El camino de Buenos Aires: la trata de blancas*, Buenos Aires: Afrodita.This book was published in English in 1928 as *The Road to Buenos Ayres*, London: Constable & Co.
Malaspina, Marquis 1902, "L'immigrazione nella Repubblica Argentina." *Bolletino dell'Emigrazione* 3: 3–24. Rome: Ministerio degli Affari Esteri.
Malnig, Julie 1992, *Dancing Till Dawn. A Century of Exhibition Ballroom Dance*, New York: Greenwood Press.
Marguerite, Victor 1922, *La Garçonne*, Paris.
Ocampo, Victoria 1965, "Carta a Alberto Salas," in Salas, 1965.
Salas, Alberto 1965, *Relación parcial de Buenos Aires*, Buenos Aires: Sur.
Salas, Horacio 1989, *El tango*, Buenos Aires: Planeta.
Tallón, Sebastian 1964, *El tango en su época de música prohibida*, Buenos Aires: Amigos del Libro Argentino.
Taxil, L. (no date), *La prostitución en Paris*, Barcelona.
Zlotchew, Clark M. 1989, "Tango, *Lunfardo*, and the Popular Culture of Buenos Aires: Interview with José Gobello," *Studies in Latin American Popular Culture* 8.

Index